Intermingled Destinies

Between A Mother & Daughter

by

Ann Palmer

CCB Publishing
British Columbia, Canada

Intermingled Destinies Between A Mother and Daughter

Copyright ©2015 by Ann Palmer
ISBN-13   978-1-77143-224-5
First Edition

Library and Archives Canada Cataloguing in Publication
Palmer, Ann, author
Intermingled destinies between a mother and daughter
/ by Ann Palmer. -- First edition.
Issued in print and electronic formats.
ISBN 978-1-77143-224-5 (pbk.).--ISBN 978-1-77143-225-2 (pdf)
Additional cataloguing data available from Library and Archives Canada

Extreme care has been taken by the author to ensure that all information presented in this book is accurate and up to date at the time of publishing. Neither the author nor the publisher can be held responsible for any errors or omissions. Additionally, neither is any liability assumed for damages resulting from the use of the information contained herein.

All rights reserved. No part of this publication may be reproduced, stored in a retrieval system or transmitted in any form or by any means, electronic, mechanical, photocopying, recording or otherwise, without the express written permission from the publisher.

Publisher: CCB Publishing
British Columbia, Canada
www.ccbpublishing.com

Dedication

Through the long distance of the Internet, with my continued friendship through the years, I would like to thank Bonnie Kaye for her understanding and encouraging friendship that includes publishing this book. We share a deep seeded goal of helping others. Added to that, Bonnie's publisher, Paul Rabinovitch, CCB Publishing has made this book possible. Thanks to Paul and his staff. To you the reader, thank you for sharing a small bit of my life with my beloved daughter.

Books by Ann Palmer

Letters to the Dead
Things I Wish I'd Said

I Know How A Butterfly Feels

Ann of 1,000 Lives
Author Ann Palmer Relives Her Own Past Lives

Intermingled Destinies Between A Mother and Daughter

CHAPTER 1

Shimmering diamonds seemed to play across the water as the hot, late afternoon sun was on the decline across the wide river. The moving bed of sparkling lights seemed an entrance to a never-never land. – Into my fourth decade, was I still looking for that fairytale world introduced to me in my first decade? Midsummer's daylight stretched well into the evening hours. The days were long and empty. Often, during my wakeful nights I would look across the still, shimmering water to the long portion of reflected lights from across the river. It was a reminder of another lonely summer eight years ago when, again, my life was at an ebb, at a turning point and another new beginning. How many new beginnings would my life include? At this point in my life, beginning again seemed to be a pattern - be it right or wrong - I never seemed to be able to change this pattern, no matter how hard I tried. To be alone was another pattern so well set in my life, it seemed futile for me to hope for anything else. This Fourth of July fireworks' display was still another reminder of that summer when I soaked up the joy and beauty of Monte Carlo and her weekly fireworks display. It was the éclat of where I thought I should be, yet maddeningly lonely! Again, the frustration of being in a special, even romantic spot in the world where I thought I would never be again, but then - alone!

I not only had the serenity of the calm, still river to look out upon each morning but often, Maggie, my-year-old Collie, and I would romp in the Atlantic surf only a short jog away. At the same time I longed to be on the Pacific beaches enjoying the Southern California climate. In the early morning the river was so satiny with only an occasional ripple of the fish hopping on the water, then by evening, it was a tossing angry sea with Florida's daily tropical storms of wind, rain and lightning. I knew I would long remember these few weeks, not only because of the excessive emotional trauma, but also because I knew this was not only another new beginning but a major turning point in this hectic life. The stigma of age in our society would allow me only limited opportunities of new beginnings in the future. Even now, I knew that every future move I made had to be done with careful calculations if I was to survive alone again in this workaday jungle. Why was I plagued since childhood with the incessant expectations of some form of success, yet, seemingly failed at each potential idea I attempted? Other people lived their normal lives from day to day without feeling the necessity to "save the world," why was I constantly obsessed with the relentless drive that I should leave the world a better place? Why should I take up air space if I could not contribute something? Was it my childhood religious training? Was it input from past incarnations? Was it ever-present personality insecurity? Was it astrological? Whatever it was, obviously it was well set in my moral fiber. It just never died or went away, if it had not done so in the past years, maybe it never would.

We suffer many deaths during our lifetime, death within ourselves, our loved ones, friends, pets, even ideas and ideals. This had been a very painful death for me. So long I had prayed for marriage. All those long years of raising a child alone, longing for a mate to share all of life's emotions, problems and joys. I had tried -- yes; this had been my third try! The first was a teenaged forced marriage, thus my daughter – the second was youthful compassion for a young man whose lies convinced me that his early expected death, due to stomach cancer, could only be tolerated by our marriage. When alone, I cried thinking he would die so young, and then finally he told me it was a lie. He was perfectly healthy. What a blow it is when you have trusted a person you love. Eventually, it had to end when he wasn't sure if he wanted to be with me, gay men or another woman. He chose another woman and it all ended. After that marriage, there had been many years of struggling along; raising my daughter as best I could as a single parent.

It was about a year and a half after my most tragic encounter with grief that Jack came into my life. It had been the most down period of my life. All of my religious faith "went out the window" and I felt spiritually empty. I worked for him in Palm Springs. He seemed to be a very nice older man; so much so, I tried to fix him up with a girlfriend. Then, in my loneliness, I thought why not me? I let down my guard and we began having an affair. Jack was not the typical guy I fell for so it took time to reflect if I really cared for him. It was a different feeling and I didn't think it would be successful, yet even some hope seemed better than none. By that time in my life, I had enough experience with men to know that everyone has faults. I had always been around drinking before, during and after dinner but not around people who got drunk. In the beginning I knew he had a cocktail after work but I did not know enough about alcoholism to recognize it until we had been married for many months and living in Florida, totally away from all my family and friends. There was that one time in Palm Springs when we were living together and had a terrible argument. He pushed me down on the bed and held a pillow over my head until I thought I was about to die! If I had been my normal strong self at the time, I would have walked away!

Before moving to Florida, we stayed in Texas with my family for a while. I was beginning to realize he drank too much but I excused it with his frustration over not being able to get a job. As a prideful, intelligent man over 50 years of age, not being sought after for a position was very hard on him. As an overly romantic, faithful, caring person, I believed I could give him the security of caring, patience and love that would help him overcome this potential crippling illness of alcoholism if that is what it was. It WAS! "You can take a horse to water but you can't make it drink!" (Especially when it is water, not alcohol!) That certainly applied to alcoholism. No amount of love, concern or compassion can do a thing for an alcoholic unwilling to even face his sickness much less attempt to cure himself. How much pain is created in our society because of alcoholism? How many deaths are caused by it? It seems alcohol in one form or another touches many people? Yet, it went on for years more as a social disgrace rather than the physical illness that it is, a desperate sickness, which requires treatment of the severest kind.

With so much of my inner strength at its lowest ebb, I too, found myself struggling to overcome another ignored sickness – – that of depression. As painful as a crippling blow, the deep inner pain of depression creeps over a person, who helplessly seems to have no control. Even when putting forth effort toward control, depression immobilizes its victim. I did not seek any kind of help or counseling. Either of those frailties was not as wide spread as in current times. I sought help for Jack's alcoholism, unfortunately the counselor was an ex-Navy man and the session became a "good ole' buddies' Navy talk" -- later the counselor did tell me I had but one choice -- to LEAVE Jack! He could see that Jack had no interest in making any changes in his drinking OR smoking obsessions. We had a Cadillac with a sunroof, which I would beg him to open just a few inches to get rid of some of the stifling cigarette smoke, but he refused and called me "Sarah Barnhart" for being too dramatic. A few years later upon having a lung X-Ray, it was assumed I had been a smoker, yet I never was, thus the results and damage that is done by the smoker to their loved ones. I cringe when I see a woman smoking, especially in a closed car with children!

The world seems to move in pairs. Facing the reality of moving back into the totally solo existence was a fact I preferred not to face. Over and again I felt I would do anything to remain in my little secure nest, yet, that nest had been years of emptiness and void of accomplishments other than making a beautiful home with my decorating talents. It was very pretty and comfortable. From early morning until he returned from work, it was peaceful but I knew if I did not have dinner ready within 30 minutes, he would get drunk and I'd have to endure another horrible! On the evenings when he got drunk, he would go to bed early but I HAD to go to bed at the same time as he said he could not sleep if I wasn't in the bed. So, being wide awake, I would lie there feeling paralyzed until I was sure he was asleep, then creep out of bed and head for the far side of the house where I could read or write. That secure nest was filled with terrible arguments, resentment, fears, and jealousy -- leaving me in state of constant anxiety. The sharing, the companionship grew into a nonexistent impasse. How little we really see into another human being, even after living with them day by day. It is so difficult to understand one another, to get behind the outer personality that is commonly superficial. I had no money and no way of getting any so I had to stay in my isolation. I read old diaries, dredging old painful memories, even listening to audiotapes of lengthy drunken arguments. My God! Why was I allowing myself to remain in this emotional cesspool in the name of "love"!! It often destroys us -- body, mind and spirit!

I don't know if my own fidelity to this fading marital relationship was one of morality or rather a lack of opportunity. Certainly, I had not so much as looked at another man since I had known Jack. With maturity, infidelity was something I thought I could cope with inside my marriage if it would end with the other woman! It wasn't the infidelity that was our breaking point but all the nothingness within it. Facing infidelity for anyone has to be an emotionally shattering experience. The fact that someone is sharing an intimate part of your life, which has been cut off from you without your willingness to give it up, much less share with another woman is shattering. When a man cannot handle his own wife's sexual and emotional needs, what the hell is he doing sleeping with another woman! Even if I could overcome his infidelity, there is the "where did I go wrong" syndrome that I think most women would feel. There was still the resentment for the emotional immediacy devastated with pain that also seemed firmly planted. I knew Jack was fond of his female co-worker, I just didn't know how much! One has to keep in mind "THIS TOO SHALL PASS." Even when a woman does all the things the books say that she should do to keep her man happy, there still exists the prevalent "seven year itch." Once a man has reached the fearful 50s, his fading macho image is a problem just like alcoholism, which must be faced and worked through, only by the man.

After around seven years of marriage, in the late spring, knowing how I hated Florida summers, Jack insisted I take a California vacation alone, since I had wanted to return there for a visit for a long time and he would not go. Instead of taking a long round trip alone, I hoped he would offer an alternate way for us to have a vacation together. We had bought a house in the mountains of North Carolina and hardly used it. He was not about to make any plans with me and went on working seven days a week, perhaps unnecessarily. Around the same time, shortly after my father's death in April, my mother came to Florida from Texas to visit us for a couple of weeks. Jack insisted I drive her back to Texas, and then visit my friends in California. I was reluctant to take that very long drive without him but since I would have a few days break in Texas, the decision was made. When I thought about crossing the country or at least half of it alone, I could not help remembering the travels Jack and I had done in seemingly happier years.

Shortly after our marriage, he decided we were leaving Palm Springs. He bought a 32' motor home to live in full time. We traveled east, then back to California but he was not happy in California so back across the country we went, ending up in Texas for those few months. During our travels, Jack would want to stop driving around 4 P.M.

when there was still plenty of daylight to drive further. He wanted to find an overnight RV park so he could start drinking! When we first got to Florida, we decided to sell the motor home and buy a small travel trailer. It seemed logical in the beginning but we had it only for a short time when he had an opportunity to get a good deal on an Airstream travel trailer, sort of the "Cadillac" of travel trailers. I well remember out first trip in it to North Carolina. It was bumper-to-bumper traffic streaming down the mountainside. The Labor Day weekend traffic was an ever-present reminder of one of my most agonizing yearly holidays. Like Christmas it was always met with extreme despair.

Along the roadside, only the young tender leaves and those most exposed to the hot summer sun's rays were beginning to turn various shades of gold, red and brown. They were sprinkled lightly among the array of green foliage -- a further confirmation that Autumn was upon us. The beauty of the Carolina mountain scenes was reminiscent of Europe and the English countryside scenery with its heavily wooded, rolling hills, thick with omnifarious foliage. It reminded me of that personal realization in the 1970's, while bumping along the German countryside riding the train through Europe, when I realized, for as much as I have enjoyed man-made beauty, regardless of how grand the palaces and castles, it was always the beauty of nature I cherished most. Prior to that trip in Europe, I worked in the film "Cleopatra" in the early 1960's for six months and on my return trip home, I took that train trip. It was too early for greenery; the train was gray, the river looked gray, the people looked gray, and everything I saw looked gray! There was still so much of my own native USA and its natural wonders I had not yet seen, thus the idea of sharing travels with a husband was very satisfying.

In Asheville, N.C. we toured the fabulous Biltmore Estate, created by George W. Vanderbilt, the grandson of Cornelius. Biltmore took five years to build. George occupied it at the ripe old age of 30. Of its 255 rooms, only a little over twenty were open for viewing at that time. The approach to the mansion and surrounding grounds (only eleven thousand acres that once encompassed 125,000 acres) was a more natural beautiful setting than any palace or castle I visited in Europe. Grand as the mansion was, it was still an American attempt to copy European grandeur. I felt it lacking a certain polish, attention to detail, artistry or some characteristic, which is present in the fine estates of Europe. Many were smaller and far less grandiose, still they had that certain presence of their past.

Lunch at the old Grove Park Inn was another slight touch with the American past. In 1913, the going rate for labor was all of 10 cents per hour. So it was no great expenditure to use 400 laborers to blast away the mountainside, to create the Inn's setting of a beautiful, lofty view of the Pisgah Forest and surrounding mountains. The Inn amassed the great granite boulders, which merged into the unique structure. Inside the main gallery, there were two enormous fireplaces consisting of some 120 tons of boulders with giant andirons weighting 300 pounds each. Being connected to America's past was apparent as we dined at another Inn, which dated back long before the Civil War. With its Georgian décor, it was like walking into another era.

A visit to Carl Sandburg's very simple farmhouse left me disappointed for the Poet Laureate of our nation. There was the simple farm beauty of the exterior of the house and nearby farm buildings. However the drab, colorless interior, furnished in early 1940's detracted from the charm of the pre-Civil war structure. It had been built in 1838 as a summer home for Christopher Menninger, Secretary of the Confederacy. How charming it could have been, furnished in keeping with the era and the farm type structure. It was obvious Sandburg was so totally dedicated to his writing and reading, he was oblivious to the drabness surrounding his daily life.

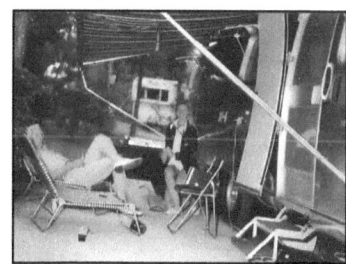

For as much as I enjoyed being in touch with America's past, I was never as awestruck as I had been in Europe, maybe because I had past lives more memorable in those splendid edifices all over Europe. So many Autumns have come and gone; yet this one had an inexplicable newness of life, perhaps because of its proximity to the beauty of nature that surrounded us. It was a long drive but we finally reached the top of Carolina's Mt. Mitchell, the highest point in the Eastern U.S.A. I marveled at how long it took us to drive to the six thousand foot level. In California it seemed a mere thirty or forty minutes to drive from the base of the mountain to the eight or ten thousand foot level. As we sat eating our very plain sandwiches in the stark, simple dining room atop Mt. Mitchell, my mind kept roving back to familiar California mountaintop haunts, which were unique and picturesque with a charm befitting the environment. Perhaps it was my Hollywood influence where everything had to be dramatized and larger than life. Whatever the case, what man had built amid the California Mountains was certainly more in keeping with the natural atmosphere than the Carolina Mountains. Even the people seemed more colorful in California, probably due to their varied sociological backgrounds. That had to be the best vacation Jack and I ever had together and it was the time when we bought our summer retreat, a home on the side of a mountain in Maggie Valley, N.C. What a thrill it was at the time but it would get so little use in our future together.

Grove Park Inn

Mountain stream

Ann Palmer

Cabin in Maggie Valley

During my many years of living in the hustle-bustle of the Hollywood scene, I took every opportunity I could to drive up into the mountain areas near Los Angeles, even if only for a day's drive. If "cleanliness is next to godliness" so it is for me amid the mountains. My daughter, Debbie, loved the mountains almost as much as I did, although our interests had been totally different. Mine was esthetic and relaxation while hers was more social and athletic. We both longed to live in the mountains, but after the summer of 1968 we change our minds. That was when we decided to chunk it all and move from Hollywood to the mountains near Lake Arrowhead. Daily drives around the hazardous mountain curves can quickly deter one's lust for the mountain living on a day-to-day basis. As fall grew near so did the mighty fog as it rolled in with such density I could not see to drive my car around the perilous roads. It seemed a warning as to what lay ahead. As the perpetual seasons changed -- spring -- summer -- fall and winter, so it is with our life cycles. First comes birth and total dependency, then childhood and reaching out for the whole of all - adolescence begets independences, often defiance, then comes having "all the answers". The all-knowing late teens and twenties, then the burst into the adult relationships between sexes, starting the new cycle of births and parenthood. The thirties may be the beginning of the realization that one cannot have all the answers or perhaps no answers at all. Each decade brings with it new situations, new realizations -- the ebb and flow, sometimes forward but often backward or seemingly into a suspended state.

As Autumn approaches, we grow tired of long hot days... the

evening begins to bring some relief with cool, nippy refreshing breezes. There are fields to be harvested by the farmers. Birds begin to fly southward. The summer's heat has parched the leaves and foliage. The leaves begin to fall, but first they turn to vibrant fire colors. As the birds chart their course toward a safe harbor, thus it should be as we approach our Autumn -- a redirection, recalculation of our course - a time to stop, think and consider what follows our fall - the winter of our lives. A time, as the leaves fall, we too must shed old worn out moirés, outdated dogma put upon us by preceding generations and discover our own personal values. As the leaves turn pure bright colors of red, rust, gold, somewhat symbolic of emotional strength, so we too begin to realize our own emotional grandeur or lack thereof before transcending into another dimension.

For some, our Autumns may be like the evergreen tree whose transition is a constant reproduction of newness. It matters not whether we shed the old, preparing for the newness or whether there is seemingly unchanged continuous cycles of new growth – – as long as we do not become barren, only to gradually die away as we begin the Autumn of our lives. Autumn is a mystical age, which can come early for some and later for others. To me, it is that magical time when one is forced to face reality as totally as one's capacity allows. It is a time to recompute the books. Ambitions must be re-examined and revalued. An honest look in the mirror tells us the hands of time cannot be turned back and acceptance must be faced. The time of competing, clawing, pushing one's way to the top, whatever that top represents, has reached a leveling off. It is time to make peace with oneself.

It is exceedingly difficult when we are living in a particular decade to simply understand those of another decade. Youth's attempt to judge their elders, at best, should only be based on a very compassionate attitude. Yet often they totally misunderstand the plight of a different generation. It just takes time to live and reflect on the past in order to reach some sort of balance -- yet that too becomes a task. For years mellow the memories of the pain and passion of Life's Spring and Summer. Still, true wisdom can only be reached after many years of life struggles through many Autumns. For me Autumn is our time to be at our most constructive and productive years before the winter of our lives is upon each of us.

Autumn is similar to the length of time needed for each human fetus to emerge into the world of materiality. Just as our Autumn can be our rebirth, a cleansing process prepares us for those productive and possibly the happiest years of our lives. The number eight represents balance, karma and harvest time. The number nine however is a representing power with higher intellect in the offing and has a vibrating magnetic quality. The only limitation is the desire and capabilities of the person. Nine represents mature judgments that may be used to help and guide others.

Autumn can be anything but most of the personal Autumns have had the same questions - "where did it all go" - "yesterday 25, today 40 - I had my goals and ideas why did it not work out the way l planned" - 'Youth is gone and I did not succeed as I believed I would." It is strange that these questions become blessings in disguise. At this point in life one stands just where he is, no longer pressured with "Gotta make it." It is time for taking stock of life, of one's self, of one's inner being -- of those he loves and even those he feels obligated to love. In truth, if the truth can be faced, the so-called loved ones may be totally disliked or inwardly hated. More than any other realization, one may conclude that the one person with whom he has been most unfair with is one's self. Yes, selfishness may have been boundless through the years, yet how many people can ever grab hold and say-" this is my life and I shall live it as I see fit regardless of what others may think." We awake to find the years have gone and we are trapped in a situation, a way of life, a partner, and a job that is just not exciting or challenging. A career we dreamed of in youth never fulfilled -- obligations, typically children with needs that preempt all else.

Possibly because the various liberation movements and increase in individual liberties, today's youth seem to be questioning the roles of life's drama they have been expected to play while the more mature adults are still afflicted by society's expectations of them. Just a few years back, any defiance to the so-called "norm" labeled one an extremist or a radical. Yet, through the ages there have always been those who did not quite "fit the mold" and some of us who defied the application of these molds. These are the "loners," the eccentric who are continually ostracized, chastised, condemned and denounced relentlessly as being wrong or bad. Some may be quite neurotic, yet, often times those of that heretic sect have been mankind's greatest creators. It is difficult to have the courage of your own convictions when you feel so beset upon with accusations that continually play upon your consciousness because of the influence of criticizing, negative and uninformed attitudes. The more highly sensitive the individual, the more preyed upon he is, but as a woman, it is infinitely magnified. Being a loner does not always mean being lonely, yet, one longs to be able to share thoughts and ideals. Failure to communicate with one's fellow man creates a measure of loneliness.

When and where does this isolation -- this detachment from others begin? In my case, I must have been born with it. The story goes that my parents came home from work one day, noticing slow moving traffic in front of their house. They discovered the reason the traffic was tied up was -- me! At the age of six months or so, I was crawling down the middle of the highway on my way, I suppose, to seek fame and fortune. My curiosity toward exploration had already. Exploring was the joy of my early springtime of life, wandering through our town alone on my bicycle; exploring nearby canyons with a friend, disregarding any potential dangers; feeling the wondrous freedom of movement in swimming and twirling and dancing, pretending to be a talented ballerina. I read and reread fairytales, fantasizing and escaping into each princess' role almost into high school years. By the age of 10 or 11, I sat at my mother's sewing machine making various costumes that I played in constantly. Once I began so confident of my untrained dancing talent, I entered a medicine show talent contest without my parents' knowledge -- only to be horribly humiliated, vanquished by a three-year-old! No fatherly consolation would ease my shame or my sense of failure. I was distraught that my father had applauded for the three-year-old! My future career seemed doomed. It may have been the beginning of my loathing of competition.

I remember those horrible spelling bees. As we stood facing one another on each side of the schoolroom, when our turn came we had to quickly spell the word correctly or sit down. As each person ahead of me participated, I became more terrified and by the time it was my turn, I missed the word I knew perfectly well. Even today, I am still terribly self-conscious when attempting to read aloud. Standing before many sets of eyes leering at me was very painful, yet as my life progressed, apparently I longed to be "up front."

Lacking self-confidence and knowing that I looked better than other girls, I loved being photographed to the point of taking advantage of every coin operating photo booth (a rarity in those days). There were hurtful words that went around --"conceded" - "vain" -- undesirable traits in the Bible belt of my childhood days. I much preferred compliments, that always seemed an anchor for me, maybe a feeling of security, yet it also attracted jealousy from other girls, so what did they do? They saw my "faults" and let me know what they were! This set a pattern that followed through all my career years, establishing my ever-constant question -- "What's wrong with me?" It followed throughout my youthful working career, sapping me of confidence.

As I grew tall and thin in my teen years, I longed to be a glamorous model but was convinced I did not possess the necessary attributes. I had endless fantasies -- I wanted to be an actress - a ballerina - travel around the world as a reporter or my talent seemed to be pushing me to be an artist, which was my college major. Whatever I dreamed to be, it consisted of relentless longing to travel extensively worldwide. Rarely did I consider being a wife and mother. Maybe it was because in those days it was taken for granted that each and every female sooner or later would succumb to that existence. It was a normal part of living. For me, it came the sooner, before I was ever considering it! Hardly out of junior college, I was in both roles of wife and mother quite suddenly; while my friends were all cheerleading, dancing and having other normal teenage enjoyments. How did I let this happen to me? There was no fairytale - Prince charming - no white horse to carry me away, not even a fake castle.

That was part of my life's springtime to summer, which came and went with its many disappointments along with many years of travel, glamour and excitement beyond my teenage fantasies or expectations. When one seeks to climb life's highest mountain, one must also face life's deepest valleys. For me, it came in the Autumn of my life but there was that one Autumn, that turned my life topsy-turvy, inside out, shook my inner foundation until it's fragmented pieces became an impossible puzzle. Pieces slowly began falling together requiring intense energy, sometimes sending fruitless results -- that Autumn, 1970.

CHAPTER 2

The hot desert wind whipped graduation gowns and four-cornered hats that June of 1969. The junior girls struggled to hold a decorative arch upright for the graduates to pass under. There amongst that array of red and white caps and gowns was my little -- a statuesque 5'8" -- Debbie in her graduation cap and gown of white. Unfortunately no one told her to wear a long white slip underneath; instead her mini skirt came shining through the graduation gown. Never mind that -- at long last her high school diploma was nearly at hand. So many years of struggle with school problems were finally rewarded. When a mother raises a child alone that diploma can seem to be a reward for perseverance. A feeling, at least, that now your child has grown to the point of self-reliance and independence so as to sustain her if the need arises.

Most graduates had mothers and fathers, grandparents, brothers and sisters at their graduation -- Debbie's family audience consisted of my niece, Sharon, a year older than Debbie, who had flown from Texas for this occasion, and a longtime friend, Art, who had driven Sharon and me to Palm Springs from Los Angeles for this momentous graduation. Debbie was very happy and proud of us for being there, almost as proud as we were of her. Art had known Debbie since she was quite young since she had appeared on his kiddies' TV show. He was easily recognizable to many of her friends and classmates having had a popular television show for many years.

Intermingled Destinies Between A Mother and Daughter

The wind and open air of the football stadium seemed to diminish the pomp, serenity and dignity associated with most graduations. Suddenly it was over, a few introductions and congratulations, Debbie and her date were eager to get off to a grad party at Disneyland. We headed back to Los Angeles with me feeling rather relieved but let down after looking forward to this evening for so many years. This was the first time Debbie and I had been on speaking terms for over a month. It was sad for me that such a joyous occasion should be marred by a strained relationship between a mother and daughter. There had been a few very awkward incidents. The worst were tickets from clothing I had found in her room, fastened together with a rubber band. Debbie had a job after school in a women's clothing store. The tickets were all from there. She had been wearing some nice blouses I didn't recognize but she told me they belonged to her best friend whose father was a well-known TV personality and could afford the best of everything for his daughter. I realized those were not the borrowed blouses but ones she had stolen from work. I was mortified and did not know what to do. I had to leave Palm Springs a couple of months before school ended as I needed to get some income coming in. She stayed with a family in Palm Springs for those 2 months. I did not have the money to pay for the blouses... If I had done the "right" thing, I would have marched her down to the police station to face her crime... BUT, she was so near finishing High School and I did not know HOW I could afford college! It was so hard to let her get by with this! I did not know what else to do! Any disclosure of this would have been so cruel for her now that her school years were ending. Another awkward situation that had affected our communications was the after effects of her having entered and placed in several beauty contests. Through those contests, a very old man, formerly in the film industry, who had "come on" to me months before, had secretly contacted her, promising her all sorts of things. When I heard his voice on the phone, I knew exactly who he was and what he was doing to a young impressionable girl, just in bloom! I warned her to stay totally away from him but I gathered that he had convinced her that I was JEALOUS of her - the furthest thing from any thought I ever had!! On one hand I was happy that the beauty contests were building her confidence but it also was creating a riff between us. I had plenty of experience with these "coming-on" men but she didn't want to hear it!

Debbie's high school years were hectic, not at all what I had planned. Having suffered greatly in my own education because of frequent family moves, I had vowed once Debbie entered high school I would not move until she graduated. As with most determined vows in my life that one fell by the wayside, as conditions were more practical for moving repeatedly. Each time I was convinced it was an improvement for her education. We moved back to Texas, furniture and all, for her schooling and after a semester, we returned to California for the same reason. There were only the two of us to consider, perhaps I was trying to over compensate since I was in a profession constantly accused of selfishness and self-involvement. It was just the opposite as I moved for a better place for her schooling, spent money on extra activities, such as dancing lessons when I needed to spend it on extensive photos, acting lessons, et al.

During the 11th grade, Debbie hated all the problems at Hollywood High. With a last desperate effort to get her in a school suitable for her last year, we moved to the nearby mountains where we enjoyed spending many holidays. As fall approached we realized the mountain school was so small it would have limited opportunities education wise, as well as socially. Besides skiing, which Debbie loved, wintertime offered little else. Most importantly, I could see no way for me to make a living. We both realized it was one thing to go to the mountains by choice on holidays, but quite another to live there full-time with unpredictable weather conditions. A few months living in the mountains had given us unexpected insight. Rather than fresh air and freedom for us it was claustrophobic with immense limitations.

In the Autumn 1968, we hopped in the car one day and drove to Palm Springs. The day was so hot it literally melted one of my old tires flat! In spite of the heat and changing tires, I answered an ad for employment and was accepted. We immediately wanted to register Debbie in school, already in session for several days AND all this before we even had a place to live.

I shall always believe that was a wonderful year for Debbie. She had been awkward about growing tall. Although the space between her front teeth had been corrected, she still was very self-conscious about smiling, awkwardly pulling her mouth downward. Even though she had attended many schools, for the first time she admitted being terrified of the first day of school. Just as I had assured her she would do, by the end of the first day, she had numerous friends she brought out to meet me when I picked her up after school.

As the school year began, Debbie and I were very close and had a wonderful relationship. She always felt she could bring friends home for me to resolve their issues. I was younger than most parents so I guess they thought they could identify more with me. In her High School years, I was still guessed to be 25ish. I was concerned that she was becoming more dependent rather than independent. I had to push her into making almost every decision. She waited until the last minute for everything, knowing I would rush in at the last minute and help her. Right or wrong, it was exceedingly difficult to play fatherly sternness and ever-forgiving mother. As Debbie became a teenager, we seemed to be closer than ever and did things together. We went together socially, visiting friends, going to the beach, skiing, movies, riding, etc. often mistaken for sisters. I never wanted to be a part-of-the-gang type parent. I was proud to be Debbie's mother and rather enjoyed shocking people, especially young, flirty men, by telling them I was her MOTHER. She argued with me that people, especially younger ones, would feel more at ease if I would let her say we were sisters. We had fun with it. After she had told them we were sisters, I would later announce that I was her mother, as I didn't like lies, but they would not believe or accept it.

In a few weeks Debbie began talking about entering a beauty contest. I felt it might be good for her. Perhaps it would build her self-confidence and give her a sense of identity. I had been aware of a bit of jealousy from her for some time from my fading modeling and acting career. As it happened, before school ended, she had won 8 trophies and had developed far greater poise, confidence and a healthy competitive attitude. It had drawn attention to her - this final year of public schooling. She was quite popular with her classmates as well as adults who knew her. She had the ability to talk intelligently to adults and was always respectful.

It was a good mother-daughter relationship but difficult to maintain a healthy balance. In her younger years, Debbie was little and I was big... size dictated authority. As she grew to my height, she resented authority, as did her peers. She was given the opportunity to make her own decisions, however I would not become subservient to her decisions. We had to share responsibilities. If she "goofed-off" in her senior year; she would have to pay the consequences in the future. If I failed to instill good values in her thinking by teen years, it was too late. One sad thing I realized is that peers have more influence on youth than parents, especially a single parent so I hoped she had good, moral, substantial, responsible friends. From early childhood, I tried to help her form fair ideology -- to look beyond the obviousness of a situation, to look with tolerance, to see and understand that there will always be two sides to every situation. Each side is always convinced that his or hers is correct. I never understood how the Bible passage was so totally ignored - "Let he who is free of guilt, cast the first stone." I tried to show her how people sit in church for one hour once a week and assume this gives them carte blanche authority to stand in judgment of the morality and actions of others. "Let your conscious be your guide." "To thine own self be true." These were old adages I repeated almost daily. I explained that it seemed laws and morals changed frequently. She must have strong inner fiber to meet the decisions she must face and face them with love and honesty toward others and mainly herself.

Debbie had a religious upbringing since birth. She and my niece, Sharon, were christened at the altar where I had my wedding to Debbie's father. Years later both Sharon and her brother would have their weddings at the same church. Debbie had sung in the choir since she was four or five years old. Church was a part of her life. In early teens it was no longer necessary for me accompany her. I was having my own inner struggles accepting organized religions that had always been a part of my life.

The first quarter century of my life had been fruitless in seeking spiritual answers in a church, yet I knew of no other avenue to search. I read a little philosophy and a bit of psychology. My mind was closed to religious philosophy outside Christian Protestantism. When a friend suggested I attend a meditation class with her and offered me a book to read during the mid 1960's, I said, "No, Thanks!" I already had enough problems being different from the religious community and certainly did not fit with any kind of "fast" crowd.

Little by little, I did open my mind to possibly find answers outside of my life's Christianity. Certainly, I resented any religion that declared theirs was the only TRUE religion! A little exposure and knowledge of "foreign" religions could never harm me; after all I had free will. Jewish people dominated the film industry. While I knew nothing about Judaism, it never made sense to me that Christians and Jews came out of the same religious source and area of the world, yet each opposes the other. Ignorance is NOT bliss - it begets fear and fear begets war after war after war!!

When in the mid 1960's, I started reading, attending meditation and discussion groups; I became very enthusiastic what appealed to my sense of spirituality. The more I understood, the more sense it all made. I told my friend that I really wish I had time to devote a month to serious reading and contemplation, if only I didn't have to constantly worry about my income. BINGO! Within a few days an unexpected residual check from a TV commercial arrived in the mail, giving me ample income for the month. I took it as an omen I should keep my word and I did just that!

The elusive answers came together like the perplexing missing pieces of a puzzle that slowly began falling in place. Like the distinctive fingerprints of each individual, no two people can, in truth, totally agree with their inner most values. In a Hindu photosphere's writing, I read a parable that said each person walks through life's beautiful garden, with many colors and types of flowers. Each individual should pick only the flowers that appeal to him, not the ones someone else thinks he should select. In this way each individual receives only the flowers (thoughts and ideas) that are for that individual's growth and development. That has always been a helpful vision for me. Most organized religions fail to allow us the right of choice. The regard for each individual's needs, as well as his intellectual ability to receive, decipher and apply spiritual values are almost totally denied. Religion is a personal journey. Without cramming it down her throat, when the opportunity presented itself, I tried to help Debbie expand her thinking. Her own nature was far more tolerant than mine, but then she was born into quite a different era than

I, as well as the opposite end of the zodiac.

Once an individual opens that inner door widely, there is no backing away. Values change by leaps and bounds. Superficialities, sometimes I seemed to be awed by, became silly and comical. Over a period of years, I had gradually reached the realization that the status called "success" is more often accumulations of one's severe insecurities and desperate need to fill an ego.

Hollywood is such a melting pot of abstract ideas; I wanted to gently prepare Debbie for any situation of which she might be exposed. I had lectured to her not to accept answers from her peers but, whatever question she might have, regarding any subject matter, she should come to me and let us discuss it to find a solution together. A few times she brought me questions that caused me to wish for a hole to swallow me, as an answer was quite awkward. On a few occasions, Debbie brought home a pregnant girl whom she hardly knew and asked me to help the girl. I appreciated her faith in my advice and counsel, but finally, called a halt to it, feeling we were being imposed upon, caught in crossfire of personal attitudes and conflicts that we had no part in creating. It was a time when a situation called for the girl's parents' intersession, not mine as a stranger.

Even though I leaped into motherhood long before I was ready for it, I vowed to do the very best in every way for Debbie. I had taken charge of her Guardianship for her good and healthy guidance very deeply and seriously since her birth. Every parent tries to compensate for shortcomings in their own parents. Childhood for me had been terribly lonely. I wanted to always be there when Debbie needed me with understanding, faith, love and affection, as well as not allow our difference in age or status of parent-child to close off communication.

I may have expected too much of myself, under the established and well-accepted definition of "success," not much had worked out as I felt it should. Being a divorced mother with no husband, I could not be a full-time wife, homemaker and mother even though it was my first career choice. Regardless of my choice, "Mr. Right" seemed never to be! My acting career would look promising, then fade away to repeat again so that I managed to "hang in there" and just make a living. My one real success was Debbie! In an era of dirty, sloppy clothed youth she had turned out to be a well-scrubbed, wholesome, pretty all-

American type of young lady with a very warm, friendly and feminine personality, which charmed young and old alike.

Having arrived in Hollywood when Debbie was 3 1/2 years of age, I was incredibly naïve. Somehow I had envisioned a fairytale world where everything was beautiful. Once I reached the ripe old age of 21, needless to say, my awakening to reality really "rocked my boat." I didn't want that to happen to Debbie. Through the years, I tried to explain everything in life as gently and as beautifully as possible. I was proud that in her late teens she had a good healthy attitude. She was aware without bitterness; she possessed a compassion and understanding toward all and appeared to have wisdom beyond her years. She seemed all of those things to me. Adults always complemented her maturity and wholesomeness. She would not tolerate boys using marijuana or any drugs. I had taught her that any habit, such as any drugs, drinking or smoking, was a "crutch" and ultimately destructive. If she grew in her own inner strength, she would never need "crutches." She was never the least bit interested in any "hippie" or any anti-movements. She had her faults -- which is what led to our not speaking prior to her graduation. If offered an easy out Debbie would take it. She did not want to work for anything. Because I had been a model and actress she assumed that without any effort, preparation, training or work, she too could be a model and actress. With all of the doors opened in the world, no one can succeed without compulsory drive, talent, ambition and hard work!

Often in her childish effort to gain the esteem of others, family or parents of friends, she created strained attitudes toward me by twisting truth or outright lies. She did not seem to be growing out of it and I was most concerned about this pattern she was setting, but made no progress when I tried to reason with her about it. By April 1969, hot weather had hit Palm Springs, tourist departed and jobs were scarce. I did not fare well in the heat. I knew of nothing else to do but go back to Los Angeles and try again. Knowing well the prospects were hopeless, still after being away for a while, I seemed to always get rejuvenated and determined to win this time.

With two months of school remaining, Debbie was invited to live in several of her friends' homes until the term ended. I hoped that this time of being on her own would help her become more independent.

After I returned to Los Angeles and Debbie felt securely set with her friend's parents in Palms Springs, she became very indifferent and totally uncooperative toward me; constantly reminding me that she was 18 and no longer obligated to comply with my wishes. The stress of being both mother and father, financial problems, not knowing which way to turn to set myself in a job offering a secure future; coupled with Debbie's indifference and an ungrateful attitude created indifference in me, too! My efforts to give motherly love and understanding with fatherly sternness may have failed along the way, but I simply could neither pamper nor coddle her with this disconcerting attitude. At this point in my life I felt totally whipped, exhausted from my own financial and emotional insecurities!

CHAPTER 3

"Survival of the fittest" is an apt description of Hollywood, but it was "home" where I had friends, if people in Hollywood can be called friends. Friendships in Hollywood are based on "what can you do for me" but needless to say - I had few friends. The only qualification I could offer was my inner strength for moral support. Many middle of the night telephone conversations consisted of my talking a friend out of a depressed state. I could be called upon for house painting, moving day, etc. Everyone is crippled in one way or another, not at all exclusive to Hollywood. Show business draws the emotionally insecure who must be constantly reassured that they are loved and adored.

If one is to learn his craft of acting, the salient fact is that acting demands extensive searching into one's inner most depths, not only in an effort to understand one's own character but also to be able to portray characteristics and characterizations alien to one's own nature; accomplished by observing and absorbing other's thoughts and personalities. It is easy to become narcissistic and to some degree it may be a necessity. An actor is not selling a product but selling himself, whether it be his acting talent or otherwise (and there's plenty of "otherwise" as selling one's self sexually for both sexes!) When you have a community of self-involved people, it takes quite a different spectrum of personalities compared to the average community. Certainly there is an abundance of so-called "phonies" but yet, as I see it, in some respect it could be viewed as a forced honesty of personalities, a certain facing up to oneself. This is not required of the person in an average community where people can spend a lifetime hiding their true feelings, not only from others but themselves as well. This to me, in many ways, is truly phonier than the so-called phonies of Hollywood. Hollywood is a vicious city, but what city isn't? Small communities, too, are hate-filled, seething underneath with the superficial smiles and greetings.

I really did not want to reestablish myself in heartbreak city, but I did not know where else to go. The film business was not the only business I knew but it was the work that I loved! The film and television industry is not a job but "a way of life." The people in it live and breathe it in their working and social time. Outsiders in a show business crowd often complain that people in the business can talk of nothing else. It is true; it is an all-consuming way of life with little time or interest in anything else. One might compare it to a "threshing floor" description in Kahilil Gibran's "Love" from "The Prophet." Regardless of which step of the ladder one is on, there's always another rung higher to climb. By chance if one should reach the very top and become a "star" - there is always the fear of falling and being a falling star. The public's fickle taste may change with no warning. Most people are never really "in" but always only on the fringe areas. Age is an enemy none can control, and even with the best of plastic surgeons, shots, and hair transplants, vitamins, etc. It is said that insecurity breeds like an over active bacteria that attacks all, from the insignificant actor who has never had a professional acting job to the greatest idols of all. Of the famous people with whom I have worked, socialized or dated -- the greater the fame the greater the insecurity! One of the world's greatest idols was the most pathetically lonely man I have ever met. He surrounded himself with "friends" who followed him like a pack of overzealous dogs lapping at his heels. He was so tuned into superficialities he could not recognize true caring and honesty. In public he never drank from an open bottle of any kind, even water. Who could he trust? He was only one of many with similar patterns. The most secure actors are those you see often, but never really know their names. They usually live normal, retiring lives with family and friends away from the Hollywood scene. The smart and happy actor is the one who hangs on to the good wages, quickly invests in businesses that will secure his future so that he need not be dependent on an acting career for survival. One may live far happier if acting can be an avocation rather than an all-consuming, obsessive drive--yet, ironically that all-consuming drive is almost always essential while the more you need it, the less you can have it. The acting profession is like a sadistic master who feeds you just enough hope to get you ensnarled in his web. Then he leaves you dangling until you are ready to abandon it all, and then the cycle repeats itself again and again and again.

Ann Palmer

The exciting life traps you. The once-in-a-lifetime thrilling exciting encounters with the famed, the beautiful, and the talented become second nature and are taken for granted. In that emotional, explosive era it was next to impossible to walk away from an exciting existence and go back to an obscure Midwestern farm or any town or city. Yet when one reaches the era of reckoning and does walk away from the fruitless mess of it all, there is a greater satisfaction in having put it behind you. It is like a pleasant memory of a high school prom, but who would want to spend the rest of their life at a high school prom?

In the era of Hollywood that I was in, when a woman was in her 30s in that youth oriented Hollywood, she must have tremendous confidence in herself. If she allowed herself to be only slightly sensitive, a sadistic man could destroy her. If she was past 25 years of age and had not "made" it, attitudes were that her career was over. This at a time when a woman was coming into her own with her greatest ability to give, to understand and appreciate, yet she was labeled "too old!"

There were the two specific eras in my life: One was when I was too young, then suddenly too old, what happened to the in between perfect era? If the woman in her 30s had not made a well-known respected name in acting or unless she could direct herself towards real character type roles, she had better do some strong reevaluating and redirecting of her goals. That was an easy decision for me as I had always been torn between acting and production work. From my observation, one needed the attitude of being willing to step on his/her own mother to be successful.

For the past several years I had worked part-time in film production and loved it. I had abundant good production credits, but jobs were hard to come by, more especially for a WOMAN. I knew it would take time to find the right career opportunity and had saved every penny I could while working in Palm Springs. Now that Debbie was pretty well on her way, for the first time in my life, I could devote full time and dedication to my career and myself. The ever-present desire for love and marriage had been with me for so many years. I finally looked upon it as a useful fairy tale dream. Somewhere along the way, I missed the boat, better to accept the fact that it's just not to be a part of my life!

Permanence grew in importance to me. I wanted to find the right job, the right apartment and hold on to the belief I could have a solid happy existence without ever finding marriage. A friend insisted I stay at his house until I found the right apartment. A buddy of mine, named Skip, had inherited a huge house in Beverly Hills from a departed aunt. I had lived in one of his apartment buildings and helped him part-time with his bookkeeping. Skip was having problems selling the house and furnishings without someone on the premises most of the time. An empty house is always more tempting for burglars. It would be a favor to him if I would stay there and oversee the house. He warned me that he personally would not stay in it, as it was so old, spooky and depressing. Depressing or not I knew it would be my only opportunity to live in a Beverly Hills mansion and give me time to look around for the right apartment while also seeking employment. As far as I was concerned, I was not afraid of anything and the house would be a joy for me. It was depressing and dark, however the address was so impressive I never had trouble cashing checks.

Just in case it might be haunted I took the least used back bedroom and bath, which had a lock on the door. Each night I took my telephone into the bedroom and locked the door. If the house could talk what tales it would tell! Skip's mother and aunt had been oil heiresses in the late 1920's and 30's with money to burn. This Spanish-style house had been built in that era. Nothing had been remodeled or repainted since it was built. The occupants had been heavy smokers. Where pictures had been removed from the walls, the results of heavy cigarette smoking could be seen. As Skip showed me the house he commented coldly that it was no wonder his aunt and uncle had died when their lungs were more coated than the walls. Little could either of us suspect what lay ahead as the results of Skip's own fickle folly.

The master suite was on the front of the house. The bedroom was quite large with a corner fireplace. The bath was black and white marble tile, with an oversized tub and separate shower, which had about 20 showerheads in it. I liked the shower but rarely went into the spooky master suite. My bedroom and bath, along with another, were located on the back of the upstairs. The back stairway led to a hall next to the kitchen. With a lot of tender love and care and a ton of money, the house could be MAGNIFICENT! Skip was soon to be married. I tried to convince him to keep this family home but when he explained the staggering taxes, upkeep and inheritance taxes that he had to raise by selling the house, I understood.

The grand entry hall had a large circular stairway; at the top was a glass dome. The wrought iron stairway and chandelier had been custom designed and built in Spain. The chandelier had a mechanical lowering device. The floor was Spanish tiles. The large living room had a fireplace, beautiful antique pieces, a grand piano, draped with an old fashioned shawl and photographs of the 1920's and 30's. The whole house seemed like a movie set. Double French doors opened from the living room onto a tile-covered patio and enclosed garden, where lovely California greenery was abundant. There was a colorful Spanish tiled fountain in the center of the garden. The floor of the living room and dining room were beautiful pegged wood, rarely seen. The den was also paneled in once well-polished wood. It had a disappearing wall used during Prohibition to conceal the bar. The mechanics of the wall had long since ceased to function. The bar was still filled with antique liquor bottles. Most of the windows throughout the house were

Intermingled Destinies Between A Mother and Daughter

handmade leaded glass. The black and white tiled kitchen was as outdated as the rest of the house. The house was quite large and restoration would be very costly. Behind the kitchen were the maid's quarters and another servants quarters attached to the garage. The garage had been equipped with an electric garage doors before they were commonly installed. The house had several basements; one was filled with possessions of previously departed relatives. One trunk had not been open for many years. Amongst the old papers, books, etc., I found some beautiful old prints that I kept. I didn't know if they had any value; I just wanted to keep something from this lovely old mansion.

Day by day I became more attached to this old house. I truly loved walking through it each day. The neighborhood was beautiful. Next door lived a famous musician with other celebrities nearby. I knew I should get settled in an apartment with some permanency and I knew Skip needed to sell the place -- still I dreaded giving it up.

Apparently my love and enthusiasm filled the house so that in only ONE week, it SOLD! There it had sat for months or more than a year, NOW it would be taken from me at the end of escrow in 6 weeks. It had sat there for all those months without one serious buyer! Even though sadly, I had plenty of time to find an apartment. A young couple bought the house and planned extensive redecoration. When the young woman came with the decorator discussing the changes to be made, I found myself somewhat possessively jealous and resentful.

After helping Skip dispose of the furnishings, knowing I planned to rent an unfurnished apartment, he offered me anything I wanted among the things that were left. With the odds and ends I had in Palm Springs and from the old house, I had plenty of furnishings and accessories for a one-bedroom apartment. I would only have to buy a sofa bed for the living room.

Spooky are not, I had begun feeling the old house belonged to me in less than a couple of months! Living in that once stately mansion for those weeks that would again accommodate elegant living plus living in that lovely area of Beverly Hills, I was given time to evaluate my own ambitions. If I could afford that mode of living, would I? My answer was NO! For the same amount of money one could own and operate comfortable accommodations in the city, in the mountains, at the desert and have the best of three worlds. I did understand why Skip found it necessary to sell it; also it did not fit with his extremely conservative and somewhat plain taste and attitude. He obviously was happy to see the END of the era of luxury. The excessive living of his wealthy family and their waste finally had come to an end.

When I returned to Palm Springs with the U-Haul trailer to pick up a few bits of furniture and household items, the heat was unbearable. Debbie was well aware of my agony with migraine headaches when even slightly over exposed to heat. The cooling system of the house was not working. Debbie knew I needed her help more than desperately, yet she informed me that she intended to swim at the home where she was staying. I could hardly drag her out, especially since she was now physically bigger than I was, so the packing I did alone. At that point in my life, I really did not like my daughter very much. I refused to pack her things and told her it was up to her to pack and transport them to Los Angeles. Since I was no longer paying rent on the house, she would have to get her things out immediately. Her attitude toward me was certainly not conducive for bringing out any feelings of love and respect toward her. When I had moving to do, suddenly my friends became exceedingly scarce, especially those whom I had helped in the past. Only one actor friend came by to rescue and help me carry furniture up the stairway to the apartment. There was not enough furniture to hire a mover, just too much for me to handle alone. I don't know how I would have made it that day without his help. Since that time he has had his own television show. A deserved reward for being a friend when a friend was needed!

The apartment complex was fairly old, small without a swimming pool, but well kept. It was clean and neat with reasonable rent and a convenient location of West Hollywood. Since I have no idea what the future held as far as Debbie and I living together, I felt the large one bedroom apartment with abundant closets could accommodate both of us for as long as needed, eventually she would leave the "nest."

My apartment certainly could not hold a candle to the lovely home in the Hollywood Hills with a large swimming pool, a full-time maid and owner who was a well-known television personality. That was where Debbie's best friend lived and invited Debbie to stay indefinitely. Since her friend's parents were working, traveling and had little time for their daughter, they welcomed Debbie.

Ann Palmer

Debbie had never gotten over having to move from a lovely four bedroom, four-bath home overlooking Hollywood in 1963. I had returned from Rome after 6 months of working in "Cleopatra" in 1962. At that time I had made up my mind to make a dedicated effort to succeed in acting. Through the years, although it went against my grain, I was forced to realize that a "show" of success was essential. To me, it was just being phony. "Honesty" when it comes to the appearance sake in show business, definitely "is NOT the best policy." The house should have rented for twice what an actress friend and I paid for it. It was owned by a construction firm. They were trying to get the property rezoned for apartments. Our rent payments probably paid no more than the property taxes. Even so, the rent was still more than either of us could have undertaken alone. By renting the guesthouse, then splitting the balance, we each could manage. We signed a six-month lease. The problem arose only 6 weeks later when my housemate suddenly got married to the man across the street. Unbeknownst to me, apparently that had been her plan when we rented the house. To keep her end of the lease, without consulting me, she moved an old has-been who-never-was actress to cover her part of the lease rent. The woman's chatter never ceased from morning to night. She had four grown children who spent a great deal of their time visiting us. No one, except me would turn a hand to clean the house or yard. The old gal made such a play for the renter in the guesthouse, he moved! Then it was up to me to clean and rent it again. I was a full-time caretaker for the house with little time to pursue my career or take care of myself. If this was the local success for me, I qualified only for a housekeeper or gardener acting roles!

As soon as summer vacation for her children was over, she moved. A girlfriend of mine from Texas came back to California and decided to move in with us. She was a pretty congenial housemate, but lo and behold within six week she moved up to the mountains to work for a man she planned to marry. The house became a monster to me with constant aggravation and work. Debbie loved it more than any place we had ever lived. Through the years, she often talked longingly about that house, always regretting having to leave it.

That house left a lasting impression on both of us. My uncanny and undeniable memory of one Sunday morning, when a dove or pigeon flew into the dining room window glass and killed itself. I had a terrible fear of some strange omen, but of what? The next Sunday the sky was overcast; again a dove flew into the glass and killed itself. Again, for the third Sunday the same thing happened! By that time I got out of the house for the day as helicopters often flew over. I was convinced it was an omen but what? Good or bad? I could never find an answer. That house was on Sierra Bonita Street, which means beautiful mountain.

After moving from the Beverly Hills mansion, I had not lived in an apartment for a long time. One Sunday morning, I sat spellbound watching TV. My telephone rang; the manager had just received a complaint about the sound from my TV. I was astounded. For the first time in our known civilization, an American human being was landing and setting foot on the surface of the moon. Over one of the greatest moments in history my petty neighbor complained. It did not take long to realize I was the only young, single pre-retiree tenant living in that building. Never mind, I would live and let live in hope unpleasant neighbors would not necessitate my moving. I liked my older but freshly painted apartment. It was constructed pre-World War II and had large rooms and ample closet space. It was just off of Santa Monica Boulevard, near La Cienega Boulevard, also called "Restaurant Row." The location was fairly central for any place where I might find employment.

During the time I lived in that apartment, I was awaken one morning by the cooing of two doves on my bedroom windowsill. I thought they were in the room. I looked out the window; a dove was not in sight. Was it just a coincidence that it happened to be on a Sunday, seven years after the dove incident at the big house on Sierra Bonita? Was it an omen? It happened twice again, each time a pair of doves and each time on a Sunday. I searched through books to find an omen for the meaning involving doves or birds but found no information to answer the riddle of the doves.

Except for that struggle of moving things from Palm Springs with no help from Debbie, making an apartment livable had been quite simple. Arranging the furniture, hanging pictures, refinishing a few pieces of furniture from the old house, I felt quite comfortable. I was determined and enthusiastic about beginning my new life of adulthood alone. At last, my time had arrived! Underneath it all I could not help feeling a little cheated out of those young adult years preceding parenthood. Nonetheless, I had tried to fulfill both mother and father roles. I felt fate had dictated parenthood for me. Perhaps it had been just as much for my growth as for Debbie's. My parents had given me a reprise from time to time by keeping Debbie for several months at a time; still the full responsibility was mine. I had always felt that since it was my choice to leave Texas where her father and family all lived, it was up to me to do without her for months at a time to be with them. Accept it, I did! Now Debbie was out of high school. The frustration of her formative years was over. If I had not done my job by now there was no turning back the hands of time.

CHAPTER 4

Shortly after her high school graduation, Debbie had a weeklong stay at the Ambassador Hotel in Los Angeles as a guest of the California beauty pageant, representing one of the desert communities. She had to lie about her age by one year to get into the contest. She never expected to win, knowing most of the girls were several years older. Those few years gave them more sophistication, plus some worked as professional models. Debbie entered with a good attitude for fun, experience, and excitement. The glamour of the weeklong activities planned for the contestants also offered an opportunity to meet new friends. Meeting new friends was never a problem for Debbie. By the second day, she had a number of "best" friends. From the first day, just as Palm Springs contests had been, the girls enjoyed the fun, excitement, publicity and the attention given to them. If I did not see Debbie each day, we talked on the phone in the evening when she would ecstatically prattle about the day's activities. Their days were filled with rehearsals, lunches, pictures taken and sightseeing. I wanted to watch the finals on TV but also wanted to be there. My good friend who had taken me to Debbie's graduation also took me to the Ambassador that Friday night. The pageant was staged on the Ambassador's lawn. A number of celebrities were judges. Debbie did well considering the competition she was up against. She walked away with a few pieces of a new wardrobe given to each contestant, with thrilling memories to cherish, but there was also a bit of sadness for the week's excitement had come to a close.

Debbie would now be walking into adult life, beginning it with excitement of being accepted and recognized as a beauty. This was good for the female confidence, yet all too well I knew the approaches and passes that Debbie and girls like her would constantly confront. Since Eve ate the apple and turned on Adam, man's intention toward the female, underneath it all, has been what you might call less than honorable. While many female's goals may be love, romance, marriage and security -- most men's goal is "conquest!" (BELIEVE, ME I KNOW!) The more the merrier! "Make this one, make that one!" Wham Bam, thank you ma'am!

If the female happens to blossom into a rather pretty or sensuous young woman the man's animal instinct for conquest is tripled. If she happens to intentionally or unintentionally get into the professions associated with glamour, such as acting or modeling, she really becomes fair game for every-need-of-ego-boosting male.

This happened regardless of his age, size, physical appearance or financial status, etc. I often marvel at how some dried-up little shrimp or fat, floppy man could have the audacity to make a serious play for pretty young girls. Some of the world's ugliest men feel they deserve the world's most beautiful women. How many homely women presume to marry glamorous men? Far less in number I am sure.

After years of my experiences and observing my glamorous friends' various relationships, I gathered that if a man can "love 'em and leave em" -- a pretty girl, that is, it is a great boost for his sick ego. All is "fair in love and war." He may have told her tales, made promises, anything to accomplish his goal. The poor girl may have fallen in love expecting love in return, possibly marriage only to awaken one morning to find he has vanished from the face of the earth -- she then asks herself what happened?

Years before, when I first arrived in Hollywood, like all pretty girls a new game had begun! I met all the phony baloney producers who were always looking for new faces to star in their next production; sometime they even had a script. They rarely interviewed in an office. His day was filled with production meetings and conferences to work you in for an interview during the day. He would ask if it were too much of an inconvenience for me to stop by HIS house or an apartment during the cocktail hour, usually assuring me there would be others there. I was never attacked at any of these interviews but I made quick exits. Generally subtle remarks are made, it seems to be up to the young woman to either give him the "go-ahead" or conduct herself in a businesslike manner. But the latter was always my choice. I never got the part either, if there was a part! Naïve as I was, when I came to the Hollywood scene, I generally could spot the phony offers. Later, I would realize this perception was more of my psychic instinct!

Through the years I saw so many young girls in the same scenario. Perhaps she had just won "Miss This or That" and was always put through the same routine. I often wondered if they had a semi-organized scheme of passing her from one to the other as time and again this appeared to be done. So often I wanted to warn the young arrivals but I knew she would not believe me. She would believe what she wanted to believe. Who was I to judge, perhaps she wanted to give her "all, over and over again!" In those days so many innocent beauties ended up as prostitutes from this introduction to the "movie business!"

One hears all the fables of Hollywood, certainly many are true but for me I either made it vertically with hard work, hopefully some talent or not at all! Taurus that I am, a Texan to boot, I was more stubborn and bull-headed than most. I was a hopeless, unrealistic optimist inwardly and very pessimistic outwardly. Perhaps this was to cover my sensitivity areas. Those qualities never left me, although they may have been my undoing. I never came close to reaching or attaining the goal of which I was sure destiny had sent me to Hollywood to achieve. If I had learned one thing, it was that no one ever makes it alone! Behind every successful man or woman actor, there is a man or woman who may have been an agent or manager (with sexual privileges), the sugar daddy, a father, an uncle or husband. If the truth be known, sexual or family ties somewhere along the line are behind 80% (my conclusion) of successful actors/actresses as well as most other phases of the business. Through the years, I observed that MANY successful people prostituted themselves, not necessarily in the physical sense, but in one way or another. This was not exclusive to the motion picture TV industries.

Having won her numerous trophies in one year, plus a taste of the attention publicity, I feared Debbie would be fair game for these lecherous men. During one of the pageants, she had been approached by an older (lecherous) "has-been" man from the film world. Debbie was terribly gullible, like many young girls but thought she would outsmart someone twice her age or more. My many warnings went astray with his flattery. By accident, I overheard the end of a phone conversation, it was obvious she tried to be sly with double talk. When I questioned her, she refused to discuss it, insisting it was none of my business. Often I could bluff a truth from her and I finally got part of the truth. The man had tried the same ruse promises to me months earlier. I figured he was pulling it on her to get back at me since I saw through his scam. He had her PROMISE not to tell me of their conversations because I was "jealous of her and would try to stop him from leading her to a quick success" with his superior know-how! You are damned right I would stop his absurd promises -- but jealousy of my own daughter? If pride is jealousy, then maybe -- NOT the case!

I don't know if it was fortunate or unfortunate that Debbie was not ambitious. She did not have the drive or energy to succeed. She did not work very hard to develop as many talents as possible. She had no God-given or natural talent that had come forth. After a few lessons of dancing, etc., she would lose interest. Through the years I had made plenty of legitimate contacts in the business that could benefit Debbie, providing she was willing to do the necessary work and preparation first. That ideal did not appeal to her, thus making her even more vulnerable for lecherous men like the one in Palm Springs -- could that be her ultimate undoing?

Debbie had made a decision not to attend college in that last year of high school. There were missing credits for college admittance. There were only a few junior colleges that accepted her limited credits. If she wanted to try to get into one, I offered to pay necessary college expenses provided she moved in with me. My attitude had always been that if one is old enough to own an automobile, they are old enough to assume the financial obligations involved. I had bought her a car in Palm Springs. When she decided that she would like to go to college, with an air of excitement, we drove to the one in Santa Monica to get her registered. As we read over the courses offered, any class that she would need was already filled to capacity. One open class was "meat cutting" -- fine if she wanted to be a butcher! Others were just as ludicrous! It was a good lesson in procrastination.

I suggested she remain at her job at the stock brokerage, save her money and wait until next semester then enroll early. We walked away disappointed. My disappointment was doubled when I realized her goal was social activities. Secondly it was to avoid work, quite common among her peers. If a person desires to learn, education is not limited to classrooms. She had never been a great student no matter how much encouragement she got. Like most mothers I always envisioned that

Debbie would meet the right young man and have a good future as a wife and mother. That was a norm in my day! This seemed to be the interest she indicated.

Everything about Debbie was suited for marriage and motherhood. Even as a tiny child, she was always looking after other children, younger or older. Naturally, I did not want her to marry as young as I had done. Yet I did not want her exposed too long to the ever-changing loss of morals from that era that we lived in. During her senior years in Palm Springs she had dated a tall, good looking blonde young man who attended a nearby Junior college. He was generally well mannered. They seem to like each other in a very special way, but neither was ready to be tied down. He had plans to go into the Marine Corps. They talked distantly about their possible future marriage plans. Their attitude seemed very sensible to me.

After the Miss California pageant Debbie spent a few days with me in the Beverly Hills mansion. She chose to stay in the master bedroom. Immediately, after Debbie's graduation, Sharon, her cousin, had spent a few days with me so that I could take her sightseeing before she returned to Texas. Both Sharon and I preferred the back bedrooms. There was something eerie about the master bedroom that Sharon and I felt but it did not bother Debbie. Debbie was not sure of what she wanted to do after graduation. We knew my stay in the old house was only temporary. Her best friend, Janet, whose father was the TV personality, was expecting a mutual friend from Palms Springs to visit for a while. She wanted Debbie to stay with them. At the time, unsettled as I was, it did not matter to me if she visited with the two girls for a short time. Janet and Debbie had been best friends since junior high school days. She had been in our home many times and had taken trips with us. I adored her, although Debbie and Janet's personalities were as different as daylight and dark. With Debbie's graduation there was reason to be jubilant. The other two girls would graduate the following year. As soon as I got settled in my own apartment, I assumed Debbie planned to move in with me. When I did question Debbie as to when she was moving into my apartment she would be very evasive regarding her future plans. She would remind me that she was of legal age to live where she pleased. At least the idea of getting an apartment inspired all three girls to seek employment that was a step in the right direction. Debbie gathered applications from all Los Angeles-based airlines. Her legal age was not enough to help her get an airline stewardess job. She found herself adding a year or so to applications when she realized it didn't work. Discouraged about immediate employment as a stewardess, we put in her application at employment agencies. Almost immediately Debbie got a job working for a stockbroker in Beverly Hills. My apartment was far nearer her work but Debbie had grown accustomed to the large home of a popular television personality and the maid cleaning and taking care of the girls' clothing.

As time passed Debbie did not move in with me. I called Janet's mother, she assured me that Debbie was welcome and no imposition. I told her I did not like Debbie's free loading. Avoiding responsibilities was too easy for her and this was not helping Debbie accept adult responsibilities. I begged her to insist that Debbie pay her share of expenses. She wasn't willing for that but she did suggest to Debbie that she put a percentage of her paycheck each week into a savings account. Debbie never got around to it. Debbie dropped by to see me now and then but usually she wanted to borrow something of mine. I don't recall her ever stopping by just to see me. Much of the strange feelings we had experienced in Palm Springs had passed, but there was still a barrier between us. I recall in the heat of an argument in Palm Springs, I told Debbie I could see through her motives. I told her I knew all too well that she was only using me for "a roof over her head" until she felt independent enough. Then it would be "to hell with you mother!" I did not know how to change her attitude of taking the easy way out. No doubt she resented the fact that I could not supply her with the affluent life style of Janet's parents.

CHAPTER 5

As for my own employment, as usual, work in the film industry was exceedingly slim. As for acting in front of the camera for dramatic roles, I had done only small parts, hardly enough to establish myself as a good actress. Not only was I too old for cosmetic commercials and not character enough looking for most housewife parts, but I'd crossed the line, from acting into production jobs, and it had created resentment towards me in the industry. At that time, it seemed to be an unwritten law that you must choose one or the other, never both, unless you were terribly successful and could do what you damn well please. Getting an interview for a commercial was now next to impossible. Lesbian females had replaced many of the men casting directors in the commercial field. I don't know why but they never seemed to like me.

I called on television commercial production houses looking for production work. I began to see that they were hiring younger women and training them for production jobs at half the salary necessary for my mere survival. I found myself being overly qualified. They were also using college students for NO pay. Regardless of the job you seek in the film industry, in front of or behind the camera, there is always someone standing in line with connections. Nepotism abounds! One needed to be related to someone or have some tie - even for a janitorial job.

Except for areas of commercial production, drama and motion picture production jobs were impossible for women to be accepted in at that time. The union also controlled the jobs! A female could be a hairdresser, wardrobe mistress, secretary, script girl or waitress in the commissary. The script girls' union was so tightly closed, even with connections of several top directors' recommendations, they would not allow me to so much as come to their office in person. That was the only job that might have led to working up to the position I wanted. If getting in front of the camera was tough, it was even more difficult in production, even more so for a female with creative ambitions.

My idealistic approach toward the film Industry was too stubborn and determined to give up! Occasionally, I came in contact with someone who once started as idealistically as I had, but had been trampled under by the "system." You conform or you lose. Since childhood, maybe because of my southern go to church every Sunday background, I have been plagued with this "missionary" drive to "save the world" or at least contribute something worthwhile to it! My mission in life was the film industry and somehow the right opportunity would come to me. I was convinced, with tremendous daily influence on the masses, the media could do so much good for mankind -- far more, than any one religion or world leader could do. No one in the business really cared, the almighty dollar was the God they worshiped, totally disregarding and disclaiming any responsibility for the results seen today in the massive increase in crime and violence. Why shouldn't the desperate person looking for an easy way or handouts take a life of crime to get what they want? Brilliant, talented minds lay out complete plans and blueprints, not missing a single detail, for anyone to follow criminal acts every night on TV.

Every time I got on the soapbox regarding responsibilities toward the masses, I was shot down with "you can't do that" and "that's trying to influence people" yet it was perfectly all right to influence viewers toward crime and violence. "Go back to Texas, you're too idealistic! It won't work!" "We only give the people what they want!" -- What choice do you have? You can flip from channel to channel and see nothing but police, crime, hospital traumas, death and special effects. This has grown beyond any possible imagining for decades now. "Message stuff doesn't MAKE MONEY!" -- Yet we have had some beautiful educational, dramatic series and entertaining shows on American TV, thanks to productions by the BBC. I never gave up. From the time I arrived in Hollywood and decided to go from just fashion modeling and acting, I had one goal in mind. It was to use this media for good. The only desire I had for stardom was so that I could call the shots and have influence. Stars were certainly in my eyes and I was blinded to reality!

In film production, the commercial production was the only possible door that I might pry open. It seemed I had knocked on all of them. I had returned to Hollywood after that summer meditation in the mountains plus the nine months in Palm Springs to attempt to get my head really together. I was bound and determined nothing would stop me nor discourage me this time. I was, however, getting a bit discouraged. Finally, when I felt the situation was hopeless, the telephone rang one day; a very strong female voice announced she was from a national advertising agency and was looking for a good production coordinator. A casting director had recommended me from a production house where I had worked. "We will be paying minimal, would I be interested in being interviewed?" I assured her I would be more interested in opportunity than pay and that I would be there at her earliest convenience. The interview went well but it would take her a few days to make a decision.

The usual anxiety set in -- the curse of show business. If you are up for dramatic parts or for a commercial, which can mean a great deal of money for you, hope is enormous! The anxiety is intolerable and the disappointment that usually follows is unbearable. After years of this conditioning, any job sets up the same effect. If I could just get this job it was a start in the right direction. If I could make my mark in the commercial field, with recognition to back me up, I could eventually move into the dramatic areas. At the time there was ONE female advertising producer who had rocked the advertising industry! If she could do it in New York I could do it on the West Coast! The woman who interviewed me, whom I shall call "Hope," called me a day early and said I had the job. I could start whenever I wanted. "Was immediately too soon?" I replied, most anxious to get started in my golden opportunity.

This was at the beginning of the highly publicized Women's Liberation Movement. Hope was one of the forerunners of the liberated career women. She was a handsome, statuesque woman well into her 50s and had been in the advertising business since year one. She had the kind of self-assurance manner I wish I possessed. I rarely listen to my own quick psychic hunches, but later was to realize I should have should have listened more where Hope was concerned.

My previous association with an ad agency or agency people was as a model, actress or employee from a production house, the "other side of the fence." This was one of the reasons Hope hired me. Too few people in an ad agency really understood film from the production point of view. Observing the fears and pressures the ad agency people live in, I had vowed never to work for an ad agency. At this point, I had to take any job I could get related to the film industry. Also the encouraging success of the New York ad agency female was enticing for me. Although my knowledge of the inner workings of an ad agency was limited, my job suited me since coordinating and organizing came very easy for me. Some of the terms and jargon of the ad agents took me a while to learn. I never let it be known that I did not know their meanings. I really enjoyed my work. It was the first time I had held a 9 to 5, Monday through Friday type of job. I actually looked forward to going to work on Monday morning. With a satisfying joy, all things seemed right with the world. My usual need to be "in love" or dating seemed redirected toward career ambition and achievements.

Only the year before, Debbie and I left the world of materialism to live simply in the mountains. Everyone has a hidden desire to escape to the mountains or a desert isle. While life on the hilltop had not worked out as I had anticipated, it was not a waste of time. Many hours of meditation, clean air, healthy foods, exercise and closeness to nature helped me grow in my inner strength and spirituality. Conditions had forced us to move quickly to Palm Springs for Debbie's final year of schooling. In Palm Springs there had been only a few acquaintances and few dates for me which gave me a great deal of time alone to continue working out my own inner problems. My childhood years had been engulfed with hypocrisy. Too much concern for what other people thought and too little thought for frank honesty that needed to be understood and redirected.

The spiritual quest plagued me more than anyone I ever knew. My method of giving love to friends, family and Debbie was not that of a martyr or an ever-sacrificing mother. Hopefully I wanted to instill a desire to make one want to stand tall, to recognize not only one's good qualities but to realize the trap of self-pity and self-indulgence. It was not very homogeneous because of the permissiveness of Debbie's friends' parents.

Often in my life, I had warned friends "Don't ask my opinion unless you really want it!" Sometimes when not asked, I gave it anyway. Being overly observant, many times I would catch a near costly error then call it to the attention of those in charge. This often seemed to attack the male ego, even though it was given as a helpful hand! To top it off, I was attractive and somewhat glamorous with a certain amount of sex appeal. I had a reasonable amount of intelligence and plenty of determination for hard work. One would assume those to be good attributes. For me, personally, they were - but it did not seem to work if I was put in an office filled with women. I could cheerfully say "good morning" and have someone bad mouthing me for the way I spoke to them. When one has worked in the glamorous field then tries to fit in with an office staff, resentment and accusations prevail to the point of paranoia! It was nearly impossible to avoid it, plus I am a Taurus with Aries in the first house of personality. That is probably explanation enough, hardly the birth position for a diplomat.

Because of the necessity of a working relationship at the agency, I wanted to be liked, as long as it did not conflict with my personal integrity. I hated the world of everyone living a lie, lying to each other and to themselves. While I had the time in Palm Springs to analyze myself and my relationship with others - I kept asking myself "what is wrong with me - why can't I ever get along with others. I searched my attitude toward life, my goals toward Debbie, family, friends, and mankind in general. Did I ever inwardly wish evil or hurt for others? Did I want destruction for anyone or anything? I knew I was my own worst enemy. I had personality traits that did not suit everyone, but who doesn't? I could never be the type of person who bends toward everyone, never standing firm for anything. If that was the price to be liked, it was too high for me. My analysis of my own personal goals came out good, positive, noble and with love. I was very tired of worrying about what was wrong with me; all things considered basically there was not a damn thing wrong with me. When I considered the pros and cons of people I had associated with through the years, I liked myself better than anyone I knew, so I decided to love myself. If I could not love me, no one else could either. If someone did not like me, disapproved of my opinion or actions, that was their problem - their "hang ups." I was doing the best I knew how to do for all concerned. My judgments were based on love and honesty. That was all that I could do. Since that moment of decision in Palm Springs to stop allowing myself to be hurt or disillusioned by others, my job at the advertising agency was my first time to test this newfound strength of self-love.

I liked everyone at the agency at first. It was a kaleidoscope of insecurity and personalities. Wanting permanency, I certainly did not want to offend anyone! I tried to be very careful of everything I said. However I have always had the faculty for opening my mouth and saying the simplest thing that later can be turned and used against me in maliciousness. I worked hard all the time and tried to learn every phase of the agency. My work seemed to be well received by everyone. The agency's Creative Director and two female producers were all women. At last, I found a company that gives women opportunities for advancement. At that time, except for these producers and maybe a couple in NYC, there were NO female producers.

After about six weeks, word was out that one of the male produces was leaving. Did I dare up ask for his job? I had been working with him on postproduction and observed the other producers and their work. Frankly, I knew the film side of production far better than they did. They had years of ad agency experience in New York, writing commercials and artwork, but little knowledge of the actual film production. Yes, I felt I could do a good job possibly better than the other producers. The producer in an Ad Agency has little creative opportunity but is primarily a go-between for the creative director and the film company. I went to the Creative Director and made a pitch. As I recall, I don't think I went to Hope first, which is what I should have done since I work for her. I do recall talking to her, at one point and she suggested I might be moving too fast; perhaps I was not quite ready. That was a little warning I failed to heed! I assured her I was capable and had wasted far too many years already and had to move fast. I felt fate would not have placed me in this position if it were not right for me to move ahead.

I shall never forget one of the happiest, most exciting moments of my life. I was working with the departing producer at a sound studio when the telephone call came to me. It was Hope wanting to be the one to tell me that I was now a PRODUCER! That was the MOST thrilling word I had ever been called! I was squeaking with joy, hugging everyone! They said timing was everything. At long last my life seemed to be getting "in tune." The long time ambition of achieving the position of a producer was at hand. I was determined to do everything right, just work hard and do a better job than anyone else. I wanted to just quietly move ahead. I am incapable of doing anything in a quiet way. I wanted to share my enthusiasm with everyone. Foolishly, I let it be known that I intended to become a smashing success just as the agency woman in New York had done. In doing so I wrote my own epitaph at the agency. How could I be such a fool to flaunt my ambition in front of other female producers at the agency! I finished postproduction work on the number of commercials for which the client was very pleased. A few odd and ends jobs came to me.

Finally with a new account I received my first set of storyboards for three television commercials. It was for well-known company with a new diet product. This would be my first opportunity to carry through a set of commercials from start to finish. Soft, female, beautiful and different was my goal. I sent the storyboard out to the commercial film production companies for bids as was required. If I had my choice, I had made up my mind to work with the film company that recommended me to Hope for my job there. I knew everyone and my way around their facilities. I had a meeting with her most creative and sensitive producer. He knew how important these commercials were to me and seemed to catch my enthusiasm. Together we came up with some great creative ideas. I could not wait to get started! The start of production grew near; everything was falling in places the way I wanted. The Creative Director had decided to go with the film house I wanted!

WHAM! The CRASH HIT! It was the cyclamate thing. The government came out with the fact that test on mice indicated cyclamate caused cancer. Today it has been proven not true but in 1969 it was a major catastrophe for many of us. Formulas for the diet products had to be changed, substituting another type of sweetener that would not ruin the flavor of the product. Thousands, probably millions of cans, labels and boxes printed with the words cyclamate became obsolete. All production on my diet product commercial came to an abrupt halt! Afterwards, when the new formula could be develop, new labels, etc. had to be designed and printed all of which caused delay after delay!

CHAPTER 6

Debbie made the decision not to attend college. If a person desires to learn, education is not limited to classrooms. She had never been a great student no matter how much encouragement she received. Her math grades were not sensational even though she had an ability to remember numbers. Her main asset was her ability to enchant everyone with her very pleasant, sweet, sincere, congenial personality. Great assets if strong enough to withstand those who would take advantage of such traits! They seemed to be good traits for working in a stockbroker's office. She had no enemies - young and old loved her. She could hold intelligent conversations with adults. If anyone disliked her, I was never aware of it. I don't know how she did it but she did not bring out jealousy and resentment from other girls. All of these qualities were advantages for her new adventure into the Stock Brokerage business. It was a field new to women at the time. Her employer liked her and planned to train her to become a stockbroker! I WISH she had followed that wonderful opportunity.

No matter what I thought, she assured me she would make her own decisions. This had been my goal, to bring her point that she could make her own decisions and live with them. Mistakenly so, we all reflect on our own youth, expecting the same capabilities or more from our own children. At her age I was on my own, naïve but quite capable of responsibilities. My prudential childhood had been terribly restricted while Debbie's had been exposed to different classes and nationalities, social graces, travel, association with celebrities and far more open-minded society in general. I tried desperately hard to teach her responsibilities. No matter how hard we try to mold our children in their teen years, their peers have far more influence than the parents who are often blamed and criticized if the child reacts to situations due to their peers. Debbie was born as a Libra with Aquarius ascending. Later, looking at her astrology chart, I understood a bit more about it. I had not realized just how hard it was for her to make decisions. At the time, I could only judge through my own Taurus attitude of independence and self-reliance. I truly believed if Debbie felt she could make her own decisions it was time to let the fledgling fly from the nest. We all make many mistaken judgments. I knew Debbie would also but totally confident in her ability to go out into the world on her own, especially measuring her with her peers.

It is ironic that Debbie, more than any other profession, wanted to be an airline stewardess since that had been my sister's profession. Interestingly my sister's daughter, Sharon, seemed consistently more in tune with my profession than had my own daughter. If a career in show business had been Sharon's goal, her personality and drive were more suited to that career than Debbie's. I had hoped that all of Debbie's beauty trophies, including the poise and confidence competitions, might also help get her a job with an airline. Her caring personality made her extremely well suited.

From my conversation with men, they may have wanted to date models and actresses but when it came time to select a wife, they would be more inclined to marry an airline stewardess. The stewardesses were constantly exposed to successful men. Since she served a man's needs while in flight, he got the idea that she would make a better wife than a model would. He assumes a model spends all her time on personal grooming. In a typical motherly attitude, an airline job represented a fulfillment career, plus offered an opportunity to find a good husband.

Debbie had liked her job in Beverly Hills at the stock brokerage during the learning stages but then the boredom of daily routine set in. She still had hopes of hearing from an airline company where she had left her applications. At that time, I don't know if they checked proof of age, as she had to add a year or so to the application. Also, more airlines seemed to be cutting back employees rather than hiring.

Since she was unable to enroll in college, she stayed at Janet's house, occasionally visiting me, especially when she wanted to borrow my clothing. The summer's excitement had worn off. Debbie's boredom was open for something to happen. Happen it did! Her boyfriend from Palm Springs had decided to take a trip across the United States. As I recall he was going to college somewhere in the South. He asked her if she wanted to go with him as far as Texas to visit her family. This was the spark she needed. She told me how much she wanted to visit the family in Texas before she enrolled in college the next semester. They assured me they would be on the road only one or two nights and would have separate accommodations. I chose to believe it. There were many parents, like me, in which the idea of their little girl having sex was appalling. Maybe I should have insisted on marriage before the cross-country travel, although it would have done no good. He was a wonderful boy and I knew they had talked of marriage after he got out of the service. They knew he probably would go to Vietnam and did not want total commitment to each other under the circumstances. Their attitude seemed to be right to me since I had been the victim of a broken teenage marriage, and I certainly did not want the same for Debbie. I liked the young man well enough for a son-in-law at some later date. In the meantime if she happened to meet some young man with a more secure future that would be okay too.

Quite suddenly she quit her job and was on her way to Texas only for a visit until college enrollment time. My major concern was to maintain my own "golden opportunity" employment. The next thing I knew Debbie and a former school chum in Texas had rented an apartment in Richardson, Texas, a suburb community adjoining Dallas. She had a job at the Gift Mart and was planning to enroll in night college classes in Dallas and she seemed quite happy with her decisions. Knowing how young hopeful girls arrive daily in Hollywood only to be used, abused and tossed away like garbage, I was not exactly sorry to see Debbie begin an adult life elsewhere.

In her usual manipulation, she left me with the ordeal of packing and shipping her clothes, etc. The greatest aggravation of all was having to advertise, show and sell her car. Even with the annoyance she had put upon me, I was relieved to know that she had decided to live in Dallas. Later, I would realize one city is no worse than any other. At that time, Dallas seemed a good progressive city for young people. Living and working among others of her own category would be a healthier atmosphere than being around me. If I was negative, jaded or had a "rain cloud over my head" I did not want my personal frustration to affect her generally positive attitude. After our past month of unpleasant encounters with each other, we seemed to grow more appreciative of each other from a distance. My theory had always been that parents and children should spend time away from each other sometimes during every year.

To talk with Debbie, she appeared wise and mature. Even parents of her friends listened to her advice. Later, I realize she was more or less borrowing ideas that I had shared with her. She could verbalize thoughts and ideas but she really did not feel nor understand them. If I had any wisdom and understanding that I tried to pass on to her, I had learned and earned it through "blood sweat and tears." You cannot give that learning experience to another.

At that time I had tremendous faith in Debbie and in general was very proud of the way she had turned out at only 18. In retrospect perhaps I saw what I wanted to see and gave her more credit for being able to make wise decisions than she deserved -- and just maybe I was too worn out and discouraged to play the mother role any longer!

CHAPTER 7

The ad agency was pressed for office space. The other two female producers were moved to my floor. Having had my office on a different floor from theirs gave me a bit of protectiveness by the separation. The lesser end rank of the two was to share my office that was larger than the one next door. That one was assigned to the prima producer as a private office. There was one secretary for the three of us to share. Neither producer could be described as even attractive. It was very obvious that both were lesbians, as mentioned, lesbians never seemed to like me - maybe because I had a strong personality.

Awaiting settlement of the cyclamate problem I occupied myself with research I felt would be beneficial to the agencies when there was nothing for me to do. I was cordial to the ladies to the point I felt as if "I was walking on egg shells" daily. Was I being paranoid or was my feeling of a conspiracy forming against me real? The more vicious prima producer was spending more and more time in the Creative Director's office and there had been an obvious change in her friendly, concerned attitude toward me.

The Creative Director called a meeting to discuss this prima donna producer taking over my project as senior producer! I would assist her as a JUNIOR producer - or in truth, to call it like it was, I was to be her "errand boy!" Explanation was, after all I was the newest of the producers. The agency would be taking too big a risk with this big new important account for a "novice" to handle it alone! I knew those words had been fed to the Creative Director by that prima donna producer. With that announcement my heart sank, I could have cried. All the creative planning the film company director and I had done was now washed down the drain! At the downtown Music Center, there were new beautiful fountains that sprang up from a flat surface and that was where we were planning to shoot a beautiful series of commercial!

I counted to 10, gritted my teeth and made up my mind that bitch was not going to get me. I was determined to bend over backwards to be totally subservient to her and do exactly what she asked me to do. I really had to choke my anger and disappointment as I saw the whole concept of the commercial being changed. In addition, she changed the film company to her favored one even though the other film company had our verbal commitment. All of which made me feel very foolish. It was common knowledge and a joke around the agency that she more or less had to work with this particular film company. They were very adept at covering her mistakes and lack of knowledge of film. To me, her plan was so inferior to our previous plan for the production. Nonetheless, I just wanted to get through this set of commercials without creating any static. I felt the slightest excuse to try to get rid of me was her determined goal. Even trying to be ever so subtle, it was obvious I was better organized and could get things done in a more efficient manner. She was smart enough to see that I was her only real threat of competition in the agency. Later, I was told she had gone to just about everyone in the agency demanding to know why I, the novice, was handling a new important diet product when that type of commercials was her specialty.

Cyclamate cost me my golden opportunity. If the production could have continued on its original schedule, my malicious coworker would have been too busy with another production to take over mine.

A substantial raise had been given to me when I was promoted to producer. My old car ran well but still had the back fender bashed in from Palm Springs. That had been one of those "someone up there must be looking over me" experiences. That bashed in fender had been a blessing in disguise. It happened right after Debbie and I moved from the mountains to Palm Springs. After paying our rent I was so broke that I did not know where grocery money was coming from, much less Debbie's needed school supplies. One night, a drunk driver bashed into my car and another one, which were parked in front of our apartments. At first it was like a tragic hit-and-run but something possessed the man to call the police and report it. He also gave them the name of his insurance company. Within three days his insurance company had paid me about $300 in damages that gave us living money until I began drawing a salary. I never got around to having the car repaired knowing it would add so little to its trade-in value.

For some time I had been considering buying a new car with the security of a regular salary, I felt I could handle monthly payments. I certainly felt threatened by this prima donna but also felt that I was in control of the situation. As long as I did my job exactly as she directed me, she could not manufacture further ill will against me. Once this set of commercials was completed, surely I would be on my own under the direct supervision of the creative director. That week I had given a great deal of thought toward buying a car and made up my mind it was the thing to do. The following Monday morning, the creative director called me to come to her office. We had a very good rapport and I liked her very much. I went bouncing in her office with general chitchat when suddenly she interrupted me with -- "There is no easy to say this so I might as well get it to the point, we are terminating you!" My mouth fell open in complete shock when I said, "They can do that?" She said, "YES, they can and they are!" I had bent over backwards to do more than what was expected of me and to get along with everyone in the agency including this prima donna. I had been the one person in the agency who could get along with their most difficult account. With everyone else in the agency, he had been difficult to satisfy but he had been pleased with my work. I could not see how I had done anything to justify my termination! "WHY?" I kept asking. She explained that the agency had decided to put one of the young art directors, at the prima donnas request, in my place. His salary was less than half of mine and the producer needed an art director more than me. This vicious bitch had succeeded in sewing her rotten seeds and now she was reaping her harvest in complete success AND gloating over it! If someone up there had guided me into this job, they had certainly deserted me now. I had totally dedicated myself to doing everything I could for the agency, while the producer who shared my office had a part-time job. She spent most of her time at the ad agency working on the other job but it was me who was fired!! She had a strong alliance with Ms. Prima Donna and offered her no competition. They had both worked on the creative director and just about anyone else who had authority in the agency. No, I had not been paranoid. There had been a conspiracy against me and now it was too late to fight it. It was all over now and so was my golden opportunity that was now sorrowfully tarnished black! (Just to add a twist, Ms. Prima Donna died only a few years later at a fairly young age.)

I had finally found a company that offered opportunities to women but I failed to have the insight to realize women do not "compete." Women do not try to beat you by doing a better job -- they simply kill you off! Their scheme was as a snake slithering through the grass unseen then -- ZAP! You are DEAD! OUT! GONE! My energy was absorbed in despondency, I couldn't even get angry. After all my stupidity was as much to blame for allowing this to happen to me. Even though some of the agency men wanted to help me, no one could "go to bat" for me. They were just as fearful of losing their jobs. When I went to my office to clean out my desk that SAME day, I looked around at my small cubbyhole. I had brought flowers, put little cute things on the wall and had loved it. It represented my ambitions and dreams had finally come to pass, now GONE. Not because of my lack of ability but the wrath of a jealous competitor! Hope called me to come to her office before I left. To gloat perhaps -- "I warned you, you were trying to move too fast!" I looked at her, wondering if the whole lot of these women were all lesbians. I was not one of them and had to be removed. Lesbians or not, what scheming bitches career females could be! I have yet to see the day when any woman has ever helped me in the work world.

What a time to be out of work! It was November; everything in film, dramatic and commercial productions always came to a near standstill during December. "Everything happens for the best" was a motto I could not bring myself to believe this time. As was the custom in Hollywood, I filed immediately for my unemployment insurance; knowing work would be extremely scarce this time of year. Unfortunately, I filed two weeks too soon! In so doing, it put me in a very low time category for qualifying purposes and I would receive less than $30 a week. By waiting just two weeks I would have qualified for the maximum. Now I was stuck with this decision for a whole year. It would just about buy groceries. Midyear my star had glowed so brightly with renewed hope of a fulfilling career, now at Christmas time my golden bubble had burst. Life was very dull and lonely. Every penny I had saved had to go on basic living expenses. I could not go to Texas for the holidays nor could I pay for the ticket for Debbie to come to California. It would just have to be a lonely gift-less season.

I don't recall exactly how I closed out the decade of the 60s.

Holidays were usually spent with married couples and their married friends. I was always the loaner, usually unescorted. If one of the men flirted with me, it created resentment. Attending parties dateless always intensified holiday loneliness but it was worse to sit at home alone. It never failed, year after year, if I had been dating someone on a fairly regular basis, he always disappeared at Christmas.

I do recall one Christmas party. It was exclusively for the ex-employees of my former ad agency employer. It seemed a great many people working in various agencies around Los Angeles, at one time or another had worked for this agency. They too had been fired. It was rather an elite group of talented and somewhat successful people. Momentarily, it eased my bruised ego to realize my experience was not unique. However it certainly did not help my depleting bank account.

It had been a year of a variety of experiences. It had begun with me having no intentions of ever returning to Hollywood. There had been good and bad times. There had been the shock of having a friend murdered. Then the fantastic thrilling moments when I was pronounced a PRODUCER followed by the memories of equally devastated hurt and disappointment when my position had been removed. Why had I been led to believe destiny was finally directing my course of life only to be dropped flat on my face?

The New Year always seemed to represent a new beginning more especially a new decade. As hard as I tried to remember I could not recall the beginning of the last decade. The 60's certainly did not bring the success I felt my destiny had in store for me in any area of my life. I wanted to feel enthusiastic for the new decade. I grew exhausted from building new hope only to face disappointments. I still wanted to believe the 70s would be my era! With somewhat renewed faith, I awaited another new beginning.

CHAPTER 8

The new decade began -- 1970. How many "new beginnings" had I made? I cannot deny my boredom with monotonous routine jobs that were the usual cause of my departure from employment. To quit a job because of my own impatience was quite a different emotional experience than being terminated! After so many years of bouncing from place to place, meeting new people, seeing new sights, being paid well for modeling and acting jobs, which I loved, plus the adulation, I was set for easy boredom. Yet, just as often as my quitting, circumstances did not deter me from leaving mundane 9 to 5 jobs.

If a glamorous type female does not depart her career through marriage (which does not come as easily as most people think) or necessity, then resorting to a workaday world and attempting to blend in can be extremely arduous. Through the years, after observing the most attractive women I knew, they often sat at home. Yet less attractive females in more ordinary career jobs dated frequently. Airline stewardesses seemed to have no trouble finding a husband. For an actress or model, it was always assumed that she was self-involved and incapable of sustaining a relationship. Yet, she may be more capable of giving her all to a husband, providing a lovely home and children! The pretty girl, regardless of her age, must constantly be on guard against ruthless males who willingly want to "wine and dine" with the goal of getting her in the "sack." If he can accomplish his goals, it raises his own personal esteem and fattens his own sick ego. He has no regard for the emotional trauma it may create in the woman. The same prejudiced attitude exists in office work from both men and women. Most employers do not want to give an ex-model an opportunity, assuming she would never be satisfied with routine work. If she does get the job, ordinary employees usually make it almost prohibitive, soloing her in their malicious jealousy. It seemed the jobs I best qualified for were usually male-dominated jobs, which made it all the more impossible. Women's Lib where were you when I needed you? There was just no source for locating jobs. There were employment agency specific jobs such as secretaries, keypunch operators, bookkeepers, etc. There were no employment agencies for "Jackie of all trades" in that era of specialization. My unions for actors did not work as an employment agency as many in unions do. About the only method of locating a job was through hearsay or leads that generally fell into a social conversation. One had to ask questions of friends and acquaintances, as well as listen for any tips that might lead to a job.

I had forced myself to get out of my apartment as much as possible for lunches, cocktails and dinners if I was to find employment. On one of those forced outings --- during the back-and-forth conversations, from the other end of the table, came the voice of a photographer promoter con man whom I shall name Jude. He said to me, "Too bad about your friend." I replied, "What's too bad about my friend?" He replied, "Your friend who got shot, the one who owned that house in Beverly Hills where you lived." Since most men are so against marriage, I assumed he meant, "shot down" because Skip was getting married. I suggested his humor was in bad taste. He then said, "Didn't you know that he was shot and killed a few days before his wedding, then the girl killed herself?" I assured him he must be confusing Skip with someone else. If anything like that had happened, I would have been one of the first to know. He insisted that it was true to the point that I became angry. I told him to prove it. I would call Skip. I rushed to the pay telephone and dialed Skip's home number. A woman's voice answered I asked to speak to Skip. She asked who was calling. When I told her, she said, "You must not have heard..." From that chilling reply, even though I was standing, I felt as though I was sinking to the floor. I had to hold back bursting forth with tears! When I returned to the table I excused myself and immediately left. Driving my car I did not know quite what to do. I had met death face-to-face for the first time only the year before when my nephew was killed in a car accident. Death was still an experience to which I could not relate. Especially, something as hideous as murder! What happened! That only happens on TV with people who mix and mingle in questionable social circles!

How could I know what a rude awakening I had in store for me? I must have upset the would-be-nearly bride. Although, I had never met her, I thought I should stop by to apologize for calling. If my ignorance had upset her as well I wanted to offer my condolences. She had moved into his house just prior to the wedding. She opened the chain locked door only a crack and asked me to leave immediately. This really added insult to injury. I drove to the home of an elderly lady who worked for Skip. She was a relative by a previous marriage. When she opened the door, I said, "Why wasn't I told?" She invited me in for a drink, explaining everything had been so shockingly sudden and chaotic. She assumed I heard about it over the TV or read it in the paper. She had been the first called and explained the gory event in details That poor girl, the prospective bride who was a school teacher, came within five days of being a very wealthy millionaire. Skip was in his prime mid-30s, never married, nice looking, and a very bright graduate of one of the most prestigious academies. He had several recent inheritances, plus his last birthday brought him into another sizable trust fund. He was disgustingly frugal. He drove an older car, spending a fortune on repairs to avoid buying a new one -- because of depreciation. Now, he lay dead and all his money would go his mother and to Uncle Sam. The irony was that it was his mother's lavish, wasteful lifestyle in his childhood that had created his ludicrous conservatism. Now all his frugality was in vain, his money would go towards his mother's resort living lifestyle.

As I drove home I recalled the last day with Skip. We had dated for some time and I think he probably had given serious consideration about marrying me. One Sunday he invited me over for a swim as he often did. He seemed to want to just discuss his approaching marriage to me. He gave me all the cold analytical reasons for deciding to marry this particular girl, primarily for reproduction purposes. She was a schoolteacher so he felt she would be stable. For him, marriage was like a commodity to be bought with little or no feeling of love, companionship or any aesthetic values.

It was that afternoon while we were in the pool that we heard the news of Sharon Tate's murder, which we discussed at length. How could anyone commit such a hideous, gruesome murder and by a group of murderers just for "kicks!" When I left that day, I was disgusted by his cold indifferent attitude and glad that we never came close to actually considering marriage. Perhaps my attitude was overly romanticizing but I really did not care if I ever saw him again! How those thoughts haunted me now. It was also pointless. His attitude was developed by years of conditioning to cover up his Cancer birth sign of sensitivity, too long withheld to ever be brought out, in my opinion. His frugality was understandable with the waste he had seen in childhood. He had really overdone his conservativeness. His "inheritance" from his estranged father had been a jaded distorted attitude toward women. Everyone has his or her own hang-ups and above all else, Skip was a decent, very honest, hardworking man who certainly did not deserve to die so young! The young woman who killed him could not have been in a serious romance, except what she must have contrived in her own mind. I knew him well enough to know he would never lead a woman on, as he was totally non-committal. His bride-to-be may never have heard the word "love" from Skip. I felt sure his proposal of marriage was anything but ROMANTIC! This was my first encounter with the murder or even the death of one of my close friends. The feelings of helplessness were enormous. No matter how much I tried to control my thought patterns and not dwell on his murder, there were reminders of Skip all around my apartment. Pieces of furniture and accessories that came from his Beverly Hills mansion reminded me that these things came from a home of many deaths. The giver of these meaningful pieces was also dead. There was something very morbid about my pretty furnishings now.

    The first of the year wore on and still no employment. I was beyond looking for the right opportunity; at this point I had to have a job - almost any job. A friend told me he knew a salesman who had an office in the Apparel Mart in downtown Los Angeles. He was looking for showroom girl. For years, devotedly I had avoided working downtown LA with this twice a day fighting with the freeway traffic. To enjoy that sort of daily activities, one needed a death wish or to be a racecar driver. Fashion modeling had acquainted me with the wholesale apparel industry. I had modeled for various manufacturers working their market for weeks to a few days at a time for several years. Showroom jobs weren't the worst work in the world. I consoled myself by thinking I could take the job temporarily until the film industry picked up. Opportunities always seemed to come after one has committed herself to another job. The salesman asked me if I would be permanent when I was interviewed for the job. I told him I could not guarantee I would be alive tomorrow. One should enjoy one's work since it occupies most of one's waking hours. If working conditions and salary were satisfactory, there would be no reason for me to leave. That was the truth, however inwardly I doubted if working conditions in downtown LA would ever be satisfactory.

Every showroom job in Dallas, New York or Los Angeles I knew consisted of dressing smartly to work with the buyers, writing orders and possibly a small amount of bookkeeping. This showroom job was sitting all day behind a partition wall in a dirty cubbyhole, writing several orders for watch repairs, working as a box boy and delivery boy. Just trying to handle the telephone complaints was a full-time job. From the looks of the stacked boxes of watches needing repair all around the floor of the office, I wondered if they sold any watches that did work. "Beggars can't be choosers" and I needed the job. The easiest way to tolerate an intolerable situation is to do something about it. I was stubborn enough to believe I could get the place in order so that it could operate efficiently. With that determination I dove right in! After that exposure to the work world I could see why the young aesthetic poet that I had replaced was departing for San Francisco. Their repair orders were months behind. The phone rang constantly with irate people who wanted to know what happened to their watch sent in for repairs months before. Usually there was no record of the watch. To say that I arrived home each evening worn and frazzled is an understatement. Dinner, bed then repeat the routine the next day was now my lifestyle. I hated clutter. I worked overtime evenings and weekends, trying to get caught up to date. Even with this disastrous employment, keeping my mind totally occupied until I was exhausted helped to keep my mind off the burdensome sense of failure. The job was exceedingly monotonous work - type service order, tag each watch, place several in the bag, then in quantity take the bags to the watch repair office several blocks away. It was too far to walk. This meant walking a couple of blocks to the parking lot and taking my car out. This was an extra cost then driving to another parking lot downtown, etc. This job was boring, aggravating and time-consuming! A messenger service would have been more practical but I could not convince the thrifty employer of this. He thought nothing of personal inconvenience for an employee.

There was just no way one person could ever get caught up with the daily new arrivals. His typewriter was nearly a museum piece. He would not buy or rent a new one. Rather than struggle with it, I finally unwillingly brought my new electric typewriter from home. Eventually, he allowed me to hire a girl who worked across the hall for a few hours. After she finished her job, she would type the service orders. From this I could gradually see hope in possibly catching up. Life was always a bore if I did not feel I was a little bit "in love." Social life seemed to be at a complete standstill. I seem to be growing away from most people I called friends. I rarely ever chatted with a girlfriend via telephone. Living in the mountains had broken that telephone obsession most women have. The ample overtime was welcome to occupy my time, plus my increased paycheck made the job more tolerable.

Even though Debbie and I were across the country from each other, our communication seemed closer through lengthy letters and telephone conversations. My letters to her were forceful, full of encouragement and pride in her adjusting to her new adult life. She wrote frequently. She so wanted to work as a stewardess but she was still a year or two younger than most airlines required. Otherwise she seemed to be doing very well. She did not like the boredom of her first job so she found another. Neither job paid her much money. We all have problems adjusting to budgeting, especially when at first on our own. Instead of using the money I sent from the sale of the car for a down payment for another, she had wasted it away. I insisted she use it for a down payment on a used car but she wanted a new one or none at all! Yeah... I would like a "new" car, too! If she could choose to spend money and do without a car, it was a decision she had to live with. I wanted her to live with me but if she chose to make it on her own that too was her choice. I felt she must be ready to be on her own. Her almost daily letters were neatly typed with little hand-drawn colored decorations at the top or on the sides of each page. Her letters were full of social events, friends and abundant dates. She was taking two evening college classes. I missed her but in my state of mind, I felt she was happier, in a more positive atmosphere than I could offer at the time.

My letter to her was always filled with advice: "Glad your social life is good, hope you don't fall in love -- you know it's nearing spring which sometimes does that to people so be careful!" Discussing friendship I referred to my past experiences. People do vicious acts with such subtlety that we don't realize what's happening. Our friends often create negativity around us, which we do not realize. There is so much to learn and realize about the mind and the way people use it or should I say, "abuse" it. (Of course, I was reflecting on my own recent experience at the ad agency.) Often, I urged her to take time to be alone and "recharge her battery" so to speak, knowing she subjected herself to constant companionship. Except for the mother-to-daughter advice most of our letters were much like two girlfriends writing to each other. I always felt we had an exceedingly open parent-child relationship. There were things I did not discuss with her but whatever I did discuss or whatever question she asked, I answered honestly because I hate lies and deception in any form. I always discouraged Debbie's nature of leaning toward deceptive practices. Yet I knew how important it was for a parent to trust and have faith in the child, which could be very trying at times.

As for attempting to analyze my own current situation I could not understand why nothing I ever tried worked out. I knew it must be my fault but why could I never seem to change it. I tried to overcome negativity. My Taurus nature is to plod along with great tenacity but the Aries personality represents change, moving, traveling. In the past I have tried to find jobs to suit both natures such as a traveling cosmetic consultant. This watch shopkeeper's job in downtown Los Angeles was one that any 18-year-old could do with mediocre intellect. Why waste my life away writing watch repair orders.

Before Easter, Debbie called saying she would be coming out to Palm Springs. I was delighted until I questioned her about the money for the trip. I could tell she was trying to hide something. When I pressured her, she told me about a very nice older man who was just a good friend, had offered to pay her way to Palm Springs. "And he was not going to be there?" was my next question. "Well, yes." I asked if she did not realize what a trap she was falling into. As much as I wanted to see her I told her she was very foolish to accept the trip. As she defended the "niceness" of this man she said, "He used to be in the Mafia." I flipped! "Debbie no one used to be in the Mafia!! It is a lifetime commitment!" I urged, begged and demanded that she immediately abandon that friendship as politely as possible. I told her, "You might end up right out in the middle of the desert dead!" I assumed she had ended the friendship but much later, I found out differently.

My tedious job became intolerability boring as I worked ferociously to bring this watch jungle under control. As it became somewhat organized the monotony was overpowering! My employer seemed to have no appreciation for the organizing and all the work I did to clean up his mess. When the unpleasantness of a job overshadows all else, the only way I can cope with it is set a goal to survive!

CHAPTER 9

Travel clubs with their inexpensive European destinations were all the rage. I joined one at the insistence of a girlfriend. I was flabbergasted at their inexpensive travel rates for a round trip to England. Now that Debbie seemed to be settled in Dallas, could I possibly think of traveling to Europe again?

Most everyone has a book inside them that they would like to write one day. I had mine but was never free of worry or had enough free time to think about it. Since my creativity was unfulfilled and my sensitivity had never been satisfied in the film arts, painting or interior decorating, maybe writing was the answer. Writing was not new to me. For over 10 years I had made attempts at writing. At first it was poetry, then articles, scripts and story ideas for a TV series. After a year another rejection slip sent all my efforts back into the drawer. Never totally abandoning writing, I recalled Rod Sterling's submissions were 40 odd rejections before he ever sold anything. Forty rejections were still a long way off. Someday, some way one of my artistic expressions just had to be successful! Painting and art endeavors in youth had not been the answer. As for modeling and acting, I just could not become totally involved with all the self-improvement required. The hours of being in beauty shops, hours of dance, exercise studios, voice and acting lessons, buying expensive clothing and accessories were a necessity.

The hypocrisy of playing up to men, I found obnoxious. This was more than I could handle. The creative end of film production had always appealed to me. However the more I became involved in it, the more I realized each person had a little pigeonhole job that must not overlap the other. There were too many pigeonholes that appealed to me to select only one. After the advertising agency I had learned the producer was hardly more than a glorified errand boy, lacking any real creative opportunities for expression. Even though a writer's work may be chopped to pieces, rewritten until the original idea may be lost, still his or her work seemed the more creative and fulfilling. Prolific letter writing had been my practice since early youth. In conversations, I often seemed to have a knack for putting my "foot-in-mouth" or saying the wrong thing at the right time. Afterwards, I was able to write logical meaningful statements that seemed to escape me in vocal conversation. For many years, to overcome basic shyness and inhibitions, alone and in silence, I seemed to be best able to express my thoughts in writing. Yet, writing required a certain freedom of thought. Privacy was needed along with freedom from emotional and financial pressures. In all my adult years, I had never before had only the responsibility of myself to consider.

If I could save enough money, I could live for several months without working. I could envision a charming little room in a small hotel in a quaint English village, surrounded by beautiful serene scenery where I could write in peaceful solitude. I took the first big step by sending a deposit to book a flight to London, with reservations for the end of June. My friend who asked me to join the travel club planned to go to Europe but wanted to wait until fall. From my previous stay in Europe, I felt fall was too late. I was recalling the cold, dreary winters that come early. Sometimes, Europeans do not decide to turn the heat on in hotels and apartments until a certain date, regardless of how cold it becomes.

My intolerable job became more tolerable with a goal to work towards. I worked all the overtime they would allow me with little thought or desire for social activities. There was time enough for making plans, selling my car and furnishings. Due to their morbid remembrances for me, on one hand, I really did not mind parting with my antique pieces from the old Beverly Hills mansion, yet on the other hand; there were individual pieces I knew I could never replace. Would I allow things to tie me down? Since this was my first opportunity be totally free of obligations, except for myself, I felt I could not let materiality hold me back now. Even though I loved the area, Hollywood had been nothing but heartache and disappointments in every respect for the past few years. There had been no reason to stay.

Generally speaking, perhaps because of the era in which I was born and childhood conditioning, I looked upon almost every man I ever dated as a potential candidate for husband. Whereas, just about every man I dated looked upon me as a desirable bed partner. Being "in love" whether lightly or heavily seemed to be a necessity state for me. Through the years there were dozens of dates accepted merely to have something to do or because I liked the man as a friend. Even so, endless challenges always began. Sometimes I wanted to scream "Can any man see anything in a woman except for sex?" I enjoyed the company of men. Their conversations were far more interesting than women's. Yet their routine was always the same. If a man invited you to his house for dinner, you needed to eat before you left home since he plied you with drinks and wouldn't serve dinner until after midnight. If he took you out to dinner, before you could finish one cocktail, he'd order another, pretending to listen to your conversation. You know he's only trying to get you loaded before dinner to weaken your resistance afterwards. It was always the same. It was amazing how unimaginative their approaches were. I longed for male compatibility without their insatiable lust for sex. Often I suggested the easiest way to make out with a woman who is sexually pursued was -- simply don't try! In this way, she would let down her guard - but alas my suggestion was never heeded. It was all the rage in Hollywood, maybe everywhere and I had been too young to see it, for a man at any age to pursue a woman under 25. Some men I considered too old for me were more interested in chasing my daughter than me. In my own age category, as well, older men were all always chasing young girls. It made them feel younger than their years in the YOUTH oriented Hollywood. I've spent many years with the handsome actor syndrome, finally realizing their self-love is all too consuming to leave enough love for a woman. Each year desirable dateable men become scarcer.

Men never understood why women dated gay men. In my early days in Hollywood, gay men were still "in the closet." In my part-time profession of interior decorating I was exposed to gay men all the time. During that period, I was dating a handsome, fun actor. He never made passes at me but I thought nothing of it. We liked each other; I simply assumed that there was no chemistry between us. I enjoyed his company without pressure or passes. We never dated on a steady enough basis to get physically involved. My dates with him were always for special events, such as the opening of a play, an awards dinner, a cocktail party, etc. Many of my most meaningful memories of outstanding occasions in Hollywood were with him. When a man has never made a pass after six or so years of dating, knowing the variety of sexual pursuits, naturally one begins to wonder. I never suspected a thing until he took me to a performance of one of his musical friends. After the performance his friend joined us. The moment he spoke in casual conversation there was no doubt about his gayness. As I looked around I realized all the men there were gay. Certainly I had been discouraged when males never seemed to accept me as anything but a sexual object. That discouragement was nothing compared to the disappointment I felt to realize my dear friend whom I generally loved was gay. God! How I wished I had not been so hung up on fairy tales as a child. It was a "fairy" world all right, but not the beautiful "live happily ever after Prince and Princess world" I had imagined!

Because of my small town Texas upbringing, it took many years of fighting my disdain toward homosexuality to accept them without inner condemnation. I could never really understand the feeling they had for their own sex. In some ways I could somehow justify the sensitive male being obliterated by some overpowering insensitive female. I could never justify female homosexuality. I could not understand that being hurt or rejected by men was justification for female homosexuality. I've experienced all of those emotions yet the idea of females making love to each other was totally gross. If I thought about it, so was the idea of two males. I tried not to envision the actuality of it and chose to ignore the aspects when it came to my gay friends. I had no contact with gay women except at the Ad Agency and that had been a disaster!

My very dearest female friend of many years was often in the company of both gay males and females. She was always defending them. She was a very compassionate person, whereas at that time, I was still a bit pious. I tried to be open to reason. Her arguments in defense and my fondness for my actor friend forced me to try to open my mind to understand their life situations. More important to me, my actor friend had always been there when I needed a friend but my lover friends were nowhere to be found. They were too busy seeking other conquests, no doubt. Once I had attended a cocktail party with my actor friend and had enough to drink to speak my mind. All conversations between us prior to that evening had been on a very superficial level, never mentioning the gay group. That evening I told him I was aware that most of his friends were gay. Obviously when two people dated, as many years as we had without the guy even making a pass at the woman, something was wrong. Even though I might not understand his choice in life, after all, it was his life. Certainly I had no right to judge. By the same token, his friendship through the years was one I valued most highly. From his honest-type conversation, I felt just as a young innocent female could be led astray under strong masculine influence, so had my friend in his naïve youth. He joined the Navy toward the end of World War II with little knowledge of the outside world. He had lived in a small remote town. In those days it was not unusual for a young man to still be a virgin. In the service, he found friends who shared his theatrical interests - unfortunately they were gay. One thing led to another, years hurried by. He just simply did not know what to do with a woman to direct a relationship toward intimacy. He was a super sensitive individual, loaded with talent in many areas with equal ambitions. He had reached a certain status of a "star" or a well-known personality. At that point in his life, a woman's rejection or making fun of him would have been an embarrassment he could not face. His sexual drive seem directly concentrated toward his career. He seemed more "A" sexual than homosexual. When you look at a man like this approaching 40, you know too much time has passed for him to change. If you love the man for the goodness and kindness he had expressed toward you and a friendship spanning years where permanency is so rare, you just have to accept him as he is. There were times when I thought if he ever wanted to marry me and if I felt I could live my life without sex, it might be a choice I would make.

At social gathering among his friends, most of the guys had dates with attractive women. Their conversations were always stimulating, interesting, creative, challenging and intellectual. Most of the females were like me, relishing an opportunity to attend an interesting social gathering without drugs. Void of men falling all over you with their insidious passes. You rarely or never saw anyone really drunk at one of the gay parties. My friends from the gay community were never the stereotype but were accepted by the general public as "normal" men. All were in film related professions and were productive, creative ambitious people. Some were bisexual and even married to females. Often one of the gay guys would marry the young, innocent girl because he wanted children. If their sexual relationships were not all that she expected, in her innocence she probably blamed herself, totally unaware her husband made love to men. It was a sad thing to see but there were sadder sights at social gathering amongst my normal "peers!" The "normal" gatherings were like entering a mad, insane jungle! When really bored with the lack of a social life, one of my girlfriends and I would venture out to attend one of their parties. Everyone there was hoping to meet someone new and their parties were generally so crowded with smoke-filled dark rooms, it was difficult to identify someone you did or did not know. The game was to get the "broads" loaded as quickly as possible and then try to get "laid!" When a woman did try to engage in interesting conversation, she would easily sense the guy was not listening but tolerating the conversation with one goal in mind. If not you, he would give up and go to the next. My girlfriend and I would get so disgusted and would leave early when the drunks outnumbered the sober ones, swearing never to attend another. It was very depressing to be 100% straight and enjoy the company of the gay socials while bored and disgusted with the superficial activities of the so-called "normal" guys.

After several years of friendship, the realization that my very best girlfriend was apparently bisexual was extremely upsetting and depressing. Through the years I had begun to look at all my friends and associates and did not know who was gay or straight! When the heterosexual person has to question her own desires and wonder if she is "normal" to be heterosexual, in these questionable surroundings, maybe it was time to move on to greener pastures - but where?

When I arrived in Hollywood many years before, I knew of a so-called casting couch routine. That meant a male pursuing a female, but now the pursuit seemed to be about 75% men chasing men and women chasing women. I definitely did not fit the Hollywood scene anymore and maybe never did. Many times a well-meaning advisor in the film world had told me, "Go back to Texas, Annie, you are not cut out for this place! You will never achieve your goals!"

At that time, I knew nothing about homosexuality. I had heard of art students called "queers" who lived in Greenwich Village in New York City and I had seen women dress like men. As far as any actual physical contact and lovemaking, I could never even vaguely imagine it. I heard words used in joke telling, which I did not understand and was too embarrassed to ask their meaning. I laughed at jokes but never understood them. I thought the word "fag" meant a cigarette butt. In my ignorance of human nature, my piety offered only rejection and condemnation. However, life forced me to take a good long look at the many facets of human desires. I even questioned my own inner desires. Why did I often find friends in the gay community? Was there anything in my inner makeup that was rejecting gays because of my conditioning? I tried very hard to face up to anything within myself that I might be rejecting - the more I brought any attempt to imagine myself in a lovemaking situation with another female, the more repulsed I got! Even as appalling as many heterosexual men might be, they were my only choice! Even though I liked many of my gay men friends, no matter how hard I tried to understand their feelings toward each other, it was just impossible for me in my younger years. Through the years, with this opportunity to understand my fellow human beings, I began being grateful. It was those experiences that seemed to test my reaction and my love for all people that had helped give me an inner wealth of character that can never be taken from me. With this realization and the realization that I no longer knew who was and who was not gay, it led to the decision to leave my longtime home of Hollywood, California. I loved it dearly but leaving seemed a necessity. Deep in my heart I knew one could never return happily to one's beginning, meaning Texas. I had tried several times to make a home for Debbie and myself in Texas. The knowledge and understanding I had gleaned divided me from the thinking, which had been conditioned in my youth and the people from that youth. Could I find a "home" for myself in Europe - would I just be another foreigner there? Europe seemed to be more adapted to the classical things such as art and music. I had the opinion that Europe wasn't as materially minded as the USA.

CHAPTER 10

I became discouraged in Hollywood of ever being able to communicate anything worthwhile through the film industry or of being associated with any film producer who really cared. After so many years of knocking on doors, working in production to learn the trade, and butting my head against the wall, it seemed a good time to leave again!

Most of the few European friends who I knew in Hollywood had returned to Europe due to being disenchanted with Americans' lust and greed, as well as their lack of aesthetic values. Perhaps Europeans did have a different set of values in which I would be more in tune. If not, I could always return and live in my parents' home in Texas. For years their hope had been that Debbie and I would settle down and live in their home, making the large upstairs our private apartment. I always felt a certain amount of guilt for taking Debbie away from my family in Texas.

Debbie and I had toyed with the idea of living in a recreation vehicle and traveling all over the United States. This had been my father's dream for our family that was never fulfilled. If one is born with wanderlust, it can never be laid to rest for long. Mine certainly began at an earlier age than anyone I knew since my family had moved about every three years. If my journey to Europe was unsuccessful, I would consider living part-time with my parents and possibly opening a small gift shop for a livelihood. If my money held out, I could buy a small recreation vehicle and travel during the hot Texas summer months. With the prospect of living in Europe I felt full of hope for a new beginning because as a mother my life had always been dictated by what would be best for Debbie. Although my hopes were enormous, I still had an alternate plan to fall back on in Texas.

The promoter, a con man named Jude, whom I'd known for years, was probably the ugliest, most pathetic man I had ever met, so it was easy to feel sorry for him. Later, I was to realize how he existed on people's pity to the point of being a parasite. He convinced me he had a friend in London in the film industry whom he would contact and ask to help me. With never any money of his own, I could not understand how he managed to know so many famous and wealthy people from all over the world. Jude found people with money, who for tax purposes, were interested in backing a show business venture. He would then introduce such promoters to well-known personalities. There was always some rich little man from Podunk who longed to touch the glamorous world of Hollywood and could afford to gamble with his fortune -- such a person became easy prey for Jude.

When he learned of my plan, he was delighted to tell me of his very best friend in London who was preparing a low-budget picture. Jude had been looking for a person with my diversified knowledge of the film business who would be a great asset to his friend. I knew London salaries were notoriously low and living expenses notoriously high. I also knew they did not allow Americans to work for English productions; however, with connections, perhaps one might get around those obstacles. This could be the opportunity to get my foot in the door of the English film business if the potential job was on the level. Little did I realize Jude had set me up. I was too naïve or stupid to even believe Jude was using me as a target for one of his con jobs. After all, I had no money as did most of his other associates.

At work I was still putting in every hour of overtime allowed to me. As my bank account grew fatter, I became more miserly even seeking less expensive lunches and taking advantage of any free lunches offered to me. I still had almost a month before I could leave my job. My employer had made me a promise to stay through the end of May. One day Jude called and insisted on coming downtown to have coffee with me in order to read me a letter he just received from the London producer in answer to his letter regarding me. Since it was written in Hungarian, he had to translate it, which would be easier in person rather than on the phone. According to the letter's translation, Al, the producer, was most impressed with my resume that Jude sent to him along with his recommendation. He felt sure he could get me a job on his production or something else in London.

After discussing all this good news, then came the pitch! For his mother's sake, Jude was desperately in need of $300. "Just until Friday, only five days!" as he held up his stubby five fingers in reassurance of the short-term loan. My heart sank! I had put in so many hours of overtime to start my small savings. He had me, and I knew it! If the job in London was legitimate, it could well be worth $300 for the contact. I did not trust him but since I knew so many people who knew him well, I could not believe he would try and pull one of his con jobs on me. With conviction, friends we both knew would help me get my money back if he failed to repay the debt as promised. If I refused him in his "desperation," I could kiss the London opportunity goodbye. It was a big gamble and he knew I had to take it!

My intuition told me I would never see the money again, and I begrudgingly withdrew the $300 from my savings account. If Jude would get out and do physical labor as I had done to earn my savings, he would not have to borrow it from me. It galled me for a man to borrow money from a woman anyway. I tried not to resent it, reminding myself I did not want to be possessed by material things. Later, Jude insisted on helping me sell my car when a Hungarian called to see it. Jude would act as translator. The man was $50 short of my bottom price, but that was no problem according to Jude. He would give the $50 to Jude when he got his next paycheck. Jude trusted the man so much that he promised to pay me the $50 out of his own pocket if the man did not pay. Needless to say I never saw that $50. Much later someone quoted to me -- "If you have a Hungarian for friend, you don't need an enemy!" Both Jude and Al were Hungarians! I learned the hard way!

Correspondence began between Al and me. The job appeared to be on the level and promising, although we didn't discuss the salary. Since I had no idea of what the living expenses in London would be, it seemed pointless to discuss money until I got there and could see for myself what the situation might be. I was not concerned with money as much as an opportunity. Al invited me to be his houseguest in his two-story downtown London apartment until I was acclimated to the city of London. I envisioned a luxury apartment large enough for houseguests and probably a live-in maid. After all, a man of Al's success living alone would surely have a full-time servant. It was probably Jude's description of Al's living accommodations that conjured up these impressions. Although I could not remember him, I did recall having met Al many years before in Hollywood when he was married to a famous European actress. Regardless of Jude's reassurance, men and their motives, I knew well not to trust. I wanted to be absolutely clear, that in no way, would I be put in the situation to be sexually obligated to anyone. Having spent six months in Europe in the early 60's, working in the film "Cleopatra," I knew full well sexual obligations were expected from most all women in Europe, not only in the film industry, but even secretaries. Fortunately for me, I had worked for an American production company, so that there was no possible misunderstanding. I stated this attitude in the letter to Al. If that would blow the deal, it was better to know it up front. His answer came back almost shocked that I could think such nasty thoughts of this poor innocent man who was too old for such pursuits, or so he said!!

I kept my expenses to bare necessities in order to save every penny I could. I began advertising in the newspaper to sell my furnishings. Money was extremely tight, and it was not a time to sell antiques. Dealers came literally trying to steal the best pieces for little or nothing and taking full advantage of my need to sell. I refused their insulting offers at first, but finally, as time ran out I had to accept any meager amount that they would pay.

Little by little my apartment emptied. I could not believe how much I had collected in just a couple of years. I gave away, threw away and ship things to Texas. There seemed to be no finality and when I was ready to move out of the apartment, I opened the hall closet to find it jammed full of clothes. At that point, I just could not face packing another box. I called a girlfriend and told her I was leaving the apartment, and if she wanted any of the clothes, to come and pick them up. Later, I found out she never bothered. When I realized it, I regretted not calling a consignment shop as I might have picked up a few dollars. I wanted to help her since her clothing was so limited. I stored several boxes in her basement so that if Debbie or I returned to California, we would have a starter set of household items. I gave her boxes of household items and clothing as well as sold her a valuable chair for only $60. Needless I say - I never saw the $60. On top of that, later she left California taking with her all of my stored household items. She was never be seen or heard from again. I had really established a "wonderful friendship" in Los Angeles!

The actual GOOD friends that I did have, with whom Debbie and I spent many holidays, insisted I spend the last few weeks in their guest bedroom. It saved a month's rent on an empty apartment. Even though I tried to buy my groceries and some of theirs, they insisted I save my money for Europe. We had both lived in Rome at the same time when I had been working in "Cleopatra." They were delighted that I was going to return to Europe so unencumbered. The wife had been one of my best friends for many years. I knew her during her first marriage, which shockingly ended in a divorce because she realized her husband was gay. Through the years, I had observed that more and more of their friends seemed questionable as to their sexual interest even though some were married couples. Once, while my friend and I were discussing birth control pills, she rather disgustingly confessed she had no need of them. That was all she ever said. Our friendship had been based on rather superficial conversations. She was not the type to open up to confess as some women do. What disheartened me even more was the realization she was keeping company with a well-known hardcore lesbian. Could the shock of losing two husbands to homosexuality have driven her to into the element of another Hollywood lifestyle?

During my stay in their home, one evening we had a Bon Voyage party for one of their friends leaving for Europe. Truthfully, I thought it was a surprise Bon Voyage party for me also, but it turned out with only a casual mention that I, too, would soon be leaving for Europe. One actor, whose face was well identified on very masculine TV commercials, took over the entertainment. He was very funny but his humor involved homosexuality. Why would this guy if he was straight, joke so frequently about gays? Among the male actors and men in the film world whom I knew to be heterosexual they did not show any sympathy nor humor toward the gay or bisexual communities. As I looked up around the room, I felt a little sick in the pit of my stomach, not really knowing who was and who was not!

With great concern to be fair to my employer, I located a replacement for my job. She was far better suited for the job than I was. After the salesman approved of her, I completely trained her so that when I left, not only was the office completely caught up and running smoothly, but she could also take over without him even being aware of any changes being made except for physical appearances. I did everything I could to leave on a friendly basis. When I was slaving seven days a week, my boss had been friendly and humorous, but now that he realized I was leaving, he was sullen, indifferent, and totally unappreciative for the now efficient operation of his once bedlam office. He showed absolutely no appreciation for my efforts in locating a really good replacement and training her so that he would have no interruption of business when the change took place. Finally, my last day arrived at work. I worked and left. That night I caught a plane flight to Texas. There had been no celebration, no Bon Voyage party, no last-minute well-wishers' phone calls, hardly any good wishes and all! HOORAY for Hollywood in the many years of established "FRIENDSHIPS."

I would like to note that this was an era when gay men or women were almost totally unacceptable to the general public. It was a time when gay men had to "stay in the closet" as they were described in those days. That was why they usually took females on dates to parties, openings, and most public affairs. They were often terribly abused physically and were shunned. My understanding and compassion grew through the years, accepting all with no judgments. We are all on a learning path; they have theirs, and I have mine.

This was the time of the advent of "THE PILL"; prior to that, there was limited adequate protection against pregnancy. If pregnancy did occur, the two people usually had to get married, (as was my case); otherwise, if an unwed woman gave birth, it was usually referred to as a "bastard" child. It was a very difficult time for women. They had NO sexual freedom as men had. Abortions were illegal, and so many women had to give their child away which caused a lifetime of guilt. In the case of "date rape," if a woman tried to report it to the police, they would have been laughed out of their offices! With "THE PILL," women began to experience the pleasures of their sexuality. Little by little, women experienced single life that included sexual affairs. This also gave them far more freedom in attempting to select a lifelong mate, experiencing how different sex could be with various men. Finally, they could find and experience the beauty of a deep, loving sexual encounter, even as a greater spiritual awareness.

Having always lived in small Texas towns, I knew nothing about homosexuality or that it even existed. After being in the fashion world, then acting and also into interior designing, I was forced to really take a look at gay men. Most were great friends and fun to be around. My most enjoyable social events were usually with gay friends. I could open up freely with them, whereas with other men, I seemed always to have to put up a guard and could not be free to be ME! Thus, through the years I worked hard to eliminate any tinge of prejudice I might have had totally through ignorance. However, I see it STILL exists within so many communities even today. Politics is so distorted with these same prejudices against gay people.

I knew nothing about sex in general, and when I had to get married, I really hated sex! It was only with my second husband that I realized the joy and excitement it could bring…later to grow spiritually with experiencing the very "highs" of sexual unity. My darling husband was a would-be actor striving for jobs and working full time. He was accepted by a notorious GAY agent and then began HIS working on any and everything he could find to be successful. (It did not happen!) Considering our exceptionally great sexual life, I could never imagine that he would participate in gay sexual encounters. Just like the young girls I had seen married to gay men only for reproductive purposes, I too, had a bisexual mate! It is sad, too, after three husbands, he was the BEST in all ways!

CHAPTER 11

Stepping off the plane in Dallas, Texas, into the hot, humid summer day, there was no way could I ever imagine this would be the prelude for the darkest chapter in my life. Since we would be in Dallas at the same time, a friend who dated a girl I knew in Los Angeles was on the business trip and asked me to have dinner with him. He met my flight, as did Debbie along with her new boyfriend, Rob. We agreed to have dinner together. At the restaurant we had to wait for our table in the bar. Although I had offered Debbie drinks at home, especially wine with dinner, this was the first experience of seeing her order a drink in a bar, which did disturb me a bit. Most of us take advantage of the coming of "legal age"; nevertheless, it is usually difficult for most mothers to see or know that her "baby" is participating in normally adult activities regardless of how open-minded she may try to be. Debbie was quite poised, took only a few sips of her drink, leaving more than half of it in the glass. Her act seemed quite normal, but to me she was like a little girl playing in a grown-up dress and high heel shoes.

Knowing she thought she was fond of Rob, I wanted to keep an open mind and friendly attitude toward him even though I immediately felt very bad vibrations. Was my psychic intuition trying to warn me? If so, I dismissed it in a typical mother reaction to "NO" boy is good enough for my child. Rob took Debbie and me to her apartment and bid us good night. It was our first opportunity to really talk to each other. Naturally, one of her first questions was my opinion of Rob. I tried to say a few nice things to please her but in my typical Taurus manner, I ended up telling her I felt she deserved much more in a young man than I could see in him. Furthermore, at her age she should be enjoying a variety of young men.

Looking back today is very difficult to put events that month into chronological order. At the same time there was no reason to believe it was any special time that I would later try to recall. I was simply visiting home and family prior to departing for Europe and not knowing how long I might be gone. Debbie borrowed Rob's car to drive me 30 miles from Dallas to my parents' home. Mid-week, Sharon, my niece, her younger brother, Keith, and I drove over to spend the night with Debbie. Debbie and Sharon had been about as close as any two sisters. Keith was closer to the girls then the two older nephews.

In the back of my mind I was hoping my life in Europe would work out so well that I would not be back in December to celebrate my parents' 50th wedding anniversary. With that in the back of my mind, I wanted to put forth as much effort as possible redecorating their home for the occasion. Hardly one of the 13 rooms did not need something done to it. For such a worthwhile cause, I felt sure other family members would chip in and help. Their intentions were good - their actions were NOT! They would start painting, suddenly remember a very special appointment, and off they would go, leaving me to swing the paintbrush hour after hour alone.

Deb was anxious for me to meet her and her many new found friends. A group from her apartment complex planned a weekend trip to a nearby lake. Debbie insisted I go with them. I insisted I would be totally out of place with young couples. All ages were going, all were not paired off, and she invited a cousin of ours who recently returned from Vietnam so there would also be family. My other excuse was that I just was not good at roughing it in a sleeping bag on the ground as they had planned. For this problem, she also had an answer. One couple had a cabin cruiser that she would arrange for me to sleep aboard. She was so insistent that I could not disappoint her.

Driving to the lake, the conversation was friendly and fun, but underneath it all, the more I saw and heard Rob, the more I disliked him more so than anyone Debbie had ever dated. It was a beautiful warm sunny day. As soon as we arrived at the lake, the girls rushed to don their bathing suits. Debbie had a new yellow bikini. Her well-formed body was generously exposed. Considering I, too, had worn a bikini for years, I could hardly tell her not to wear them. The years had given me quite a different attitude -- there are bikinis and there are bikinis! She filled hers out so well that a man would have to be dead not to want to start grabbing. I just shook my head and warned Debbie, "In that suit you are asking for trouble!" Was my exclamation another psychic warning that I failed to heed? I knew Debbie's attitude was too trusting and naïve, just as mine had been at her age. As usual she ignored my warning. After all, no matter how youngish I may have been, I was still a parent and all parents are "old-fashioned" to their own children.

Everyone boarded the boats for the trip across the lake to the lovely remote sand island. Most everyone had planned to water ski but found the water was a bit chilly. It was a very long day for me even though I had brought books to read. About the time everyone decided to eat, a terrible windstorm came up quite suddenly. There was a deluge of lightning but only slight rain showers. There were no shelters on the island. The water had become far too rough to take the boats back to the mainland. The people with the cabin cruiser did not show up. With this, when the sun sank, the wind was bitter cold. No one came prepared with long johns and ski jackets as were needed! The bonfire was built with such intense heat you could not get near it. While on one side you roasted, on the other side you froze.

The evening hours dragged by endlessly. Debbie got a fishhook caught in her thigh that was in the sand. They had to cut away the leg of her blue jeans to remove it. She hardly flinched but I was worried about infection. Not one person failed to bring their beer, but not one remembered to bring a first aid kit. The sleeping bags and blankets were spread in one mass palette for warmth. That was how we were to sleep. I lay there on my thin blanket, gazing at the stars and I could feel the cold wet sand oozing through it. In a short time, every part of me ached from lying on the cement-like wet sand. I don't think I ever spent a more miserable night in my whole life! At best, I could not have slept more than two hours the whole night - the longest night in my life. To top it off, while Debbie slept on one side of me Rob was on the other side of her. Innocent or not, it was still "asleep together." I would gladly have paid $50 for a short ride to the mainland but the water remained too rough all night for small boats. When morning finally greeted us, everyone was tired and ready to depart this small remote Island. My cousin had cleverly slept in the hull of one of the boats out of the dampness and wind.

Debbie wanted me to stay with her at the apartment while she worked. She thought I could socialize at the pool. I had quite enough socializing with her friends. Perhaps I was blinded to her needs by thoughts of my plans for all the painting and work needing to be done at my parents' house. I suggested she try to get down to their house on weekends and as many evenings as she could, so that we could spend time together. I just had much too much to do to sit around her apartment alone all day long. Her friends were acceptable as young adults go. I understood their need for socializing. At their age I felt the same way. Some traits of Rob seemed all right. I did not know if I was misjudging him, but I had a terrible resentful feeling toward him and really did not wish to be around him. Should I have given greater credence to those strong feelings of dislike for him?

As soon as I finished painting one room, the new paint made the next room look gray and dank, so it had to be done also. There seem to be no end. I spent far too much time behind my paint brush, concerned with the needs of my parents' home and far too little time realizing Debbie may have needed me emotionally more than I could understand. Looking back, at the time I assumed she really had made adjustments to being on her own and seemed to be enjoying her new found adult life. Sure, she made mistakes, but hopefully I had instilled enough wisdom in her to meet life's trials and tribulations. Maybe I could not comprehend her needs because selfishly I was looking forward to getting a fresh new start myself. I wanted to see life working out well for her and that's what I saw! I was tired! I was totally discouraged with none of my goals working out well for me. As unmotherly as it may sound, in some ways I felt like a prisoner who had just been released after serving nearly a 20-year sentence.

Through the years I had often recalled at Debbie's birth the quick flash of frightening thought that I would have to raise this child alone. I shared that fear with no one, but it had all come to pass. Coming out from under the anesthesia, I made several seemingly silly statements that amused my family but later turned out to be psychic predictions. Motherhood was thrust upon me long before I was ready for it. Youth today would hardly understand that in my youth sex, pregnancy and related subjects were so totally hush-hush, that I as well as thousands of other women felt completely alone and in the dark having no one to whom we could turn. "Ignorance is not bliss!" Pregnancy was definitely not an enjoyable experience as some mothers claim. For the first six weeks I was sick most of the time and the rest of the time so often uncomfortable. I must admit when a female begins to feel that fluttering movement within her body, the realization that God's Universal law of creativity is at work within her is doubtlessly a joy and spiritual experience that is without description and yet all the while, the constant fear of death plagued my inner thoughts. Although pregnancy seemed to last forever, suddenly that fearful day arrived when the labor pains began. There was no backing out! Those last few months had been filled with overpowering fears, knowing there was no way out of facing the experience of childbirth. There was a life inside my body growing day by day that sooner or later had to come out! I knew my fears of not surviving childbirth were quite normal especially among firstborn mothers, but it did not make it any easier. Fortunately, today a mother-to-be and her husband can join a prenatal group that seems to be quite successful in removing most fears other generations of pregnant women experienced. What seems to be "fears" is generally ignorance of the unknown. I never had a serious illness, bad cuts, broken bone, and rarely ever visited anyone in a hospital. I knew nothing of a hospital, medications, or anesthesia. No alcohol beverage had ever touched my lips. The thought of subjecting myself to anesthesia or drugs was terrifying. I feared what I might say or do without conscious control of my mind.

    I remember being taken through two large swinging doors in the delivery room at the hospital. That was the last I was to see any familiar face except my doctor's until afterwards. After the usual preparations, I was assigned to a bed in the labor room of four beds, but I was the only occupant. This was a time I really did not want to be alone; any stranger would be welcome. I was trying to be very brave, cool headed, and adult, but I was scared to death.

    My labor pains were growing intolerable. At last, my doctor arrived. I was so happy to see him but not for long. A few seconds after he arrived, he broke my water which then seemed to create one continuous labor pain. He and the nurses departed leaving me totally alone. I kept expecting the breathing space between the contractions but there was no break in the continuous pain. A nurse wandered by just as I was about to throw up. I begged her to give me something to ease the pain a bit. She gave me a shot in the hip but the pain was just as bad. The shot seemed to make me sleepy or I just was getting worn out from the night's ordeal. At that point I did not care if I lived or died. Death felt so near. I don't care how natural everyone told me it would be; it was a grossly, horrible experience with no joy or wonderful feeling. Exhausted from the constant pain I turned on one side and pulled my knees up that ease the pain slightly. I felt I could take a few breaths in this position.

I must have dozed off, for the next thing I knew the nurse was shaking me and telling me angrily to turn on my back as the doctor had told me because I had stopped my labor by turning on my side. I felt terribly guilty that I might have harmed the baby. Apparently she was wrong because suddenly there was a flurry of activity. They were pushing and pulling at me. In the delivery room I remember raising up on my elbows and seeing my reflection in a large lit circular mirror and thinking what a mess my hair was. With a sharp burning pain I wondered why the doctor had stuck a torch to me! Finally I saw a small nose-mask coming down on my face and thought, "At last, sleep!" I took such a deep breath the nurse cautioned me to take it easy. Now I thought there would be hours of sweet slumber but alas "no rest for the weary." The next thing I knew they were pushing me down a hall and into an elevator, then pushing me onto a bed -- Debbie's father's face was a few inches above mine, saying, "We have a little girl!" Just as though the stork had descended from heaven and dropped her there! I thought but didn't say, "You stupid ass, don't you think I know after what I've been through!" There seemed to be endless family eyes staring at me. If they had taken the time to drive to see me, the least I could do was to talk to them, but all I wanted to do was just sleep for a while. Everyone stood around the room smiling, and I knew I was supposed to be happy and excited with this miracle of birth, but all I felt was exhausted. The next three days in the hospital felt more like three weeks.

In the beginning I had hoped for a boy, but my in-laws had taken it upon themselves to decide if it was a boy, he would be named "Jack," my husband's stepfather's name and a name I disliked. I was happy it turned out to be a girl. At the time, in the silver screen actresses were endowed with the names of Debbie, Debra and Deborah. Thus many girls Debbie's age ended up with one of those names. The name

Deborah was biblical and Dianne was classic. With those two names she could shorten her name in many ways and pick the one she preferred later. She always liked Debbie and by high school, she insisted she had the right to use my maiden name as I myself had done for years. Having spent so much time with my parents, their surnames seemed more suitable for her. Her father in Texas had expressed little concern with her upbringing in general.

Before I ever saw Debbie at the hospital, doctors and nurses kept telling me what a beautiful daughter I had. All the babies in my family were beautiful. When I finally saw her, I thought, "That's not my child--it is a miniature of my mother-in-law!" I assumed the intimacy of nursing a baby brings instant motherly love, but my doctor encouraged bottle-feeding from the beginning. I felt I should feel more love, but I did not feel much of anything. Debbie was a small stranger, not a toy doll from my childhood years but a frightening living being that cried and whose diapers had to be changed. It was only after we were home alone together that love began to blossom. It was like having a real live doll and how I love my dolls! Debbie was such a good healthy baby, and each day seemed filled with new growth and development.

That love seemed to have a slow beginning then grew through the years with the closeness of just the two of us together. By the time she was in high school, I felt so much love and attachment for Debbie I thought I could not face life if anything ever happened to her. If it did I thought I surely would die. I had no premonition no ominous fears; quite the contrary, I felt so sure of Debbie's future. Since she was a small child and loved smaller children, I felt she would marry happily and have her own children to love. I did not see her in any sort of career endeavor nor a divorce but a normal happy life.

Whatever good feelings I had for Debbie's future certainly did not include Rob. He was much too possessive and jealous to cope with Debbie's flippant attitude. There was something about him I could not put my finger on but I felt fearful for her. I was not terribly concerned as I felt her interest in him dwindling during my month in Texas. She seemed to pay little attention to my advice, but alas, as a mother bird must watch her fledgling spread its wings and attempt to fly, so I must have faith that Debbie would make her choices wisely. She would have regrets as we all do, but hopefully she would have realization of learning from the mistakes and try to use them as to an advantage. All I could see was that she intended "doing her own thing in her own way." In no way did I sense that she might need me more then, than when she was a helpless baby.

Debbie had won another trophy in a beauty contest and was chosen to represent her area in the Ms. Dallas contest. She had many friends and was thoroughly enraptured in her young, adult apartment dweller life. There were parties every week. I attended one. Debbie and I looked enough alike to pass as sisters. No one would believe that I was her mother. I may have blended with the group but I was with a mass of boring beer-drinking kids attempting to have fun. Debbie always behaved in a lady-like manner that made me proud. I felt the social involvement was quite normal for her age. She drank modestly. I was not concerned with her getting drunk. She did not smoke nor was she interested in using any kind of drugs.

I was preoccupied with redecorating of the house plus a letter from Al in London gave me a writing project on which to concentrate. His letter assured me he would meet my plane, and he would not hear of me staying anywhere except as his houseguest. It definitely sounded as though I would have a job with his new production. Upon my arrival in London, he personally would hand me the $300. American money to repay his good friend's debt. Now Jude was off the hook to repay the loan before I left the United States.

When I was with Debbie, she chatted about so many people I hardly listened. Later, I would strain my memory wishing I could remember more about each one. Growing up without fatherly guidance, she always sought friendships with older men who seemed to give her a fatherly presence. Again, she told me of her very nice friend who "used to be in the Mafia," and again I warned her it matters not how nice a man may seem to be; she was treading in dangerous waters!

Never, never in my foggiest dream could I envision I might never see my beautiful young healthy, on the brink of beautiful womanhood daughter again. I looked back with deep regret for not having taken advantage of those last moments--those precious moments that would be gone forever. My mind draws a complete blank when I try to remember my last sight of Debbie on that visit. I can't remember what she said, what she wore or even her being at the airport to see me off!

To fly to London from Dallas via Los Angeles seemed a bit backward, but my charter flight from Los Angeles, which would have only one stop in Bangor, Maine for refueling. At long last, the day arrived for my flight, my "dear" friend, Jude, who had arranged everything in London, met my flight from Dallas. I had a few hours layover until the flight to London left. I don't recall those hours of where we ate in a restaurant near the small terminal or where the chartered flight group gathered. Jude was, at best, merely an acquaintance and one whom I did not sincerely trust. None of my long-time friends came to see me off on my most important venture. The terminal was a congested muddle. Passengers were herded like cattle through alphabetical lines. It was lonely seeing other passengers' emotional farewells; I just wanted to get on board the plane. Finally, I was seated aboard tightly packed seats of the stretched jet. "What am I doing here?" "Why am I going to Europe alone?" I had traveled through Europe alone before and sworn never to travel alone again. I had enjoyed and felt peaceful while staying at home with my family and Debbie. The charter flight company would not refund my $150. "Was that my only reason for going or was fate pushing me toward a better life?" That hope began turning to fears of traveling alone so far from everyone and everything I knew. The flight was airborne there was no turning back now.

CHAPTER 12

The stretched jet did not seem very stretched after a cross-country flight from Los Angeles to Bangor, Maine. To accommodate as many passengers as possible for the special charter flights, more seats than a usual commercial airliner were added. After the lengthy refueling, back on board, next stop, London, England!

All I remember about the flight was that it was terribly long. My knit pants suit never quite lost the shape of my backside after the trip. "Why was I going halfway around the world?" was the question I kept asking myself. I remembered how I hated traveling alone; yet, I really wanted the solitude for writing that had always been impossible for me. "Time" was the magic word that could be an answer to my prayers. I was leaving behind the confusion and frustration of making a living, struggling against the impossible odds of a Hollywood career, as well as a social life. Such an atmosphere created chaotic conditioning for the creative freedom required for writing. There was just never the time I needed. As long as I was around family or friends, I was constantly diverted away from writing to do something with or for someone else. Self-discipline was not a trait I could claim. In Europe I would be away from the everyday hustle and bustle, from everything and everyone I knew. Those were living conditions I thought would inspire my writing. Now this special time was at hand!

Lifelong circumstances that made me into a loner now helped me to realize there was limitless learning to be done, most of which must be done alone. I felt terribly lonely as the jet circled for a landing. A strange man was to meet my flight in a strange land. I had agreed to be his houseguest, but for all I knew, he could be some kind of horrible maniac. Looking out the window, the countryside was beautiful with its imposing, tranquil old castle-like estates. It was like looking down upon a fascinating era long passed, if only for a few brief moments, because the next thing I realized was the jet airline was descending for the landing.

Passengers and their greeters came and went. I saw no one who resembled the man I had in my memory. Having met him in Hollywood long ago, I hoped I might recognize him. Finally a gray-haired, short, stocky stern-faced man approached me. I felt very awkward and uncomfortable riding into London with a strange little foreign man whose broken English was difficult to understand and the meanings even more difficult to decipher. I felt even more apprehensive upon entering his house. It certainly was a far cry from the palatial downtown London apartment my Los Angeles friend had described. There was no live-in housekeeper but there was a pungent odor of very unpleasant cheese that permeated every corner of the apartment. The odor was so overpowering it made me slightly ill. This strange little man escorted me up a narrow stairway to his bedroom where he said he was giving it up for me. I insisted that he allow me to use the guestroom as I would feel more comfortable than taking his bedroom. As he discussed experiences with his former female houseguest, I got the impression I was supposed to invite him to stay in his room with me! This ill-at-ease feeling was very irksome for I had clearly stated my feelings along those lines through our correspondence and felt he should have no misgivings. I was so tired that all I wanted to do was get a few hours of sleep. It seemed I had been up for days. For me, jet lag is very real; getting accustomed to changing day to night can be most difficult.

 I listen intensely as Al discussed his new project that was to be a horror movie. For promotions of the future production, he was sending out bottles of red wine with special labels on them. Pasting labels on wine bottles seemed like a strange, mundane job for "producer" of the film! I was anxious to go to the studio, but since it was Saturday that would have to wait until Monday. When I tried to discuss my work possibilities, Al became very invasive and negative, not at all like his letters or Jude's promises. Al was a weird little old man of Slavic descent. He lived on past glory of bygone days. It seemed his main claim to fame was having once been married to a movie queen of yesteryears. I wondered how she could have lived with this pathetic little creature even in his younger days.

 Al had failed to meet the plane with the money for our mutual friend's debt he owed to me as he had promised to do in his letters.

Because of the weekend, he said he had not had time to get the money from the bank but would do so first thing Monday morning. It was a very long time until Monday morning. After a nap, I was anxious to see a bit of London but my host made no effort to offer to take me sightseeing, so I took a stroll around his neighborhood. It was England of 100 years ago. The one truth I found was that his apartment was conveniently located. It was in the shadows of one of the largest international hotels in the heart of London. That evening, our dinner was meager and the conversation that followed was very discouraging regarding my assumed job. Every question I asked was met with a negative answer.

Sunday morning my host was very grumpy complaining bitterly about his uncomfortable bed. He could not sleep and had stayed up most of the night. Since he did his work of pasting labels on wine bottles in his small guestroom, it would be impossible for me to sleep there because he sometimes got up in the middle of the night to work. I offered to sleep downstairs on the sofa so that he could have his bed and his work area and privacy, but he would not allow that either. I grew more ill at ease. That day seemed more like a week, but I was much too tired and confused to search London for a hotel room and I had no idea how to make plans with Al's total negativity. It seemed doubtful that he had any intentions of helping me find a job by putting me to work on his project. It also seemed questionable as to whether he really was a producer or more of a handyman. I was totally lost as to what to do.

Monday morning solved the question for me in a hurry! Again complaining about his sleep accommodations, he began insulting me. Since my arrival, I had tolerated his insulting insinuations because I was a houseguest. I was aware of the insecure male's putdowns as an attempt to elevate his own stature. I was tired and felt I had tolerated his put down attitude quite enough. Tempers clashed and I returned his venom. He told me to get out and I told him I had every intention of doing just that. As he went storming out to go to the studio, I asked about the money Jude owed me which he had promised to pay. He told me to contact Jude! It was not his affair! I was still too confused to see and realize the whole set-up which I had been subjected to by these Hungarian lifetime friends.

Since I came to Europe to stay indefinitely I had a large piece of luggage which was too heavy for me to lift so I left it behind while I searched for a hotel room. Unfortunately this was during the height of London's tourist season. I was to learn later that my luggage had been thrown out on the street in my absence. I set out to find a reasonably priced hotel which was quite a task in London. As I walked and walked for hours, I became more terrified. My very first plan had gone asunder. I started questioning myself. "What do I do now? Where do I go?" "Should I stay in London?" I was still tired and so confused I did not realize how far I had walked. Finally I found a room in the Earls Court section of London. The first room the hotel offered as a single was so small I could not get all of my luggage in it, so I had to take a double, which was 3 feet wider than a single. It was beyond my comprehension as to how it could be called a double. It had one small table, one wardrobe (not a build-in closet) and the shower had been installed right over the carpet. There was a lavatory, a window, and the entire room was painted stark white. At least it was clean. I wondered if prisoners in the United States had better accommodations for free. The bathroom was always at the far end of the hall. The room was on the third floor and there was no "lift" (elevator). With London packed with tourists, I was lucky to find any room at all without having made any reservations. The desk clerk showed me a map so I could return to Al's apartment and claim my luggage. I was overwhelmed at the distance I had walked in my angry daze. The only logical method of transportation for my luggage was a taxi so I did just that.

In that summer of 1970, I heard more American accents and saw more American clothing than the British. The bus and subway system were utterly confusing, mainly due to overcrowded conditions everywhere. It was one of London's busiest tourist seasons. Earls Court was too far from the center of London to walk. With my undying determination and having a map of the subway system, I set out to conquer the "underground tube" as it is called. Even with a map book constantly at hand and my keen sense of direction, I seemed always to be going in the opposite direction from where I wanted to go. My sense of direction did not function well underground. I would walk out of London's tube system to find myself far from my destination of the American Express office to check for mail from home. I would walk and walk and walk until I was ready to drop. After only a few days in London, I had done more walking than in the past two years altogether. My main concern was to get my mail and parcels that I had sent before leaving the United States, and then forwarded from this madman's house since I did not know what he might do with it all. The movie he planned to produce was to be a monster movie, but it appeared that he was the real monster!

For as bad as our Postal Service, telephone, and utility systems may seem to be for many Americans, they were very refined compared to Europe's. It was quite an ordeal to simply forward my mail. When traveling outside the United States, the American Express office becomes a refuge for most Americans. Some days I waited 30 minutes in line only to be told there was no mail. Each time I searched the entire American Express office hoping to find a familiar face from Los Angeles, but it was the college student knapsack season!

I finally became adjusted to the time change and knew I had to get some sort of plan going. I contacted a few people I knew in London, only to find that the film Industry was even slower than it had been when I lived in Rome in the early 60's when working in "Cleopatra." The few people I knew were from the days almost a decade past.

European film productions are very strict regarding hiring Americans. The only hope was to locate an American production currently filming in Europe. Since those were rather sparse, I began reverting to my original plan for coming to Europe to find an inexpensive lodging and get to work writing my book. After all, this was my real reason for being there - time and quietude for creativity.

As miserable and confused as I had been since my arrival, there was something about London I dearly loved. It seemed more difficult to get around London than it had been in Rome where everything is built in circles and piazzas like the hub of a wheel. Before I left London, I wanted to contact everyone who might be hospitable. An English couple I knew in California still had family in London. The young handsome brother came to take me to have dinner with him and his mother at their home. It was lovely to explore English home life. Afterwards he asked me what I most wanted to see in London. Since I could not go out alone at night, I took advantage of his masterful masculine companionship and told him I would really like to see a typical English Pub. He took me to a couple of pubs that were not quite as Hollywood betrayed them. I enjoyed the evening immensely since it was my first pleasure in London, except for the thrill of sightseeing and absorbing history. On another evening he took me out of London to an unbelievable picturesque pub near Henley-on-Thames, owned for generations by the same family and friends of his. The barn, hundreds of years old, had been converted into a nightclub. Next to it was a very old pub with its charm too much to describe. The 10 o'clock closing hour came much too soon for my most pleasant evening in England.

With the crowds and confusion, most of all the high cost of staying in London, which was as expensive as any American city, I knew I must depart London if my small savings account was to last for any length of time. I also knew it was extremely doubtful that I would ever see the money I had loaned Jude, cutting off about a month of my planned stay in Europe.

Henley-on-the-Thames was just the type of picturesque community I had envisioned with its neat, frilly private room in an old English cottage with a thatched roof. Upon discussing my plan, I was informed that Henley would be just as expensive as London. It was famous for the Henley Royal Regatta, sculling races that had been held there for over 100 years and just completed that week before I visited. Surely there would be another Henley type of community I could locate outside of London and I decided I would find it.

Buckingham Palace

White Cliffs of Dover

CHAPTER 13

If I wanted to find a quaint community I needed a car since I had no friend to help me with my search. By renting a car, I could explore the countryside to find my special dwelling place. An automobile would afford me the opportunity to get away from London's subway system and its hordes of tourists.

I knew exactly where to go and just how to get there; only I got the wrong train in the underground. Fortunately, I realized it by the first stop and quickly departed the train. Never mind I was used to making mistakes by now. I would simply get the correct one – only it never came five – 10 – 15 – 20 minutes went by. The platform was filled with people wondering why the train that usually came by every few minutes was so late. Obviously there was something wrong, so up the stairs, onto the street I went to wave down a taxi. I waved and waved and waved from several different streets finally, lost, lonely, confused and completely frustrated, I burst into tears right on the streets of London. If I had been 18 years old and this had been my first trip to Europe, my actions might have been justified. Feeling very foolish, I finally gained control enough to walk into the hotel and ask if they would be kind enough to telephone a taxi for me. "Take a bus -- take the tube -- we can't telephone for a taxi for you!" With a not so sincere "Thank You!" back onto the street I broke out into tears of frustration again.

Back down to the Tube was the only hope--again--no train! Finally in desperation, I took any train going anywhere on the next track. I had spent one-and-a-half hours just to go no more than a few blocks from my hotel. I got off at the Westminster stop. It was difficult to appreciate Big Ben, Parliament, Westminster Abbey and all the famous government buildings as I walked past them after the morning's confusion. The car rental office was nowhere near, but the American Express office was, and at that moment, a letter from home would certainly give me a much-needed lift. After standing in line at the noon hour, I was informed there would be no mail delivery until 3:00 pm. All I could think of was to get in the car and get out of the city of London before 3 pm!

If my senses would never master writing left-handed, how then would I manage an automobile and streets, opposite to my total driving experience? It had been years since I had attempted to drive a gearshift car without power steering or brakes. This car had four forward gears plus reverse. With a deep breath and much determination (as well as fear) I started the car. I felt like a bull rider on his first bull. The first half block was around the circle called Marble Arch where I sat for 30 minutes trying to go about two blocks. By now nothing else would get me down. Finally I reached the hotel. I felt quite successful mastering my very peculiar driving experience. Checking out of the hotel with my luggage loaded, I could not get the key of the ignition to work nor could several hotel employees. Just as I was ready to call Avis, I accidentally turned on the engine. At that point I did not care if there was a malfunction as long as it was running, I would not stop until I got safely out of the city of London. Then, I would worry what to do about the car if it would not start again.

It was terrifying driving on the wrong side of the street. One's whole equilibrium is thrown off-balance. Once out of the city area I was somewhat apprehensive for if I should have a car trouble or have to stop, there was no place to pull off of the street. The streets were just wide enough for two cars, coming and going, with a curb on each side and no place to pull off. Eventually the roadway seemed somewhat normal. I came upon a picturesque teahouse where a famous writer had lived and composed. Did I dare stop the engine? Sooner or later I had to face it. The dining spot was just as charming inside as it was outside. My tea time helped me relax after the total confusion in London. I had to get on my way, not knowing if the car would even start. After many attempts it finally started again. Much later, I discovered that by jiggling the key to a certain spot, and then quickly pulling the steering wheel out of the lock position the car started immediately. Within 24 hours I conquered the left-hand side of the street driving--with the exception of going over a few curbs at corners, highway signs, the "turnabout," the gear shifting and even a temperamental English automobile.

Getting out of London was certainly the right thing to do. I drove in and out of small towns with no particular destination. The beauty of the forest, the rolling hills, the quaint villages... just everything in sight was thrilling, and I began feeling very happy and at ease once more. Since I had rented the car with unlimited mileage, I just drove and drove until I ended up at the sea. It was Brighton-By-The-Sea. It was much like an American seaside resort community, filled with tourist. This was not what I was looking for, so I continued along the sea for a few miles. It was late afternoon, and I thought I should find a place to spend the night. Along the roadside, I saw a small hotel that looked like a nice, clean old home. I was the only guest when I registered. It was operated by a charming older couple who had a new color television at a time when color TVs were not that common.

The only good place to eat, I was told, was at an Old Inn in Rottingdean, a nearby community. When I saw the charming Old Inn, I was sorry I had not found it first. During dinner, at a nearby table, was an American explaining to his English host his problem of driving on the left side of the street. It seemed he, too, had problems hitting curbs on corners. I was amused since I had shared the same problem. After dinner, I sat in the lovely rose garden alone, sipping a glass of wine. I read until well after 9 pm since it was still daylight and no one was sitting in the garden except me. Even though I kept telling myself I wanted to be alone, this evening had been so lovely in a romantic English countryside, that it was very lonely.

When I returned to the small hotel the owners were engrossed in their new television. British radio and television program fascinated me since this had been my field of endeavor for so many years. There were no commercials. The government owned it and at certain times you could listen or watch an educational program as there was nothing else offered. I thought it was a good idea to feed the masses a bit of wisdom since when left to their choice on American television, we seemed to become gluttonous for the gory not very evolved from the Roman days of gladiators, lions, and Christians' mastication.

An early start was needed the next morning if I was to find a place to stay outside of London. I would need to unload my luggage, return the car to the rental agency in London and take the train back to wherever I would find to stay. I did not know which direction to go. I hoped inner instincts would direct my path. I was influenced by the fact that an English actor friend from Hollywood was in Europe and expected in London any day to visit his mother who lived south of London. Since there were no freeway systems in London, I wanted to be somewhere in the area hoping that through David, there would be people I could meet and have some social life or business contacts.

Driving back to London, I found an inexpensive room in a guesthouse in Dorking, 45 minutes by train from London. It was within walking distance to the station. The rental cost $14.50 per week, a bargain price anywhere; however, with a lifetime of movie makers' illusion plus the creativity of my own imagination, these "quaint" spots can never match our expectations. If one was willing to accept similar living conditions in the USA, probably the same price and bilious decor could easily be found. For years I had not only redecorated each of my apartments but had worked as an Interior Decorator to supplement my unpredictable acting career income. With my keen sense of color, design and coordination, to look around the room stretched my imagination enormously to keep in mind "quaint" England!

There were five different types of wallpaper designs, flowered curtains, and another floral design on the chair, a striped bedspread and at least seven different carpet scraps with a different design. The fireplace had been blocked out for an electric heater that had stones of glowing plastic. It was necessary to put in a shilling ($0.12) for measured time of electricity. For a bath, which of course, was located at the far end of the hall, I had to make reservations one hour in advance and pay an extra 30 cents. At least I had inexpensive ways to stay with a clean bed and heat provided I would keep the Schillings around.

Outside of the house was a striking contrast to the ugliness inside. The house was adjacent to a lovely park. Just down the hill, within easy walking distance, there was a pay phone, the railway station, restaurants, shops, and even a coin operated laundry. The window of my room overlooked the community of Dorking, located in the Box Hills of Surrey, South of London. All I could see in the background of Dorking were soft rolling very green hills. There were no advertising signs to be seen anywhere, only two-story red brick houses with sharply slanted roofs, chimneys, white windowsills, and always there was a small rose garden at each and every house. The houses carried no street numbers. The mail was delivered according to the name of the house. The stores were small and very individualistic. There were no supermarkets in Dorking. Everything seemed a lot more personal. It was like living 25 years to 100 years in the past.

Without the harshness of the sun, nature's foliage was very gentle and tender. Fruits and vegetables were more tender, as were the flower petals. Everything seemed to be several shades greener than in most of the states in America. When the sun finally shown its face one day, I lay on the grass in the park reminiscing and contemplating my future plans. There had only been a week of gray, sunless skies, but I realized with my childhood in Texas and adult years in California I had always lived in sunny climates. Sunshine was a necessary lifetime condition for me. July in England had seemed more like cool winter days in California.

In all the confusion, frustration, and extreme loneliness, I really felt no inspiration for writing. A mere letter from home would give me a boost, even a bill. I knew my address change was delaying my mail. Even a letter sent within London had taken a week to be delivered. With difficulty, I had located the necessary converter for my typewriter, so that I could convert England's 220 current down to 110 or 115. My typewriter seemed to run too fast, but it was usable. The working typewriter, the sunshine, the beauty and serenity of the English countryside, even meditation could not stimulate any creativity. I was just not inspired to write.

The more I thought about my parents' ample, comfortable home in Texas, the more I asked myself why I was in England. Ever since the plane had landed in England, each day I just wanted to go to the airport and go home! In one letter to Debbie, I wrote: "I thought I knew exactly what I wanted, but I feel so desolated; I just wish I was home in my own bed! I love the English countryside; however, if David doesn't come along with help or suggestions, I am seriously ready to pack my bags and come home. I don't enjoy traveling or sightseeing alone. It is a very empty experience. Maybe I am just too old to put up with the inconvenience like no bathrooms. When one is younger, it's a fun and new experience. I don't feel like putting up with all these problems. I am just very unhappy with myself right now. I am not happy anywhere it seems. I am DOWN right now for the first time in a long time! By next week, I will have made some decisions as to where I'm going. I would always hate myself if I really packed up and went home without seeing more places than just the London area. I am really a creature of a romance, without any love interest, life is a bloody bore no matter where I am. It has been such a long time since I have cared for anyone, I feel like I'm too old for a man to even look at me anymore, and I feel no one will ever love me which causes nothing to look good to me or make me feel good. I'm really tired of being alone. I knew better, but here I am. Maybe my next letter will be more cheerful. Much love and please write, you don't know how one needs to hear from home when you are so far away from family, people and home. Mom"

No amount of self-analysis or rationalization could overcome the loneliness. I knew California wasn't the answer and seriously doubted that Texas would be either. I had tried Texas before. I felt I had grown away from idealistic and childish ego drives that had held me in Hollywood. There was so much about California to really love, especially when I first arrived in Hollywood. But after years of struggling in the TV and film industries, when a heterosexual person must keep asking herself "if she's normal" when so many friends are either gay or bisexual, I felt it was time to get out of the what I perceived at that time as a "sick society." I certainly did not fit in the new mode of Hollywood nor did I fit in my parents' hometown.

Now that my hope of finding a place for myself in Europe was rapidly dwindling, I felt like a worldwide misfit. I had leaped into the adult life before I was ready for it, filled with hope and visions. Through the years when one thing failed, I tried another. Nothing ever got me down for long, always recalling my father's advice: If you don't succeed the first time you try something, just try again, then try again. Each time you get better and keep trying until you finally master your goal. Never give up in defeat! My interests were so varied, if one aspect of a chosen field in film and television was not progressing, I would shift gears and try another. The only problem in those days were women working in the production end of the business were few and far between. It was only the beginning of the Woman's Lib days. One might say I was one of the few women plowing the way, creating the ripples that made it possible for future generations of women to be accepted in films and television production jobs. I love acting and like most starlets dreamed of a performance worthy of an Academy Award nomination, but I was realistic enough to accept the fact that I had missed the boat somewhere along the way. Regardless of talent and prominent connections, one must also have a phenomenal luck. The actor is at the mercy of the decision of a casting director, the director, the editor--even re-editing for television where the small parts are cut out for commercial time. During my struggles for production jobs, there were few offered to women--maybe a Script Girl. It was hard to get jobs, and the union seemed to be closed to new members, hairdressers or wardrobe ladies, or secretaries.

By this time in my life I grew very weary of "New Beginnings!" I always had to energize enthusiasm on each interview, only to face another disappointment and defeat. My love life followed the same pattern as my career. When I did flip over some guy, because it was all consuming, it usually scared the poor prospect off before the romance really got off the ground. So many marriage-less years had passed, it seemed that pattern would not change. Once Debbie passed the age of 12 years, my interest in having another child waned, also. I had read enough "peace of mind" literature to know the fault was mine, yet knowing and doing the right thing to correct traits, sometimes gets all mixed up. In truth, I really liked the inner me more than those qualities of the people who were successful in dealing with others. I just could not see any inner character in the people I knew that was any greater than my own. "To thine own self be true" was my motto to live by. Maybe I was totally narcissistic--perhaps my rationalizing did not suit others, maybe I've lived in illusion, but for me my inner world was filled with truth and honesty-- never selling myself out in an industry noted for just that! I was aware of my own deep desire for learning, for purpose, for caring, and great inspiration of beauty in all things. Those qualities I had not sensed in those who advised me to change my ways. This stand against other's attitude sets me apart from others. Unfortunately we all need people no matter how we try to convince ourselves we don't and can be self-sustaining. I had times of loneliness in California and in Texas, but Europe was all consuming.

I seem to have reached the bottom of the barrel and had no more reservoir of energy for new beginning and explorations. For a woman alone with no support or encouragement from others, I managed to

Ann Palmer

have quite an exciting life traveling, seeing many marvels of the world, being exposed to the famous, the rich and successful. To take a good honest look, I had met with a certain measure of success more than I dared dream possible in my youth. Maybe my goals were set too high for me to reach. Debbie was definitely my one great sense of accomplishment. Nonetheless, there was still an ever-present feeling of unfulfillment. Those who have no ambition are truly blessed to live peaceful lives. "Ambition" is merely a word to people like me, it is a tenacious master, a pledge for which there is no antidote, only temporary treatments, then a spark and it ignites once again with a burning desire to do--to accomplish or as I wrote in a poem… "to will this earth something that would not have been, had I not been born." -- the unanswerable life's quest!

My answer was not in Europe; perhaps it was nowhere except - within myself. The logical answer seemed to be to take it advantage of the fact that I was in Europe and should make the most of it to sightsee in London and then travel through Europe as long as my money held out. I had to learn something from my travels and new experiences. My writing could be done in Texas, living at home with my parents in comfort rather than a shabby room under conditions I would never tolerate at home attempting to imagine that it is "charming and quaint." Inspiration is necessary ingredient for any form of creativity. Since everything in England had gone wrong, if I left for France, perhaps inspiration would come to me yet again.

CHAPTER 14

Many Americans happily make their homes outside the United States, but many, many more, like myself, could never make the adjustment unless it was absolutely necessary. There was no question in my mind that I do love the charm and beauty of England in spite of the chaos and confusion. Yes, I doubted if most Americans or I could adjust to permanent full-time living there or most other countries. We are spoiled with conveniences we take for granted. Such simple items as hot water heaters, central heat and air-conditioning, major and minor electrical appliances, large one-stop shopping centers, with wide roadways and freeways and so on and so on. We never give a thought to living without these conveniences. The European hot water heater is generally inadequate. Most kitchens have an unsightly exposed water heater installed above the kitchen sink with exposed plumbing and electrical wiring. Usually another small heater is exposed in the bathroom. One good bathtub of hot water is the most one could expect to get, and then wait for hours for it to reheat in most small, inexpensive hotels or homes that accommodate guests. A far cry from the instant recovery water heaters Americans take for granted.

Furnishings are often ugly, uncomfortable, and expensive. To deny the fabulous antiques that come from Europe would be ludicrous, but that is not the average run-of-the-mill furnishings in European homes. At that time, automobiles usually needed to be small, with simple designs and were very uncomfortable for traveling. Traffic tie-ups on inadequate roadways can cause hours of delay. Streets are so narrow I often stopped to watch a truck maneuver around the bend or corner of a city street. Back then; gasoline was almost a dollar a gallon. It was expensive for the time but would be a delight in the present time! Repairs or service for just about anything was an impossibility. While small shops and outdoor shopping are unique and fascinating, this type of shopping grows very tiring and frustrating for Americans accustomed to more convenient shopping.

Ann Palmer

There was so much I wanted to do and see, but alone, I was disposed to putting it off for another day. My room became a hermitage. Sometimes I felt like a turtle in a closed shell. My English friend, David, was no help. He seemed to disappear more quickly than he had appeared. My only social engagement with him was to ride several miles by car to a private rifle shooting club to sit and watch him practice for hours. This prestigious private club would hardly measure up to the simplest American private club or country club.

I forced myself to go into London several times a week. My refuge in Dorking seemed quite far away about midday when I grew tired of walking and the crushing throngs of people in London. When the English sun does come out, it does so with a vengeance. On one sightseeing bus ride I took, there was no air circulation. With an outside temperature of 86° in stagnant air inside, everyone was irritable. One woman had a seizure. The bus stopped and waited for an ambulance for over 15 minutes. I found it more impossible to be homogeneous in hordes of people. London parks were so crowded it looked like swarms of ants, as did Piccadilly Circus, Trafalgar Square, the American Express office and everywhere. London streets were filled with smartly coordinated from head to toe American women, but like male birds strutting with their proud plumage, the well-dressed English gentleman with a bowler, cane or umbrella was a common sight. The buildings of London varied from ruins from World War II to modernistic skyscrapers, small by American standards and were new to the London skyline at that time. London seems strikingly clean for its massive daily flow of humanity. The English believed in their afternoon teatime but with equal fervor for their fresh flowers. An American city dweller is overwhelmed by London's array of flowers. Hardly a building is barren of some sort of flower box, beautifully filled with hanging vines of colorful flowers and often they were red Geraniums.

I managed to stroll through Soho and the theatre district, the Mall and see the changing of the guards at Buckingham palace. When I had been in London years before, I had seen the Tower of London, St. Paul's Cathedral, Westminster Abbey and other traditional sites. This trip I wanted to see sights I had missed on the last visit, such as Hampton Court, the fascinating Windsor Castle with its splendid St. George Chapel which is the locale of many nobilities' repose. I had always been attracted to the Rocco period of the 17th and 1800's of France but there was so much to be said for the heavy polished woods of English castles, their heraldic insignias, their heavy drapery and upholstery. It all seemed a part of a long forgotten past of my own for which I felt an all embracing personal affinity for certain items and sites of special periods. Had I lived there before? The unexplainable feeling of irritation that was a powerful emotion for what I felt were lies presenting as historical truths. As I gazed upon a prominent reproduction of Anne Boleyn, I felt the woman in the picture was not Anne at all but a substitute because she wore a necklace with a "B" on it. When I looked for her effigy, there was none. When I asked where she was buried I was told in a rather obscure church. I looked upon her daughter, Elizabeth's eloquent crypt and contemplated how Anne's tragic life had changed the face of England and Roman Catholicism's hold on Europe and England. She had been such an integral cog in the wheel of English history and religious freedoms yet so abused by historians. I had the feeling I wanted to get away from England and go to France. It seemed more and more that reincarnation was factual, had I lived as Anne in another era? (At that time I knew little about past lives, yet I had such a strong "knowingness" about Anne Boleyn.)

American Independence Day for me was spent wandering in and out of the various historic rooms, chapels and courtyards of Westminster Abbey, observing the effigies of the English royalties and the famous by listening to an occasional tour guide or the English people probably deliberating over their past. It made me realize one of the major problems in the United States today is our waning national pride and trust. Great Britain was master of the world for many hundreds of years. The United States has been a major world leader for only a few decades primarily since World War II. With only a short time in England I could see and feel the pride of country among the youth as well as the elderly. We had that pride years ago. To me, those who have brought on radical political violence and general insecurity in our country have damned our nation's pride. If national pride can be broken so can the nation. England's national pride had never been broken and it is hard to imagine that it ever would. Yet, a nation cannot live on past glory alone as many countries of the old world attempt to do, but must advance toward the present and future. This advancement should not include giving up national pride. The U.S. has made preeminent contributions for modern man, yet national confidence teeters. America has a fascinating beginning, as did my native state of Texas. I could not believe that this should ever be forsaken but held in respect and pride in understanding for the rights of all.

American history appears not to give today's youth the same sense of pride it gave my generation. To have that pride is not to deny others the same right of pride and respect. American Heritage is a part of the English heritage and is not to be denied. It was astounding to hear parents explaining their various kings, queens and their accomplishments to very young children who listen intensely. If they did not instill that pride, their nation might not survive. It takes more than just hanging out an American flag on special holidays to establish national pride. It takes knowledge and pride of our past heroes, accomplishments etc. The English take great pride in education. I was fascinated at how quick, alert, and eager to learn the English youth were and yet theirs' was a struggle as in most countries. Most Americans under the age of 40 really don't understand what hard times are. I was reminded of our gross waste of time, energy, education, money and everything. I wished a knapsack generation of Americans in Europe would go home with a sincere appreciation for the opportunities in the U.S. where a farm boy becomes a millionaire or a peanut farmer the President of the United States--almost an impossibility anywhere else in the world except America.

With my poor aching feet propped up on the seat across from me on the train returning to Dorking, I realized I had celebrated the Fourth of July in quite a unique way of roaming trough Westminster Abbey. It gave me a rebirth of appreciation for our American pioneering spirit heritage. Most Americans were just getting up to celebrate the fourth with picnics, boating, water skiing, fishing, beer drinking, and a watermelon feast. I wondered how many would ever give thought to why we celebrated the Fourth of July or even momentarily appreciated their land of opportunity.

There was more sightseeing to be done than I had strength to do. Necessities I felt I had to carry made sightseeing burdensome. It was impossible to go into London without a raincoat, umbrella, guidebook, maps, a camera and the usual necessities women carry. One tour book was "Europe on $5 A Day" that I used constantly. On one tour a man humorously suggested when he returned home he was going to write a book on how to tour Europe keeping your tips to only FIVE dollars a day.

Upon leaving London, if my intentions were to sightsee and tour, I knew it was impossible take my entire luggage. Victoria Station became the focal point of my frequent visits in London. Fortunately, there was a storage department at the station. I planned to take only essentials while touring and store the bulk of my things including my typewriter. My first agenda was Paris. I would take the train to Folkestone, near Dover, then the boat and pick up the train again in Calais, France. I don't remember the reason for deciding to leave on a Saturday, possibly there were reservations for my room in Dorking, and I had to move anyway. It was too late to book passage through the American Express office, so I had to secure my tickets at Victoria Station. I waited in line for over two hours until I felt faint and weary. The line started outside and went through two rooms in the station before getting to the room where tickets were sold.

There was still so much in London and England I wanted to see, but if I got out of England maybe my luck would change. Ironically, after reservations were booked, clothing separated for storage and traveling, David became attentive with potential plans. Even strangers were more talkative, too. It seemed I had gone for days without a word from anyone, and now that I was leaving, everyone became friendly. That day I took my luggage to Victoria station for storage, a lovely English lady on the train talked to me all the way into London, and then even helped me with my luggage while an English gentleman passed us struggling with the heavy luggage without so much as a glance. I don't know how I would have made it without her help. There were always porters at the train station, but I could never find one when I was loaded down with luggage and desperately needed help. If I had no luggage, they were always nearby. I seemed always to be on the car that was furthest from the central loading area.

In general, when I was there, English people were quite reserved and not prone to extensive conversation with foreigners, yet often, shopkeepers were very friendly and took more personal interests than in the U.S. When I returned to the U.S. I planned to open a small gift shop in my parents' home. I wanted to pick up many small antique items possibly for the shop. Dorking was noted for its many antique shops. I found the shopkeepers in England quite honest and willing to prepare and ship. They might even escort you to a nearby store if they felt you could not locate it. Many of them expressed that wonderful dry wit sense of humor attributed to the English. Even when the English or European people are friendly, most Americans are not.

I would say goodbye to England for now. It was a fascinating country in every respect and very beautiful. It was a thrilling experience to study and be a part of the grandeur that England once was. The English lust for culture and learning is inspiring. London has such charm with its oldness yet cleanliness. The new modern structures seem ugly and out of place amid the timeless quality of the magnificently designed older classics and with few advertising signs and no gaudy neon signs. The cars driven within the city at night use only their parking lights which added to a peacefulness amid the crowds and chaos.

On the train to Folkestone, I talked with a very pleasant young English woman traveling alone to Switzerland. When we arrived, she went through the custom lines for Great Britain, and I went through the one-marked "Foreigners." When I got on board the ship, I explored it a bit soon locating my new found friend. We wandered all over the ship while awaiting embarkation. The crossing would take only a short while but was delayed another hour-and-a-half for people to get through customs. The bar would not serve drinks until the ship left the harbor. Pulling away from the docks there was a picturesque scene with a serene White Cliffs of Dover in the background. There were quaint old buildings snuggled against the cliffs. There was a small old fortress and below the fortress I could see a swarm of men along the hillside who were doing what else on Saturday afternoon but playing golf!

My new friend and I had just sat down at a table when the rather nice looking customs officer who had checked my passport at length appeared with several of his custom officers. They informed us that we were sitting at their table. I was about to get a little annoyed when I realized it was only the English wit again. The five with enthusiastic prattle was a welcome relief to my muted years, hungry for conversation. It was the first time I had really laughed since I arrived in

England. The next thing I knew we were arriving in Calais. The boat was docked before I realized it. We continued our carefree humorous conversation over a glass of French wine at the station in Calais to avoid the waiting line for French customs. Our English custom officer friends were trying to help us, only we talked so long, the French custom officers left and we entered France without the official entry stamped on our passports. The three Englishman convinced us that Saturday night in Calais would be more fun than sitting on a train, plus the fact it was much later than we thought because of our delays. It meant I would be arriving in Paris on Saturday night without reservations well after midnight with no knowledge of the French language. It made sense recalling my previous arrival in Paris years before without reservations and almost not getting a room. As overcrowded as London was with tourists so must it be in Paris. They also assured us that, as official representatives of her Majesty the Queen, there would be no way they could be rapists, murderers, or thieves. If they conducted themselves in anyway but a gentlemanly manner, our complaints could get them fired. They help us find the hotel. While we freshened up, they did the same in an apartment they rented in Calais. Without a date situation, the five of us went out together for dinner then on to a few unique French bars. It had been a most fun day since my plane landed in England. Now that I was on French soil, perhaps my luck was changing in France.

The next morning the custom officers who had checked my passport promised to meet me for coffee and help me locate the right train. The English girl had a much earlier train. We hastily had our coffee since he had to take the boat back to England. My short-term never-to-be-seen-again friends could not know how meaningful their friendship had been, no matter how fleeting. And there I sat again alone Sunday morning in Calais, France on the continent of Europe!

It was a couple of hours before my train left for Paris. My friend suggested I sightsee in Calais. For centuries Calais had been besieged with battle since it was nearest to England. World War II had obliterated it. As in many areas in Europe, when they rebuild, they attempt to duplicate the structures exactly as they were. The focal point of the town was a tall steeple at the town hall. It had been destroyed during the war, yet it was restored exactly as it was before according to photos of before and after. It was a work of art. The large cathedral of Calais still stood as an empty shell, a constant reminder of man's capabilities for destruction.

The buildings and homes were quaint and typically French. Most of the time was spent in the park near the train station. The French have a marvelous way with their manicured gardens. I was astounded by the perfect floral designs. This magnificent beauty of nature was in sharp contrast to a German bunker, now a museum. Inside the cold concrete walls were war mementos and grotesque photographs taken of the concentration camps, hideous reminders of the very dark period of man's inhumanity to man!

Outside again I preferred to wait under the beautiful rose arbor, admiring the picturesque array of flowers with flowerbeds that reminded me of a lavishly decorated cake. While enjoying the moments of peaceful beauty and serenity, I was feeling a bit lost, lonely, and frightened, especially in not knowing the language. Contrary to public opinion or travel books, the English language is not spoken everywhere you go. Now on top of everything else that goes with traveling alone, there was the language barrier. I tried to think of nothing more than the beauty of the garden around me and the wonderful smells of the roses while waiting my soon to depart train to Paris.

CHAPTER 15

At long last came the time for me to board the train to Paris, and I climbed on board the first car. Hardly anyone was in that car. I suspected by the looks of it, it might be first-class and my ticket was for second class. Taking full advantage of my foreign ignorance, I managed to enjoy the first 50 miles or so of my journey before the conductor invited me to travel in the next car. It was really terrible. Most of the youthful knapsack travelers in second-class created an overcrowded condition in an old uncomfortable car. I admired their youthful simplicity of traveling. For me, I had to have things such as makeup, accessories, and a change of clothing with matching shoes. No matter how I tried to convince them, I still had too much heavy luggage to manage at the train station without a porter that never seemed to be found in France either.

The French countryside, like the English countryside, was very beautiful. The small villages and homes were similar but yet you knew that you were in France. The red tile roofs were similar in both countries, but the general construction in England had been red brick whereas in France it seemed to be plaster or stone. The train stopped in each and every community. I thought I would never get to Paris, and I nearly did not make it to Paris!

The train pulled in at Amiens. Everyone, except one girl and me seem to be getting off the train. We both sat there until the conductor finally chased us off. Unbeknownst to us, we were supposed to change trains. At least it would be an opportunity to get something to eat at the station, assuming there would be no dining car on the train I was to board. I had not eaten in Calais in order to use up some of my travel time for a meal, thinking it would be in a dining car. I forgot that some trains in Europe did not carry dining cars and I was starving.

Off the train alone, I really felt mute without knowing a few words of French. The only way I could get anything to eat was by pointing to it at a trackside concession. I ended up with nut bread, cookies and chocolate milk even though I wanted a sandwich and a cold drink. Oh well, c'est la vie! I wished I could remember a few words of the French language recordings I had tried to study before leaving the states.

When the train finally pulled into the station in Paris, as always, I was on the furthest car from the station and there were no porters. After much huffing and puffing, I located a locker where the luggage could be stored while I searched for a hotel room. I picked out a hotel listed in my European travel book and had been expecting to have to call several hotels. What luck! With my first call, I located a room for $3.60 per day only a block from the Arc de Triomph, a perfect centralized location. Maybe this was an omen that France would be a happier place for me than England had been.

The taxi driver could not speak English, but again, a bit of luck, he was Italian. With my limited vocabulary of Italian we carried on quite a conversation. The only problem was that while I was able to make him understand me, I failed to understand almost everything he said. I smiled and nodded my head as though I understood.

In the hotel my few words of Italian served me well. The room was no worse than the one in England. At least this one overlooked a busy Parisian street. After a rest, and a small degree of freshening up, I ventured out for a walk on the Avenue des Champs Elysées. My inner excitement was now growing by the minute. It seemed ironic that a city like Paris, famed for its freedom of attitudes, where prostitutes were able to walk the streets freely, that a foreign woman alone may walk without fear of being compromised or attacked in any way unlike in our own country where violent crimes run rampant in every city and even within smaller communities. I was not afraid, but rather fascinated! There is an atmosphere about Paris that is very electrifying. London is stately and impressive but Paris is filled with of vivacity unique to Paris alone. One cannot help feeling joy, a gaiety with a Maurice Chevalier melody running through one's head. He was symbolic of the living, breathing Paris.

Since my few words of Italian had carried me so far, I decided when I found an Italian restaurant that would be the spot for dinner, assuming I would be able to make myself understood. Sure enough, my confidence was unfounded as the menu, written in Italian, looked like a bunch of foreign words. While I could converse slightly, reading the language was more difficult for me. Nonetheless I ended up with a nice dinner.

Sometimes it seems one can almost converse better without a language, for then you are forced to reach, sense and feel what another is trying to say. So often communication is lost with words. We failed to sense the real meaning of one's wishes to convey because of getting too involved in the superficialities of words. On the other hand it can be very frustrating when you cannot ask for a fork, a glass of milk, ice, or the simplest necessity.

My second day in Paris found me completely exhausted. I spent most of the day just resting, venturing out only for lunch and dinner. For my dinner, I decided to walk down to the Seine River and see if I could get on board the dinner boat. It was already filled but I could take the boat trip that did not serve dinner. It was not quite dark when the boat pulled away from its mooring at 9 pm. Without question, this was the most thrilling experience of my European visit so far. There stood the Eiffel Tower with a full moon back lighting it magnificently. As it quickly grew darker, I became awed by the beauty of the crystal clear brightly moonlit night as the moon nipped in and out of the background of spectacular fetes of architecture grandeur found only in Paris. We passed the Louvre, Place de la Concorde, Notre Dame, under the bridge built of cannons Napoleon captured, and sites too numerous to recall. It was the best $1.80 I had ever spent!

Paris must have nearly as many tourists as London but somehow Paris seemed to swallow them up. They did not seem as conspicuous as in London. Thousands of people milled up and down Champs Elysées-- its wide street and walkways seem to gulp them up, creating a living painting. The Arc de Triomphe stands so magnificently facing the Champs Elysées--the most famous street in Paris. As wide as it is, it is also a very short street terminating at Place de la Concorde.

Napoleon had designed Paris so that all roads leading into the city came together at the Arc so it becomes the hub of a gigantic wheel where twelve streets terminate. It is called Etoile, meaning star. The air of excitement for me was even greater knowing my room was only one block from the Etoile. The excitement grew that evening when I heard fireworks, singing, and much noise outside my window, down on the street. At dawn it would be Bastille Day! Totally unaware the significance of the day, I found myself in Paris on France's Fourth of July, only it was July 14th. As I stood on my small balcony on the fourth floor, I watch the antics of a group of young French boys. They were performing much like circus clowns. I was laughing even though I did not understand a word they were saying. Fireworks were blasting. Many people were milling up and down the street at nearing midnight; the excitement was contagious. At midnight there were far greater fireworks. The next day I found out that the firework display had been on the Eiffel Tower, something that I would love to have seen. I knew there would be a parade that I planned to watch.

Bastille Day came with its entire military splendor. On the way to the parade, I met a young American schoolteacher, Lynn, also staying in the hotel. Her French vocabulary was far better than mine. We decided to watch the parade together. It was only a short walk. We arrived early enough to get a fairly good view, only as the crowds grew they pushed at least five deep in front of us. Street vendors were selling cardboard periscopes, and that seemed to be the only way I would really be able to see the parade. At least it would afford me a momentary glimpse of Monsieur Pompidou, France's Prime Minister. After the parade was over, I asked where Pompidou was. Lynn informed me that he had passed while I was buying the periscope to see him. The parade was totally military and obviously France's answer to Russia's May Day show of arms.

As a parade of jeeps, tanks, trucks various military machines, and missiles passed, the most thrilling site of all was a jet streaking overhead leaving red, white and blue vapor trails in perfect formation over the Champs Elysees. Every piece of military equipment in France must have been in the parade. It quickly became very boring. I don't know if that sort of military show of arms has ever been held in the United States but if it had, I felt sure there would have had a few bands and female prancing, too! This was strictly male chauvinism with not one female in the entire parade. The street was lined with soldiers and sailors. As the last piece of military equipment passed in review, the massive number of men gradually fell into formation bringing the parade to an end. As I watched the viewers of the massive show of arms, I sensed a great national pride among the French similar to that in England.

Lynn and I decided to share a room at the hotel cutting our room rent in half. For afternoon sightseeing, we would go our separate ways. She had already visited many of the places I planned to see. We moved into a double room. While riding the Metro subway toward Notre Dame, I marveled at the near desperation of being in a foreign country alone when two total strangers would move into the same room, trusting that each other would be honest simply on the basis of both being Americans, although from totally different backgrounds and parts of the United States. Lynn was far closer to my daughter's age than my own.

London's Westminster Abbey was so overcrowded with tourists; one forgets that it is a place of worship even though regular service is held. Notre Dame radiates a more worshipful atmosphere than the Abbey. I could feel the serenity of the Cathedral. It was beautiful and had many interesting relics. The interior was far more spectacular than the Abbey. Notre Dame's fame is more for its extraordinary exterior architectural design. I was unaware that the pictorial view of Notre Dame usually seen is of the rear view.

I walked in and out of streets in the old city and the flower market. Many buildings I wanted to see were closed on Tuesdays. As it began to rain and feeling tired, I returned to the hotel. Lynn was not there; she told me she had plans for the evening. As evening approached, I decided I would splurge for dinner not caring how much I spent. I walked both sides of the Champs Elysees looking along the side of the street trying to find a restaurant that had a lot of atmosphere. It was still drizzling rain but I was well prepared in rain attire. I decided to be very daring and before dinner, had a cocktail at the George VI Hotel bar. One of Paris' most famous hotels was a bit disappointing. The bar was too brightly lit, as were most of the European restaurants. The Hotel was not spectacular nor did it have any particular interesting atmosphere. Regardless how mature and worldly wise I thought myself to be I still had my hang-ups and felt rather foolish sitting in a bar alone. After one drink, I was ready to search elsewhere for atmosphere. I stopped at a restaurant, "Fonguet's," where there were well-dressed patrons entering. Struggling through the menu, I ended up with a glass of wine, trout and French fried potatoes, costing about seven dollars. As for its atmosphere, it was Paris! I went back out into the drizzly weather and to my hotel.

On my previous visit to Paris years before as well as this visit, I had viewed the stately Arc de Triomphe only from a distance. I had never crossed over to look at the tomb of the Unknown Soldier. As Bastille Day was drawing to a close, it seemed a fitting thing to do. Hanging from the top center of the Arc was the most gigantic French national flag I had ever seen. The access to the Arc was to go underground through the subway tunnels and then come up under the Arc. I seemed never to end up there, so I decided to try and cross the Etoile. Several people were attempting to dart across the street traffic that consisted of about eight lanes of traffic. Sadly, there were no lanes. Autos were darting from the inside lanes to outside ones, with other zigzagging in opposite directions. THIS method of reaching the Arc was taking your life in your own hands! I made it along with others. It was well worth the effort. I stood underneath the huge billowing red, white, and blue striped flag and watched it flutter in the wind while the search lights shone through it illuminating the colors. I then went to see the eternal burning flame of the Unknown Soldier which was pulsating with life with the Champs Elysees as a background. This had been the ultimate experience for ending Bastille Day, 1970, in Paris, France.

Chapter 16

The rest of the week was filled with sightseeing ventures I had missed on my previous trip to Paris. When I visited Du Tombeau de L'Empereur, I was convinced Napoleon would not have been very happy with his tomb considering his lust for grandeur and splendor. It was a huge pinkish marble crypt in the middle of the basement with 12 large angels surrounding it. I thought Napoleon would have at least desired his laurel wreath crest with the large "N" on the tomb. Fortunately, someone had the foresight to have the floor of the church cut out so that you could look down upon the crypt. The upper floor with its beautiful altar and dome were more impressive than Napoleon's crypt. The admission ticket included two military museums, but with my luck they were closed during the noon hour, and I was not interested enough to wait an hour or more.

I could see the Eiffel Tower nearby, so I walked toward it. Standing under or away from it and viewing the vast network metal and bolts was an incredible experience. One cannot help but just stand in awe of such a gigantic metal structure. Attached to each of the four bases is an elevator that goes up and down with the slant of its legs. The ride up was not so bad, but on the ride down one has the feeling of being pitched forward, and it was a little frightening. It reminded me of the funny feeling in my stomach writing the Palm Springs tramway in California. I could ride all the way up to the top of the first level which was quite enough for me. My ticket permitted ventures up to the second level, so I finally mustered the courage to take it to the second level. It was well worth the trip as I could walk completely around the tower getting a full panoramic view of the city of Paris or as far as the eye can see. I could go to the top of the Tower to get a spectacular, stunning view of Paris and its monuments; however, with acrophobia, I couldn't face it!

Up and down the streets walk - walk - walk - and as in London, thorough confusion of the Metro, so I found myself walking along the

Seine River, observing people. Parisians reflected a more affluent society than I had witnessed on my previous trip. My observation of the general public in England had been a very uptight society, filled with national pride, and not overly fond of strangers. Credit must be given to some of the English people at their attempt at humor. The general public in Paris seemed much more relaxed, and much less inhibited. They talked and they laughed. A young man was apt to give his girlfriend a kiss in public. The French people's skin tones were definitely different from the lily white English. European men in general have slighter built bodies than most American men, with smaller chest cavities and more rounded backsides. I attributed this male physical structure difference to American men with their lust for athletic excellence, perhaps overly emphasized in America and perhaps lack of emphasis of intellectual fetes. I did not find the French people to be particularly friendly nor did I find them to be unfriendly. On my previous trip, I had numerous opportunities to attend social gatherings where I could get a more personal first-hand look at the residences of Paris. All those contacts were now gone.

Fontainebleau was a must see that I had missed when in Paris before. It was a 40-mile ride out of Paris. I was off to the American Express office to meet my tour bus for a planned day of sightseeing with other tourist. As always, I made my usual check for mail but by this time I had given up hope convinced that no one in the United States cared if I was dead or alive. The bus ride seemed like endless miles of city. Unlike any other city I've visited, I saw no houses, only more and more apartment buildings apparently needed to accommodate over 8 million inhabitants of Paris at that time. Finally, outside of Paris, I began seeing the old unchanged villages through the centuries; the charm of Europe and the countryside was fairly flat farmland. Shortly before we arrived at Barbizon on the way to Fontainebleau, the tour guide pointed out the spot where the artist Millet had painted his famous "Gleaners." We toured the tiny hotel for artists who lived there and sold their works. The hotel had housed many famous artists since the revolutionary days in France when artists like Millet, Jack Charles Jacque, Rousseau, Jules Dupré, and Diaz had taken refuge there.

Fontainebleau's exterior is far less grand than I had remembered from the photos slides I had studied in art history class. It was a composite infusion of additions by various royal occupants. Fontainebleau was long known as a royal hunting lodge with its beautiful wooded countryside and ample game. One becomes at a loss for descriptive words for the grandeur of European palaces, castles, cathedrals, and art. The ceiling art alone could present an entire area of study. Most ceilings are covered with great paintings, frescoes, with carved gold leaf decor working its way down from the ceiling, often to the floor. The walls may be covered with great works of art, tapestries, and woven silk, gold and silver fabrics or sometimes heavy-carved wood panels. In France the wood panels were usually painted with gold-leaf whereas in England the wood panels were heavily painted with oils using natural colors.

Marie Antoinette's bedroom was my favorite room of the first "queen or king" sized bed which I had seen since leaving the US. Napoleon's bedroom was not as grand with its tiny bed. It took a few steps for Napoleon to get into it, indicating just how physically small he had been. The tour guide said he slept in a sitting position, as was the custom in those days. He never gave us the reason but I assumed it was because Napoleon lived in constant fear of attempted assassinations. Where his uniforms were displayed, he must have been only around 5' tall and very small. Of course, Josephine's room was beautiful, too. Versailles had an impressive library filled with 18,000 books.

When you "see one Palace, Cathedral, Museum, etc. you have seen them all" as it becomes increasingly difficult to recall just what you saw and where. Today when I see reproductions of these great works of art, I am not sure if I saw the original or not when I saw so many. On my previous trip to Europe, I made two trips to Versailles. It is Europe's--perhaps the world's--grandest palace with its sculptured gardens, statues, lakes, and walkways far surpassing anything I had ever seen before.

The whole European trip would have been much more pleasant if I could have shared it with Debbie. For months I had begged her to save her earnings and I would share mine in order for her to make the trip with me, but instead she had squandered every cent she made including the money I sent for the sale of her car. I had scrimped and saved, sold everything including meaningful antique pieces in order to have those few months in Europe, not knowing what the future I was facing when I returned to the States. I had sincerely wanted to find a new life and stay in Europe. I was so tired of the materialistic lust and greed in the United States; I thought I would find greater aesthetic values among Europeans. Instead, eventually I had to face the realization that our materialistic lust and greed is only a bit more refined than in Europe. I wondered if the American way had created it there, too.

Lynn and I saw little of each other. We talked very briefly. I knew only that she was a schoolteacher, engaged be married, and Europe was sort of a think it over last fling for her. We decided to see the Basilica du Sacré Coeur in Montmartre together then visit the Latin quarters on the Left Bank by early evening. Sacré Coeur is the scene so often captured on artist canvas. Approaching the church was an exciting sight except for the extensive stairs to climb! It looked like a stairway to the sky, adding to this, five domes spiraling toward the heavens. There was a service being held inside which made me wonder if the angels heard the singing voices as they echoed through the dome.

As we rode the Metro toward the Left Bank, we noticed a very emanated young Frenchman staring at us. When we got off the Metro, he was still following us. I was beginning to become annoyed but Lynn was intrigued and wanted to encourage him subtly. We stopped at a sidewalk café; he stopped and sat a short distance away. Soon he started a conversation to which I was rather brisk but Lynn was very friendly. I thought, "Oh well, each to her own." While they became better and better acquainted I found him to be unattractive, but he seemed rather nice and appeared to be harmless. He was a law student and knew only a few words of English. He asked very politely if he might accompany us to show the more interesting areas of the Latin Quarters. As a local tour guide he was most welcome. He took us through the old streets so narrow that only foot traffic and pushcarts could pass through.

There were many interesting restaurants and shops seemingly untouched by centuries. When we tired of walking, we stopped in another sidewalk café for a glass of wine. By now we were old friends. As we sat chatting, a handsome blonde Frenchman bound up to our table with great zest and begin exchanging words with the law student. They seem to know each other. Apparently, he was inviting us to go to a party with him. Lynn asked me what I wanted to do, and I asked her because I did not know what to do. When in Europe before I had been to a number of social gatherings and found them much like parties at home. I did not wish to return to the hotel so late alone. If Lynn wanted to go to the party, it seemed we were safe in numbers and our new law student friend seemed to offer some masculine security, plus it seemed a bit adventurous. (An UNDERSTATEMENT!)

As we piled into a small sports car, there were at least two more females creating a packed sardine can car. The blonde driver sped through the streets of Paris. I thought he lived in the Latin Quarters, but he drove further and further from the central of Paris. The further we got, the more ill at ease I became. "Dear God what have I gotten myself into?" I was soon to find out! We arrived at a fairly new apartment complex and we untangled ourselves from the car. When we went upstairs and opened the door to the apartment, there was only a very dim light in the living room. One look in the living room explained immediately what sort of "party" we were attending; the lamp was the only piece of furniture! The floor was covered with plastic pillows: "Oh my God, we have walked into a sex orgy!"

For all my years in Hollywood I had heard of such happenings, but I was totally disinterested in any sort of experimentation! Now, there I was! And what's more at the FAR outskirts of Paris. I knew the Metro stopped running by that midnight hour, and I saw no telephone to call a taxi. The only thing I could think of was to head for the bathroom and try to get my wits focused! After all I was not an innocent young girl; I was an adult with a grown daughter while some within this group were probably near her age. I felt no fear of being physically attacked; I just felt terribly embarrassed and very out of place. Even so, I had gotten myself into this situation I could get myself out, hopefully without making a scene.

What these people chose to do was none of my business, and under these circumstances, I was a "foreigner." I stayed in the bathroom until a group of French girls were pounding on the door wanting to get in. I quietly slithered from the bathroom to the adjoining kitchen attempting to remain unnoticed so that I could neither see or be seen. Several of the young men came into the kitchen to refresh their drinks. They spoke no English. To any of their gestures I said "No, thank you!"

Universally understood.

One interesting observation I did make, since I found myself in a very unwanted situation, was that none of the males paraded nude. All of them wore some particular particle of clothing while the girls were totally nude with no obvious feeling of shyness or embarrassment. It became amusing as more of the males gathered in the kitchen around me - fully clothed, attempting to carry on a conversation with a few common words. The nude ladies were showing annoyance, urging them back to the living room orgy. Finally, a rather nice looking Frenchman, clothed and a bit nearer my own age, came into the kitchen. He studied in the United States and spoke fairly good English. He assured me we could sit and talk and remain clothed in the bedroom, as it was not being used. The party was strictly in the living room and one other room.

He gently began sympathizing with me since Americans are too shy and inhibited and wish to hide their very natural act of sex. I proceeded to explain to him that my choice of noninvolvement in their orgy had nothing to do with shyness or inhibitions; it had to do with values. For me, intimacy between one man and one woman was very special, beautiful even a spiritual experience that deserve total commitment which was impossible in such an atmosphere. To me their actions were empty, superficial, and shallow attempts of having fun--it was abusing a gift of God. If this was his "thing" then go do it, but not mine. He wanted me to just watch, but I assured him I was not a voyeur either. I would have never come to the party if I had any idea it was an orgy.

I asked if he knew any way for me to return to my hotel. He reaffirmed there was no telephone for a taxi and the Metro had stopped running but as soon as it started running again in the early dawn hours, he would take me to the nearest station. He seemed sympathetic toward my attitude and remained with me as we chatted about my travels. A very beautiful young French girl with a perfect form body kept coming in the room arguing with him. I urged him to return with her. He need not spoil his evening because of me. He confessed he was bored with the whole thing. Later, after we left the apartment, he told me in amusement that the young French girl was interested in ME, not him! Finally we left as dawn was almost breaking. By that time most of the participants had left. Lynn, her lawyer student, and I were taken to the

Metro line after having coffee with the Frenchman. He had conducted himself quite gentlemanly and was my salvation throughout the horrifying night. He asked me to go out with him that evening, but I was exhausted from no sleep and inwardly outraged at the night's activities I had been subjected to without any means of removing myself from the revolting event. I was too hesitant to make any plans but suggested he telephone me later in the afternoon. He was seemingly gentle, kind, and nice looking. He worked for an American International company. After my speech regarding group sexual activity, I was a little afraid I might have merely challenged his masculine ego. If he could not score in the group, he might only wish to try again in privacy. I was not interested in any one-night affair in Paris. It was not on my list to complete my sightseeing in Paris, although admittedly Paris is a very romantic city!

Lynn and I rode the Metro back to our hotel, too tired to talk. I had no idea just how much Lynn had participated and really did not care but obviously she and her lawyer had been intimate. I thought of her as a sweet young thing; however, my opinion had changed considerably overnight. I was thankful to be of an age when I did not feel the need of approving my feminine sexuality, especially group wise! The only thing I felt good about was that I had the courage to speak out to make a firm stand when confronted regarding my values. In my youth, I was never one to "go along with the crowd," but I also had not spoken out regarding my ethics as I had on this occasion. Even though I had developed into somewhat of a believer of "don't knock it until you try," there were many experiences where I drew the line. Sex orgies had been one of them. Now I had accidentally experienced one without participation! Surviving it untouched, I was more convinced one needs not experience everything first hand but some knowledge and understanding can never harm you. It is total ignorance of the unknown that create prejudices, hate, and intolerance in any race, nationality, or religion.

I had hoped my travel through Europe would be a learning experience. Paris had been a learning experience. I doubt if any real values had been accrued because of the sex orgy, yet experience had confirmed my belief that such activities were for the insecure, shallow, and insensitive animal-people of the world. I longed to be with people after the magnified loneliness of solitary travel. I had been unhappy alone, but as this experience proved, I was far unhappier with people under such extraordinary circumstances.

After a few hours sleep I decided I had enough of Paris. I felt dirty; the fresh air of the countryside would help cleanse my memory of the last night of Paris. I was not finding much hope of Europe being a refuge as I had imagined it to be. I felt like a ship on the lonely sea without a port to call home. My beautiful memory of Paris still remains and reminds me of my alone boat cruse in the River Seine; still it is somewhat empty when the soul tingling experience is not shared with someone you love or even like. A woman traveling alone is more prone to become acquainted with a man she would never so much as converse with at home, as was to be confirmed in the near future. I doubt if the sweet Midwestern schoolteacher would even be caught in a similar activity in her hometown. Lynn was also leaving Paris the same day.

During that week I had checked on the television production companies thinking I might talk to them about potential work. Realizing there would probably be a work permit problem for an American, an even greater problem would be my inability to speak their language, so I gave up on another idea as a lost cause.

I took the metro to the American Express office to make my final mail check; as usual there was nothing. I also purchased my train ticket so I could make stops in to Dijon, Lausanne, Geneva, Marseilles, and Nice. The word "Marseilles" had always had a romantic ring to it, but as I discussed my travel plans, others advised me against going to the shipping port alone. Fortunately it was quite easy to change my train ticket and receive a refund for not using it. If one has never traveled outside the United States, he or she cannot appreciate what a "security blanket" the American Express office becomes for an American. It seems as if it is always there to serve most Americans needs.

I had a couple of hours before my train time, so I decided to take a quick trip through the Louvre. There is no such thing as a quick trip to the Louvre! I had spent hours there on my previous trip to Paris. In my opinion, there is just far too much antiquity for one museum to possess. It is impossible to appreciate the world's greatest artists when so many are amassed in one spot. Maybe the creations could be digested if one could spend many days taking different sections one at a time. I had not seen the Egyptian section as thoroughly as I wanted, so I made a quick trip through that section. They have the rental-taped guides. While it was a great assistance, I wish I had remembered more Egyptian history. I rushed from room to room viewing indescribable antiquities. If only one half of the Louvre's works of art could be moved to another area of the world, perhaps London or New York City, so many more people could share and enjoy the past Masters. The Louvre would never miss it. There would still be too much to assimilate. You see so much you can't remember it all. It is like eating too much sweets then getting sick from them.

Suddenly, I realize my watch was slow. I rushed to the Metro on feet so tired and painful that I could hardly move them. I had yet to pick up my luggage, then rushed to the train station. If I did not make a perfect connection, I would miss the last train that day and would have to look for another hotel room.

CHAPTER 17

Now I really had to rush to get to the Paris train station, and asked the hotel to telephone a taxi for me. The driver tried to speed through the traffic, and I was sure I would miss my scheduled train. I rushed into the station and for a change the nearest train was mine. Again, I climbed aboard the nearest car, again first-class. By the time the conductor sent me to second class, the train was well on its way out of Paris. In my very poor Italian I tried to tell the conductor I would pay the difference to stay in the first-class, but he sent me five cars away. The second-class section was packed, and even the aisles were filled. After tremendous difficulty squeezing through to these second-class cars, dining car, and others while making two trips to get my luggage to the crowded cars, I finally got settled in the seat only to decide to go back to the dining car for dinner. It was not crowded and a relaxing, enjoyable way to travel. Looking out the window was like watching dozens of beautiful pictures flashing by. I lingered in the dining car so I would not have to travel for long in the overcrowded second-class section.

When I paid my dining check with American Travelers checks, I finally realized why my money was going so fast. It was my usual habit of accepting change upon paying the check without counting it. When I looked at the change the waiter gave me, I realized he had most of the $20 Travelers check. I called him back pointing to the check and the change. He merely threw his hands up gesturing that he could not understand English. I was getting more infuriated. It seemed obvious what he was trying to do. A French gentleman sitting across the table from me could speak no English, but he too realized the waiter was trying to cheat me. He explained to the waiter what I was trying to say and then in all innocence the waiter gave me the rest of my change with apologies. I thanked the man across from me. The simple meal had still cost seven dollars; even so, I would gladly have spent more if the conductor had allowed me to move to first class. Dijon came and went.

I just could not see fighting my way to get my luggage just to spend one night in Dijon. If there was something special other than the mustard manufacturing, I did not know what it was. So I decided to stay on the train. I had enough of France.

Again with luck - one phone call located a room near the train station in Lausanne, Switzerland. The hotel was a converted beautiful old home, and I loved it. The room was crispy clean and feminine. I would have relaxed there for days, but they had no room available except for one night. The next morning was Saturday, and I walked around Lausanne visiting the ghostly old cathedral upon the hill. I had a good inexpensive lunch and walked through the clean narrow streets, built on the hillside of Lake Lausanne. It also borders Geneva where I headed by train in the early afternoon.

I could certainly tell I had crossed the border out of France. Besides all the shops built with clocks and watches, the Swiss people were so much nicer to me than the French had been. Everything seemed crispy clean and less expensive. As I traveled, each country became more beautiful with Switzerland unequaled. Geneva is the worldwide business center but seems to offer little for sightseeing. I saw no reason to stay overnight. I decided to bypass Marseille after hearing so many warnings. It was an overnight train ride to Nice going through the Alps. By this time I was so tired of overcrowded trains, I decided to splurge and fly to Nice. For a few dollars difference there was no comparison to the time saved. Air travel was only 45 minutes while the train would have been all night. I was so near the long awaited French Riviera--my enthusiasm began to bubble.

I took advantage of the two-hour wait for the plane to see Geneva. I walked down the hill from the train station through the business section toward the lake and a small park. As I stood in the park studying the very large Memorial, the large fountain began shooting many feet of water high in the air. I noticed a round object moving across the sky. I walked toward the water's edge for a better view. It was a parachute water skier. Across the lake were three-story old European style buildings. Modern neon type signs diminished their charm.

It was after 6 pm before the plane was finally in the air. There had been a delay at the airport. Thank God, I decided to fly! The view of the snowcapped Alps from the air in late afternoon sunshine was an

Ann Palmer

indescribable spectacular sight that would be engraved in my memory from that day forward. As I looked back toward Geneva, I saw the familiar dark smoky layer hanging over the land, just as I have seen every time I had flown. And people thought Los Angeles was the smog capitol in those days! I wondered if enough attention had been given to the layer of pollution in the air that jet aircraft creates. I was mesmerized at the beauty that lay below. How grand it would be if one could drive up into the tiny villages that dot the top of the Alps.

Off in the distance I could see the top of the mountain shaped like the Matterhorn at Disneyland that I assumed it was. We flew over Mount Blanc, which is higher than the Matterhorn. The tiny villages dotted the Valley and the mountainside. Houses were scattered throughout the valleys, on the mountainside and atop the mountains. Many were located where there was no trace of a roadway. Some of the mountains were totally barren with no sign of life. At 23,000 feet, one gets quite a panoramic view of the Alps in Switzerland. To think I would have missed all of this on the overnight train. After just a glass of orange juice and cookies, the pilot announced our landing in Nice. There was a view of the sea and at long last my dream was about to come true. I was about to set foot on the French Riviera, the jet setters' playground. I now felt a far greater excitement than at any other time on my trip and a fluttery happiness was growing.

As I walked out of the airport, I realized that I was really at the French Riviera! My luck held out with the first phone call locating a hotel only a block from the beach in Nice. The city was built along the wide thoroughfare of palm trees and flowerbeds named, Promenade des Anglais, with nothing but hotels facing the water. Those hotels were far more expensive than the one I had taken just a block behind one of the oldest and most famous hotels, the Neglesco.

It had been a long day. I took a short walk along the promenade then found a small Italian restaurant near my hotel. The next morning, after the usual breakfast of cold, hard bread, butter, jelly and coffee, I took a walk on the beach side of the promenade. The air was warm and pleasant. Almost hypnotized, I walked toward the castle like building or monument on the cliff quite far away. I had not intended walking so far; the nearer I got, the more curious I became. When I arrived at the cliff and looked back, I realized I had walked several miles. I climbed the stairway to the top only to find a small Maritime Museum of ship pictures and marine objects. It did not look interesting enough to pay admission for, so I stood atop the cliff admiring the view. My curiosity made me continue around the bend to see the small harbor. I continued to walk around the harbor and found myself in a rather uninteresting looking residential area. My feet were so tired I knew I must find a taxi back to the hotel. I started to walk back hoping to see a taxi then finally stopped for coffee at a sidewalk café overlooking the harbor. I watch the yachts and boats come and go while resting my tired aching feet. I never found a taxi, fortunately benches were scattered along the promenade so that I took a very long time to return to my hotel, three hours to be exact, I was anxious to take in the sun on the beach but so tired from walking, I fell asleep. Late afternoon, I slipped into my bathing suit and headed for the beach. Much to my surprise there was no sand, and the gravelly sort of rocks were quite uncomfortable to lie on or when trying to walk on without shoes.

That evening I walked along the promenade with many tourists, trying to decide on the place for dinner. Most of the hotels had sidewalk restaurants and bars. Selecting a dinner spot always became a problem for me since I hated eating alone. With my bad experience padding the bill, confusion and trying to figure out menus, I dreaded mealtimes. At least European restaurants had their menus posted on the outside so if the prices were outrageous I could avoid embarrassment. Nice was so overcrowded with tourists and extremely noisy with motorbikes and the loud gear shifting of trucks and cars, I decided to travel to a quieter spot. I was so anxious to really see Monaco, Monte Carlo and the Riviera in general; the only logical way was by renting a car. In this way I could go in any direction that looked interesting. I wanted to find the right spot to just stop traveling for a few days.

Early morning on Monday, I went to the crowded American Express office and made arrangements for a car. By the time I got the car and my luggage from the hotel it was nearly noon. There was a very handsome young Frenchman eyeing me over at the car rental agency. He could not speak English and I could not speak French. Driving on the wrong side of the road in England had been confusing, but now I was not able to read the road signs and asking directions was equally confusing. Most of the warning signs were simple lines drawn and self-explanatory. Once out of the traffic of Nice, driving became easy with roadside pull off areas to view magnificent scenery. A pleasant drive, then the sign "Monaco!" Even though it is a separate country within France, there were no border stations with customs and passport inspections. I was totally unaware of leaving France and entering Monaco. As I drove down the hill, I could see the old palace where the American Princess Grace lived. It was fun to be in her domain since; when casting directors wanted a "Grace Kelly type" I was called in for interviews. Driving by the harbor there were exquisite yachts especially the huge Revlon Ultima II. Elizabeth Taylor and Richard Burton's yacht was amongst the many. Up the hill and around the corner, I was in front of the famous Monte Carlo gambling casino. I wanted to see it all later and kept driving. Much to my surprise, in a matter of minutes I was out of the city. I would come back but I was anxious to see what lay ahead. Next was Menton (pronounced like "Mahn-tawn") with its lovely beaches.

San Remo in Italy was only a few miles further. The guards at the frontier (border station) were true to the Italian male reputation and quite flirty. It was amazing how after crossing a simple border everything changed so drastically. It was like leaving United States and entering Mexico. In San Remo, the streets, the houses and buildings were dirty with paint falling off the exterior walls. The people obviously lived in poverty conditions. San Remo was pretty but nothing to compare with Monaco. I liked the beaches in Menton. Perhaps Monte Carlo's glamorous publicity influenced my decision to return there.

The highway I traveled was the old highway along the sea. It was referred to as the "Lower Route" even though it was high above the sea cliffs. Nestled among the beautiful cliffs were many villas. I have seen a signs "Autostrada" - a highway that appeared to be totally suspended by bridges high up on the mountainside. On my return, driving through the great vineyards, I located the "highway in the sky" which was carved through the mountains of solid rock. Between the mountains there was a bridge to the next mountain tunnel. I could just zip along as though on any expressway in the United States. Huge fans were mounted in the tunnel, and arches were cut out for some form of ventilation for the long tunnels. Along the way, I could see old villages interwoven in the mountain areas seemingly untouched by modern days. The Italians collected from you to use the Autostrada, as did the French, so you pay the toll fees twice.

Nearing Monaco, I caught sight of old Roman temple ruins. I tried to drive toward it but got lost. Later, I found out it was built by Emperor Augustine. Never mind, I would go back and see it during my stay in Monte Carlo. I could see Monaco directly below, yet it took me over 6 miles of steep winding roads to reach the city below, which indicated the height of the cliffs behind Monaco.

I started searching the streets for hotels listed in my tour book. I decided to park and walk to the hotels. Each one I tried said, "complete," meaning filled. Back in the car, up and down the streets of confusing traffic. The car kept dying, so in frustration, I parked again and walked until I found one hotel listed in the book with an available room. No wonder I could not find this particular hotel. It was at the end of a dead end street. I then continued down the walkway for about a half block. It was dark and dingy, but I was getting nervous that I would not find a room and was willing to take any. If I did not look up and see the paint falling off the ceiling while having to walk the dingy stairway then the room was not so bad. At least it had a nice tiny view of the sea. After resting, I had dinner in the hotel that was included in the price of the room as well as breakfast for about five dollars a day. After a very nice dinner, I was ready for my first night in Monte Carlo!

That first evening in Monte Carlo introduced me to a very important area - the Post Office. It controlled most means of communication; including payphones, long-distance calls, and telegrams. As usual, the operator spoke no English. I wanted to send three telegrams but the price she quoted was extremely high. Totally unable to communicate with her, a voice behind me said, "Perhaps I can assist." He was a handsome young man who was a well-tanned Scandinavian Monte Carlo resident who spoke English. With his help, I was able to send one telegram. I got the feeling the operator was trying to pick up a few Franks for herself as seemed to be the custom for those dealing with foreign tourists. The young man asked if I could join him for a drink at a nearby sidewalk café where we later were joined by several of his friends. He then invited us all to go aboard the yacht he skippered for a nightcap. I was not afraid that it would be another of those "parties" as in Paris since the harbor was easy walking distance to my hotel. When my new Skipper friend found out that I had been in the motion picture business he told me of an English producer living in Monte Carlo who he knew quite well. If I would get one of my resumes to him he would see the producer received it. A small ray of hope for work only added to my happy, exciting introduction to Monte Carlo AND a good looking blond yacht Skipper! I was in love with Monaco!

CHAPTER 18

The next morning I returned the car to the rental agency in Nice where the handsome young Frenchman insisted on checking in my car. He knew very few words of English and a bit more of Italian. He managed to ask if he might come to Monte Carlo to see me. He was younger but it would be nice to have a male escort now and then, especially a handsome, vibrant one. I told him the name of my hotel not really expecting to ever hear from him.

The frequent trains run from Villa (town) to Villa at the base of the mountain with each station centrally located so that it is easy walking distance to shopping areas in each town. There was also a bus that made frequent trips between communities. The fares were very inexpensive on the bus or train. It was actually easier to go shopping by public transportation than by automobile.

My first few days were spent on the beach, resting and reading during the warmest hours of the afternoon. Sometimes I took walks exploring the town. Dinner in the evening around 7 pm and a walking excursion around Monte Carlo or "people watching" at the outdoor café was my evening social life. With a wonderful night sea air and no danger of being out alone, I could spend a minimum amount of time in my dingy room. The hotel's inexpensive room, good food and conversation appealed to me, not its drab décor. There were very few inexpensive hotels in Monte Carlo. This was one of them. At first I said I would stay three days--then I asked for a week--then for a month. The most time they could offer me was through August 3rd since all the hotels were booked well in advance, often even a year, for the month of August. It was the established time for the Parisians to come to the sea. The antiquity of the hotel and its narrow street was in sharp contrast to the very expensive modern apartment structures rising graciously above the sea. I dreaded trying to find another hotel but I was determined to remain. I really loved Monte Carlo. The central shopping area was only one main street a few blocks long that could easily be reached by walking up the long flight of steps next to the hotel.

I became acquainted with a rather quiet reserved French gentleman who was in his 15th year vacationing away from Paris, where he lived with his mother. Pushing 50, he had never been married and could best be described as a spinster-type bachelor. He worked for an American company and spoke perfect English. Often he would help me with the hotel dinner menu; then we would occasionally take our evening walks together.

There were many beaches on the very clean promenade along the seaside. There was a not-so-attractive waterworks along the beach, but between nine and ten o'clock each and every evening it presented a fascinating live performance of dancing waters in brilliant colors in tune with classical music. One could become completely enraptured in these performances. This, along with the beaches were free to the public, a difficult thing to find anywhere in many area of France!

The beaches of Monte Carlo had been reclaimed from the sea, by hauling tons of rocks from the mountains above and building it up above the sea level. This project was brought about by Prince Rainier to create far more land for the construction of expensive high-rise apartment buildings and hotels. Since the mountain behind Monte Carlo was a sheer cliff, thousands of feet shooting upward, it was impossible to build in that direction.

A protective seawall on each side of the fairly narrow opening, forming a perfect swimming area, was constructed to prevent the surge of the sea from reclaiming the land. As in Nice, the beaches were small rock pebbles, hard to lie on and hard on everyone's feet! It was necessary to buy a grass mat to lie on while sunbathing and wearing beach shoes. The water flowed over nothing but rocks making it crystal clear and quite cold when I first arrived. As the weeks passed, the water temperature grew increasingly warmer.

Along the public beaches, the promenade floor was constructed out of huge slabs of travertine that also formed the roof for beach shops beneath. It was 50' in width and equivalent to a city block in length. It was available for meetings, theater, and dance areas. At one end there was a large lit metal sculpture fountain. There were chairs scattered about the well-lit area. Some evenings I would go there to sit and read or write until 10 o'clock. Everywhere along the beach area, as well as most areas in Monte Carlo, were immaculately clean.

Within the little principality of Monaco, there were four sections of the old city of Monaco, Monte Carlo and two of lesser significance. The Old City sits high on the cliffs, almost like a separate island, accessible only by a stairway and one narrow road. The tightly crammed four or five story buildings and narrow passageways make it impossible to travel except by foot. There is a small open-air theater facing the sea. Nearby was a large museum of Oceanography, built by Prince Rainier's great grandfather who was a world-famous oceanographic scientist. Its stately façade facing the sea is more impressive architectural achievement than the Palace at the opposite end of the Old City where Prince Rainier and Princess Grace reside. The palace was a somewhat unimpressive orange structure. At night with the light shining on it from the cliffs below, the palace became a living picture that cannot be captured in photographs. Attached at one end of the palace is a very old medieval castle, dating back to the 13th century. The south side of the palace is Italian Renaissance style and can be traced to the fifteenth and sixteenth centuries.

Many legends have been handed down through the centuries about Monaco dating back to Julius Caesar who used the harbor while waging war against Pompeius. He was quite familiar with the area, and when he completed his conquest of Gaul, he boarded a ship at the port in Monaco for his return to Rome. In Monaco, the Port of Hercules went by that name far back into ancient times. In Monaco there is a temple dedicated to Hercules. St Devote or Devota is the patron saint of Monaco. She was a beautiful and extremely pious 16-year-old girl from Corsica who was martyred. Her body was to be burnt, but other Christians placed her remains in a boat and put it out to sea bound for Africa in 312. On the way, as she predicted, a dove flew out of her mouth and guided the boat to the port of Hercules in Monaco. The boat was dashed against the rocks and the crew drowned but the body of the Saint was recovered by some local fishermen and placed in a Christian chapel that was already there devoted to St. George. Later a chapel dedicated to her was built and it still stands in Monaco to this day where flowers planted in her honor bloom out of season on her feast day of January 27.

Actual documents, tracing Prince Rainier's Grimaldi family tree goes back as far as 1133. Many Americans, like me, are fascinated by one's lineage, which can be documented so far in the past, especially in Europe. A problem can be that many Americans, especially those involved from farming pioneers generally could barely read and write, if at all, and written record of lineage is limited, except those who kept old family Bibles. To my amazement, I found that Italians, French, English, and others only attempted to trace a few generations to claim their nationality. For many decades the Romans ruled the British Isles. Most European countries having been conquered at one time or another, so nationalities have been mixed. Their heritage is as amalgamated as the Americans' heritage. Those of us who can trace back to the 1600's and before usually include Native American ancestors.

The topography of the peninsula of the Old City of Monaco perched atop its cliffs and the hills of Monte Carlo form a perfect "U" along the seawall create an excellent yacht harbor. At the base of the "U" is an Olympic size swimming pool with grandstands for water shows built by Rainier for the people of his country. Behind it, along the promenade are several sidewalk cafés where one can sit mesmerized by the goings and comings of the world's most elegant and expensive yachts. Tourism began with the onset of gambling in 1863 for which the present Monte Carlo Casino was built by architect Garnier, builder of the Opera House in Paris. The ruler at that time was Charles III, thus the name "Mount Charles--Monte Carlo. From its beginning, it was always an international playground for the rich and famous.

As you drive up the steep incline from the harbor and round the corner at the top, the magnificent palatial Monte Carlo Casino comes into view. Around the side of this white structure, you are suddenly in front of it. Across the wide thoroughfare sits a pretty park where one can stroll or sit on the bench and enjoy the surrounding beauty. The park was filled with large old trees that look much like magnolia trees except for their bulky trucks. The interior of the Casino is like the grand palace with its beautiful ceilings, huge crystal chandeliers, and the velvet draped walls. Since I was always alone, I never ventured beyond the Grand Hall into the gambling rooms. I love the manmade beauty, but there was so much natural beauty to enjoy, too.

Beneath the casino where this shoreline curves, it was an arch within an arch interlaced with walkways. Cement had been poured into the huge rocks which created the ever-constant sound of the sea slashing against the rocks. Walking back towards my hotel on this promenade, I met young and old, people walking their dogs, lovers strolling arm in arm, stopping to look at the shimmering path of gold laid across the sea by the full Moon. There was the warm sea air, crystal-clear water, twinkling lights, and the occasional fishermen along the rocks all creating a beautiful serene serenity beyond expectations. I had found my very special spot in the world!

I really began to feel I wanted to remain in my kingdom by the sea for as long as my money would hold out. The hours, the days and weeks lose their meaning where the Majesty mountain stands like a gigantic rock castle protecting the city nestled in its bosom--from the red tiled roof of pleasant dwellings to the Prince's Palace, then it finally kisses the sea. This is a land where beauty and serenity reign in sweet harmony. I could not imagine leaving this to return home to the daily tension, depressive negative or competitive hustle-bustle. It takes getting away to realize just how much we Americans are bombarded daily with the world, national and local news of dire misfortunes that create a very negative influence in our daily lives. Since I did not understand the language or could not hear the news nor did I buy any English newspapers, I did not wish to spoil the peace and serenity that was slowly engulfing me. I felt Monte Carlo must have many English-speaking people with whom I could make friends. One Sunday I attended St. Paul's Anglican Church. It was a lovely, large clean structure with hardly 20 or so people in attendance. I read aloud the congregation's responses from their prayer book that included blessings of the Sovereign Queen. It was a strange feeling for an American unaccustomed to blessing the Head of State as the printed part of a religious service. Alas, I have no common bond amongst these few English-speaking people except the similarity of language.

Much to my surprise, one day my young friend from the car rental agency called and asked if he could come to see me that afternoon. His attractive presence on my daily jaunts to the beach might be fun, so I told him it would be all right. When you live in such a peaceful atmosphere, you forget to fear strangers. If there was crime in Monaco,

I was unaware of it. I felt totally safe and secure anywhere at any time. The knapsack and hippies were rarely seen in Monaco and never for long. My handsome friend and I were going to the public beach; no harm could come from that. However, when he arrived, he suggested he show me the surrounding areas in his car.

What a wonderful opportunity to see the sights with a native that I would otherwise have missed. With his pleasant harmless smile and childlike enthusiasm plus an invisible angel riding on my shoulder, I still felt no fear about going out for ride with this total stranger who could hardly speak my language nor I his. We had such a problem with communication, yet it was a comfortable feeling. He would help me learn French if I would help him learn English. We drove up the mountains toward the old ruins, which I had wanted to see the first day in Monaco. I don't remember why we did not stop there, and unfortunately I never did get to see the ruins up close. We stopped in an old community at the top of the mountain and had coffee at a sidewalk café.

This excitement was building as we laughed at ourselves trying to understand one another. My full-of-life French companion stopped and bought a bottle of wine, cheese, and a loaf of uncut French bread. We continue to drive back into the mountain area passing old unchanged villages, winding around mountain roads, through an arch that was carved out of the mountainside, and past other old Roman ruins. We stopped where there was a plateau with a fantastic view of the valley below. After spreading a covering over the green grass, we sat, he opened the wine, and we happily enjoyed our bread, wine, and cheese. We shared many laughs at our inability to understand the other's language.

A very warm rapport had been building between us, so it seemed quite natural for him to gently hold and kiss me. That simple afternoon would be marked indelibly in my most cherished memories. Our attempt to teach each other our own language may not have been too successful, but there was a sweet, tender, and wonderful communication that transcended any words that could have been spoken. Before traveling to Europe, if a woman would conger up a "PERFECT" fairytale afternoon of meeting a young, handsome Frenchman, going for a ride in nature's antiquity at its best, then this picnic would have been that perfect fairytale! Yet, still under forty at that time and my state of mind, I might rather have been swept off my feet by a handsome man who owned one of those luxurious yachts in Monaco's harbor!

My Frenchman was able to get across to me that the American actor, Charles Bronson, was filming a movie in Nice where there was a film studio. It was an English production company. He told me he occasionally worked at the studio as an extra or bit player. He explained as best he could how I could find the studio myself. He especially wanted to see me that day because he had to leave the next morning and would be gone for 10 days; otherwise, he would have taken me to the studio personally. It seemed that when tourists rent a car, they could also rent him as a chauffeur and guide to tour the countryside. He wanted to know if I would still be in Monte Carlo when he returned from his trip.

CHAPTER 19

My bachelor friend from Paris was always at dinner to help me with the menu when I needed his help. He was never pushy to sit with me or to go for walks with me since he sensed my desire to be alone. He tried to help me learn a few words of French. We shared many similar beliefs since he taught yoga in Paris, and I studied all religious philosophies. I told him that I would be unable to find a hotel room for the month of August, if I seriously planned to stay in Monte Carlo for a time. My friend suggested that I rent a reasonably priced apartment. He had only one day left but he knew people who owned apartments, and he would help me try to find and rent one. Up and down stairways we walked, searching to no avail. There were also several rental agencies I could use for a fee.

My friend wrote a note in French for me to give to the agents to help communicate with them. The first rental agency he recommended had only one apartment in my maximum price range. The apartment was very conveniently located. It was in the building housing the post office and communications center with access through the lobby. It was only a block from the casino and restaurant area. The other end of the building opened onto the main street where the shops were located. There were also shops within the building. The apartment was basically what I needed but more money than I wanted to pay. I looked at a few other apartments but none fit my needs as well as this one in the Palace de la Scala, (Palace of the Stairs), the first one I had seen. When I told the agent I decided to take the apartment, he then told me I must sign a three-month lease. The rent was doubled for the month of August. I refused to pay the double rent but would pay half a month's rent more and sign agreement. Since I had to put up two month's rent in advance and an extra half-month, it was a sizable hit in my thrifty pocketbook. I was also anxious to get the keys and just get settled in my own little home, but alas, nothing can disturb the French custom of a two-and-a-half hour lunch interlude. I had to return at 2:30 pm to sign the rest of the necessary papers and pick up the keys. It was a very tense feeling signing legal documents in a foreign country without being able to read them and having no one to translate. It was probably very foolish!

By the time I was settled in my one-room efficiency, my bachelor friend had returned to Paris with his vacation ending for another year. He also made reservations for the next year before he returned. The apartment had a sitting dining area at a large double window some 8' in height, overlooking a portion of the yacht harbor with that fabulous view of the Palace where Princess Grace lived. The matching French provincial furnishings were quite pretty and would be outstanding pieces in the States. The bathroom had a large tub, so big that when I filled it, I could float in it. The ill-equipped kitchen's refrigerator was so small that I could hardly keep more than a couple of days' fresh vegetables. Never mind, it was a welcome sight since I could now prepare any food I chose. There would be no more not knowing exactly what I had ordered from menus I could not read. My fourth floor apartment was easily accessible by elevator, one of the few I had seen in Europe.

I looked out the window to see if I would have any of that horrible street noise. As I looked about, I realized I was directly across and equal in height to Grace's Palace. I had to laugh to myself thinking of the name of the apartment "Palace of the Stairs" so I had my palace and Grace had hers! So often in my career in Hollywood, I have been compared to her. If I ever had a female idol, perhaps it was Grace Kelly. She captured Hollywood's highest crown, the Oscar, having worked with the top leading male stars, then "thumbing her nose" at Hollywood when she was at the pinnacle of her career to go off and marry a Prince. She lived in a storybook kingdom, had several beautiful children and remained a beautiful lady through it all. (This was before she died in a car wreck.) My palace nor my career could not in any way compare with Princess Grace's, yet how well I knew life is not always as it appears for the rich and famous after my years of exposure to them in Hollywood.

When I lived in Rome in the early 60's, working in the film "Cleopatra," Al Capp, famed cartoonist and gossip columnist interviewed me regarding my personal viewpoint on living in the world's most glamorous city, working in the most expensive movie ever made (at that time), and my attitude toward Elizabeth Taylor. He was expecting that I would want to trade places with her. "No way!" was my reply! I went on to explain how I enjoyed my freedom to think, go, and do as I pleased. Certainly the famed become imprisoned within that fame and fortune, a price I was not willing to pay. No, even with life's trials and tribulations, I still preferred to be me and live my own life as it unfolded.

Aloneness was part of my total life, yet in many ways, I was happy with it, as it was a state of mind I had always lived with. Only a few years prior, I could never have adjusted nor accepted many things in my new life. When we lived amongst family, friends, a common language, with autos, telephone, television, radio, newspapers, and constant noise--and suddenly to be cut off from everything familiar-- requires some mature adjusting. I thanked God for whatever struggles life brought to me, for it has also brought me independence, solitude, and a certain amount of inner peace. I felt I was ready to accept responsibilities for creating a philosophical book regarding very deep thought and consideration. These conditions seemed necessary for that accomplishment.

Again, doves found a place on my windowsill--and the dove was the symbol Monaco. The meaning of the doves for which I have long sought must be a good omen. Possibly the fact that I had come to Monaco and liked it so much was the only meaning, if there was any meaning of the doves in my life at all. As soon as I began getting settled, I wrote David in London asking him if he would mind shipping my luggage to me, which had been stored at Victorian train station. I was especially anxious to get my typewriter to start writing. This necessary peace of mind and inspirational atmosphere was engulfing me now. I wrote everyone I knew giving them my semi-permanent address. In spite of being a bit lonely with no dates or friends, I really felt ecstatically happy.

I had to buy linens for the apartment. When I saw the prices of linens, I decided I could make pillowcases by hand until I realized the price of cotton was about $10 a yard. My shopping was a game of charades, mostly done by pointing. Now I did enjoy foods like fruits and vegetables and salads, eggs for breakfast, ice tea and all the milk I wanted to drink. Funny how we take the simplest foods for granted until they are unavailable for a time.

When I lived in Rome I put forth little effort in learning the language not knowing my six-week contract would be extended to six months. I would not make the same mistake again, so I signed up for twice a week French lesson class with an American-born British accented female teacher. She had lived in Monte Carlo for many years. As some people are tone deaf, I thought surely I must be language deaf. Her method was good. It was audio/visual with a book, then recording your own voice, playing back with the teacher interrupting with corrections. I learned sentences such as: "Take off your coat, hang it there." "No, she is playing with her doll." "Fourth floor on the left. Take the elevator." (That one I could apply to my apartment except it was to the right) "Yes, these are toys everywhere on the floor, on the bed, on the furniture, on the walls, even on the ceiling." All of which were of no help at all when I went shopping. My mind was too slow to pull out the words from the sentences I had learned, translating at the same time.

Each day, I would practice with the Concierge sitting at the front desk at my apartment building. He was always so happy to tell me when I had "post" knowing how eager I was for mail from home. At long last current mail, as well as forwarding mail from London, began catching up with me. Only a pittance of correspondence arrived from Debbie with no earthshaking developments, only descriptions of the ever seemingly superficial social world of her returning to California, boys - boys - boys and wishing me well. If there was any animosity toward me it was not apparent in her letters.

I still did better with my few words of Italian and charades than I did with my new French. About twice a week I would go shopping in the morning at an outdoor vegetable market. There was also a "super" market, about the size of an America convenience store. I was amazed at the prices, even cheese, which I assumed to be from Europe (the really good one) seemed more expensive than in the United States.

I began to get a routine of life. After breakfast, I would try to organize my thoughts and write until I was tired which was at about noon. After a light lunch, I would go to the beach, which was a pleasant walk from my apartment. About two o'clock I would return to my apartment. I would rest during the heat of the day, and then back to writing until dinner. After dinner I often continued my writing. Since my tenacity was become a bit of a hermit, I sometimes forced myself to go out for dinner. Monte Carlo was very pleasant in the evening. Sometimes I would have a glass of wine at the Café de Paris, near the casino and just sit and watch the potpourri of people streaming by.

I truly enjoyed having dinner in my apartment looking out my window viewing the palace with its bright orange lighting against the midnight blue sky on the other side of the yard harbor. Some of these palace walls seemed to reach down several stories and were artistically lit with the orange lights. Each set of archways was lit with softer shades of orange. It seemed too lovely to be real with this beautifully combined green foliage, stone, orange walls, and movie set lighting effect. The hillside of the Old City was covered with green foliage, broken only by the gently sloping of one street with its symmetrical street lighting. There were sparsely scattered lights in old Monte Carlo at night. Toward the sea, the old fort of gray stone was also lit with gold lighting; beyond that was the shimmering moonlight upon the sea.

The palace was definitely a more beautiful view from a distance at night than it was during the day, especially from my apartment window. Facing the palace, there were sidewalk cafés, souvenir shops, and a hard surface parking area. Two guardhouses were at each end, and a few potted plants were the only décor for the simple orange colored structure. There wasn't even a contrasting trim on it. Along one side were permanently placed cannonballs and cannons. There were no obvious advertising signs in Monaco and no large flashings signs. I assumed there was a law against them. I recalled walking through the beautiful gardens surrounding the Oceanography Museum with my friend from Paris. He was like a tour guide showing me points of interest of old Monte Carlo streets. It had been a fascinating evening. I would never have attempted it alone.

For America's Independence Day, I wandered through our parent country's history in Westminster Abbey. In Monte Carlo it happened on France's Bastille Day, NOW celebrating the master of all pyrotechnic (fireworks) display is undoubtedly Monaco! Each and every Friday night between midnight and two or three o'clock in the morning fireworks blast and blazed near the summer Casino. The natives learned to sleep through it but I awoke almost every Friday night. I never found out where the custom originated, but apparently most of the communities along the French Riviera have their fireworks displays.

Fortunately I was in Monaco during the yearly International Fireworks Exposition. Twice a week for several weeks a month different countries put on fireworks displays competing for a prize. There were posters all over the town announcing it, but since I did not read French, I was not aware of the pending Exposition. One evening I was sitting along the beach promenade when it started. The beautiful explosions in the sky beckoned me nearer – red, green, blue, gold, and white fantastic beautiful explosions as I walked closer. Each good vantage point was crowded with people. Just as I entered the tunnel of the arches, a blast overhead was grossly magnified and echoed in the tunnel. As I reached the area where I wanted to view the display, it was over!

In the United States I would never have put forth such an effort to see fireworks displayed after my childhood years, but in Monaco it was an event I eagerly anticipated. The fetes were so spectacular that if each country does not exhibit a really fantastic display, the crowd's reaction is quite dispassionate. The night for Great Britain's exhibition came. I walked down the hill overlooking the port of yachts. The loud speaker was blaring upbeat Swiss or German accordion music creating a festive mood for everyone. A man and his son skipped past me in time to the music. People were gathering in every vantage point facing the port. I took a table at a sidewalk café centered in front of the port. The music stopped - streetlights and all lights facing the port went off and the fireworks began! The fireworks were shot from both sides of the boat's entrance into the port. Words fail to express adequately the excitement of those displays. I had always associated firework displays with children's enjoyment, yet no child could have enjoyed these displays more than adults like me. The displays were shot off simultaneously from both sides of the U-shaped port. A great burst of white followed by a burst of blue then green and on and on it continued. There were stardust, upside down shooting stars and orange gold explosions in the shape of giant palm trees or flowers which then held their shape for a moment. Some were so bright they lit up the whole area, some floated slowly down into the sea; some wiggled, others flashed colors in every direction. For the grand finale, each side threw everything they had in the air simultaneously, creating thrilling excitement throughout the crowd. I wished all the children and adults as well, throughout the world could have seen this spectacular sight. The 30 minutes passed all too soon. The audience applauded, the boat horns blasted, and those with searchlights flashed them across the harbor in an enthusiastic salute to Great Britain!

During my dinner hour in the apartment one evening, the fireworks display began. The building to the left almost totally blocked the view, but I could see some of the display. Preparing my dinner I kept running back and forth to catch a glimpse of the display. When I finally finished preparing my dinner and rushed to the table to enjoy the display, again it was over.

Brazil's exhibit was fair, but Great Britain's was still the best so far. The final exhibition was to be given by Portugal. Since this was to be the last, I went early and took a table at one of the sidewalk cafés. Again there was the festive music, then the lights went off and it began--this time, not from the port entry but from numerous positions inside the port. A beautiful small display started simultaneously shooting one at a time, then at the two entry points, then the grand ones began. They shot higher and higher, wider and lit up the sky more than any other exhibit had done. Their primary method used was similar to an atomic exploding in all directions. With various size explosions and magnificent colors, this exhibition was indescribably fantastic! There was so much going on in the air, the crowd was mesmerized and thrilled, "ooing" and "ahing." For as much as I enjoyed Great Britain's exhibit, this far exceeded anything I had seen in my whole life. From the ovation of the crowd and the boat horns blasting when it was over, it was unanimous for everyone, and so it was for the judges. Portugal WON!

Each and every day I lived in Monte Carlo I loved it more. I knew it was the excitement of living in the world's most glamorous playground, and its newness might wear off. At least, I had three months to enjoy it, and at the same time put forth maximum effort in accomplishing my goal of writing a book. Maybe the time had never been right for me until then. The doves continued their vigilance on my windowsill. I felt very settled in my "home" in a foreign land. As I began working, my book moved along very well. Words seemed to flow from an unseen force not from me but through me. Everyone had said it was impossible to find a room for August when I looked for a place to stay. Then it was August, and I was very much in Monte Carlo- -difficult perhaps, but not impossible!

CHAPTER 20

Walking became such part of my life that the half-mile hike to the train station was nothing. Trains ran frequently. The first venture outside of Monaco was an attempt to find a film studio my friend from the auto rental agency had described. With photos and resume in hand, I set out to follow his instructions. To my surprise I found the studio with no difficulty. Within the studio I acquired about the production starring Charles Bronson. It was an English production company, and as with all European film companies, they could only hire one or two American actors in major starring roles and none in production. The people I met, associated with the production company, were cordial, inviting me to have lunch at the studio and assuring me they would contact me if anything came up; however, I left with little or no hope of ever hearing from the studio.

Another trip was made to Nice when I received a notice that my luggage had arrived from London. I had quite a time locating the warehouse where it was stored, then getting a taxi and unloading the bulky pieces at the train station. As I stood on the platform awaiting the train, a rather non-descript man in his late 50's or 60's asked in English where I was going. I answered his questions in a protective hurried manner. In a pleasant response he told me that he was an American living in Monte Carlo. He had just driven to Nice to take a friend to the airport. He would be happy to help me with my luggage and drive me back to my apartment in Monte Carlo. Assuming my protective Angel was still on my shoulder, plus the camaraderie of a fellow American, I really needed some help with the luggage even though I was a little apprehensive about a total stranger. An example of trust is just because the other person is an American, whereas under similar conditions in the U.S. I would never accept a ride from a stranger. Driving to Monte Carlo he told me he lived there for many years. He managed a band that played in one of the one of the nightclubs. He suggested that he show me around Monte Carlo on another day.

Since I had no telephone, the only way to reach me was to stop by my apartment or leave word downstairs with a concierge. Late one morning, after I had been writing for hours, my helpful friend from the train station stopped by to invite me to have lunch with him at the Old Beach Hotel and to bring my bathing suit for there was the best beach in Monte Carlo. A break was most welcome. We had a nice lunch on a lovely poolside patio. This was obviously the gathering spot for most Americans visiting Monaco. Almost everyone was speaking English for a change. It was a lovely spot with permanent cabanas, sand instead of a pebble beach, and rafts placed at different distances in the bay that made swimming quite far out safe. There was also a large salt-water swimming pool. This very gentle man put forth maximum effort to introduce me to everyone he knew. He invited me to return to this beach at any time and to tell the guard at the gate that I was his guest. He also told me of the free bus that made regular roundtrips from in front of the Casino. It was for hotel guests, but no one ever checked. Most of my future beach visits were made to this beach rather than the public beach. The more sophisticated atmosphere was more to my liking, plus I enjoyed swimming in the pool. At first, conversations that I could understand were pleasant to my ears, but shortly thereafter, the New York accented people always discussing dire misfortunes--which grew a bit tiresome while sunning in the world's most famous playgrounds. Occasionally I saw the young yacht captain and his friends. This was obviously a spot where the affluent played. It was my impression that the local young men searched out wealthy lady tourists like a pack of hungry wolves.

My American friend offered to show me some of the "in" night spots in Monte Carlo, which he did, including the Sporting Club Gambling Casino. The society gamblers gathered there during the summer months while the Monte Carlo Casino was swarming with tourists. The Casino was surprisingly non-luxurious compared to the lavishly decorated casinos in Las Vegas. These gamblers were so deadly serious without the drinking and gaiety seen in Las Vegas. After I was told the amount of money at stake around some of these tables, I understood. Around one table alone, literally millions of dollars were represented. What a waste! One visit to see the jet setters gambling was enough for me.

One day when I answered the doorbell, a tall, gangly longhaired young man dressed in a T-shirt and jeans stood asking, "Are you Ann Palmer?" Assuming he was a delivery boy, my mind raced trying to figure out what he could be delivering. He introduced himself as a young English producer to whom I had mailed my resume. I invited him into my apartment. We had a quick rapport discussing film production. He had the most mystical eyes I had ever seen. For less than 30 years of age, his wisdom was beyond that of a man twice his age. He had just returned from filming in Malta on his way to Hollywood for the next six months. That left little hope for any film work through meeting him. Hours flew by, and after he left I realize how good it felt to be able to just talk to someone again with whom I had so much in common.

Unannounced, the next day he stopped by with an American friend who looked like a typical looking film businessman. Again, we talked for hours about the film industry. The Englishman was terribly young to have attained the status of a producer; however, I was told that he had a limitless checking account and that certainly can't hurt anyone seeking a film business career. He was obviously quite bright and enormously talented. The money behind his ambition had helped attain a rapid success. They asked me to go for rides in his unusual automobile. Unusual it was! It was a very expensive antique convertible that turned heads as we drove by. When he dropped me off at my apartment, in a quick manner, he asked if I had a long dress with me. I told him I did. If I would like a glimpse of the local society, be ready in 30 minutes, and he would take me to a birthday party. As fast as I tried to apply makeup, it melted off in the summer heat. Nonetheless, I managed to be formally dressed in 30 minutes. Here a man, young enough to be dating my daughter, escorted me. His attire reminded me of Debbie's her dates but was quite a contrast to his daytime attire. His shaggy hair was incongruent for his evening clothes.

The evening was wonderful--to see the petty, phony social climbers at work was amusing, especially with my escort's humorous tongue-in-cheek remarks about each one. He gave a background for each guest, and then pinpointed his or her social ambitions. Humorous as he was, his observations seemed very astute with deep understanding for a man so young in years. Compared to the social climbers I had observed for years in Hollywood and Palm Springs, these were petty amateurs, but then they exist everywhere even in the smallest community or town. To me, their whole existence, their reason to live was built on trivial allusion. While Princess Grace's Philadelphia Society background might have been a contributing factor, people in Europe appeared to seek social acceptance even more than in America. To my thinking, it was a very empty, unrewarding goal. When the young producer suggested going to the outdoor Hawaiian nightclub for dancing, I was ready to leave. The birthday party was held poolside at the Old Beach Hotel and was more or less a coming out party for a teenage girl being honored. I hoped it had been successful since her parents must have spent a small fortune on the dinner and rentals. I was happy to have the opportunity to observe firsthand the lifestyle of the so-called jet set. Once again, life had presented me with seemingly glamorous and desirable circumstances for which most people lust and crave. It all seemed pointless from my contemplation and evaluation of these peoples' trivial values. It only confirmed to me my own inner wealth and riches which could not be lost by stock market crashes, recession, business failures nor any of my mistakes in life.

The young English producer, the yacht captain, the young Frenchman in Nice, and other young men in Monaco offered a composite of younger male jet setters. The older gentleman was typical of the male population in yesteryears, but where were the men in the middle years in Monaco--all married, I assumed. Often scanning the yacht harbor, I had not seen one man that I would care to know. The rugged, handsome, mature yacht-type was only another of Hollywood's creations that were non-existent in Monaco.

I had no female acquaintances either. I had written two girlfriends hoping one or the other could come to Monte Carlo. Realizing I would eventually return to Texas, I wrote to Debbie, now in California, to tell her I planned to try to open a gift store in my parents' sunroom. While she was old enough to make her own decisions, I told her I felt that if she were to find a happier normal life, her chances would be far better in Dallas than in Los Angeles. Little did I know how that advice would haunt me through the years to come. I finally realized that even if I did meet people in Europe that I could become friends with true friendships take years to develop.

Ann Palmer

One day in my apartment I became very sick with no telephone and no friend to call even if I had one. Alone, the chilling fact was that I could die and no one would even know it or even find me. It was such a very lonely and lost feeling. Solitude was an atmosphere I wanted for writing my book after the years of hectic struggling, but I realized there is great difference in being alone by choice and being alone by NECESSITY! At my parents' home, I would have my own apartment upstairs and could be alone by choice not necessity!

As any writer soon finds out, every now and then I desperately needed to do research either in my own books or those in the library. The Monte Carlo library would not help me with research since I cannot read French. To be completely cut off from family, friends, or even strangers with a common language can become overpowering. I had the solitude and the surroundings so glorious that anyone should be inspired, and I was, for a while. But then the loneliness seemed to begin to dim all my creative endeavors. Day by day the remoteness, the desolation and isolation consumed me like an infectious plague. Like a defensive child, I kept telling myself I did not need anyone after so many disappointing love affairs, yet this total solitude was driving me crazy. I really wish I could be mature enough, self-sufficient enough to handle it, but all I could feel was like an abandoned waif. If we are responsible for growing into total independence when we seek maturity--I failed! I truly hated to NEED anyone, but need I did!

(Hotel de Paris - Outstanding Famous Old Hotel - Just to the left of the circle was the Monte Carlo Casino, Opposite the hotel was the Café d' Paris where I often had drinks and dinner. To the right was a street, where a half-block down that street was the Post Office Apartment where I lived.)

CHAPTER 21

For the first month or so my writing had moved along exceptionally well. I had been able to reach deeply into my mind attempting to bring out deeply buried perceptions. It had been slow to come since my arrival in England but finally it flowed fairly freely in Monaco. There were times I felt my brainpower was much too limited for that which tried to flow through it. How could I unlock this area of my mind? It was as though something was there I knew it was there but no matter how hard I tried, I could not bring it to the surface. One part of me wanted desperately to reach into the unknown realm of my subconscious mind to bring forth a small portion of enlightenment to be shared through my writing. Through the years, in meditation quick flashes of thought would come to me so strongly that they stayed with me as though possibly an enlightening memory from another time. I would research these thoughts and was astonished at their correlations. However, during my stay in Monte Carlo, the harder I tried, the more my female emotions got in the way. The loneliness and being so totally out of touch with familiarities was taking over me. I kept wondering why I was there – spending my money I had so laboriously saved by selling all my belongings, when I could be home writing with little or no expenses. There, too, I would be able to converse with people at least once in a while at my own choosing. I knew there would be many distractions and yet wasn't my remoteness even more distracting?

Subconsciously, I was still seeking my fairytale romance with Prince Charming. Perhaps part of my desire to visit Monte Carlo was the ever-present hope of finding some rich, charming handsome man on one of those beautiful yachts that would come along and sweep me off my feet and whoosh me away to his castle in Never-Never land or at least aboard one of the fantastic yachts in the Monaco harbor. Psychiatrists would have named it, maybe basic insecurity, not accepting reality--whatever "reality" may be – escapism--I was probably guilty of, I also knew that all human beings only use a small portion of their brain power and no one person has the answer for everyone's personalities. We all have our "hang-ups" in one form or another.

Long before I had any plans for traveling in Europe, "Malta" kept coming to mind. I read all I could find about it. The only significant thing I could find was that it was a stop over for the Crusaders or was it the Maltese cross that was an important clue? Was there a mystical power in that cross? Used by religions and royalties, it symbolizes virtues or maybe regeneration. At that point in my life, I could certainly use regeneration after the years of hope, disappointment, failure and frustration. When I found myself in Europe with this ever-present Malta symbol in my mind, I hoped to travel there. When I first arrived I drew a straight line on the map with equal distance from Monaco to Malta. I then drew two more lines to form a triangle, a common religious symbol. The third point of the triangle landed near to Oran in Algeria. When I had the drive and picnic with the young Frenchman from Nice, he told me he had been brought up in Oran, a place I had never heard of before, but now it was the other part the triangle. The young English producer had just returned from filming in Malta. There had been the doves on my windowsill along with a seven-year period of searching for some meaning of the doves – then to realize the dove was a symbol of Monaco – on the crest of Monaco is a Maltese cross and the dove. The puzzle was intriguing--why was I in Monte Carlo? Had some power brought me to Monte Carlo as a part of my destiny or was this connection from a long past life? Was some brilliant and enlightenment to come to me if I could remain open to it? With total dedication and commitment perhaps, but alas, my hopeless romanticism always got in the way.

With no social contact, I began to appreciate just how very active my social life had always been and how I had taken it for granted. There would be no social activities if I lived in my parent's community. In Monte Carlo, I did not know one person I could call. It was only a matter of a few weeks before a girlfriend from Los Angeles would arrive in England. We could travel around England, Scotland and Ireland together but traveling with her on the continent would only be retracing my own travels. One of my longtime friends from Texas was living in Spain with her husband and children. I did not know if I would be a welcomed guest. I had never been there and hoped to see her on this trip, but I did not know if I should travel to Spain alone.

My parents could not understand why I was even in Europe alone. The few letters I received only made me homesick. I was just too long an American to become a permanent resident in Europe although being a fatalist, if a job should appear, it might mean I would stay. The film industry in London had been a bust. I did not tried to make contact in Paris realizing the language would prevent me from finding employment there. The studio in Nice had been a washout and there was only one spot left, Munich. Germany was supposed to be the most active film area in Europe. Munich was also preparing for the Olympic games. By now David had returned to Milan, Italy, which was close to Germany. I became so disgusted with his lack of concern during my stay in England; I really did not care to see him again. For months he had known of my arrival time in England, since we corresponded frequently. Even in Hollywood we often talked of writing together as a team. We had dated off and on for a number of years. Then when I finally arrived in his native England, he was too busy to help me or to see me more than the one time.

On Saturday I had an extremely good day writing. Artists and writers often admit their creations that come through them not from them. This had been a day of writing coming fast and furiously through me, not from me. By late afternoon I was mentally and physically exhausted. Getting out of my apartment for dinner was imperative. I soaked and floated in the huge bathtub relaxing then I dressed leisurely. The Café de Paris was a nice spot for outdoor dining. After a quiet solo dinner, I took my glass of wine to one of the front tables to "people watch." As I watched the throngs of people passing, a blond, well-tanned Scandinavian-type of man sat at the next table. He had a strong resemblance to Steve McQueen, who I worked with in the film "Love With A Proper Stranger." With nothing better to do, I studied his face. I played a mind game guessing his background. He had such a remote look, I was sure he had just gotten off a ship that had been at sea for a very long time traveling the far corners of the world. He had a strange haunting look I had never seen before. He appeared to be well over 30 and under 50, a novelty in Monte Carlo, which warranted staring. Hollywood had made me feel "old" even though I was not yet forty.

There was really no desire to meet him as someone to date, only curiosity as a character study. I imagined the sort of a life that had created this long voyaged seaman's appearance, if indeed he was a seaman! After a while he asked me questions in French. I said I did not speak French only English. In perfect English he asked if he could join me at my table. He was no seaman at all! He claimed that he was an artist and was from Germany. He had lived in Monte Carlo for several years. All that I had been thinking about his rugged, sea faring background had been a waste! "Artist" had a ring of romanticism--later I was to find out he made a meager living laying bricks, hardly the work of an artist!

Just behind the casino was the English-speaking outdoor movie theater. The Café de Paris was next to the Casino. Being only steps away, he asked if I would like to go to a movie with him, I accepted. Considering the near proximity of the theater, I did not feel it dictated any fear of this seemingly gentle stranger. After the movie we had a drink in one of the nearby bars. It was good to have someone, just about anyone - someone to walk and talk (English) with. Even thought our ages were quite close, Eric seemed very childlike or seemed to have a very innocent and youthful attitude. His goal in life was much less complicated than mine. That was the end of my loneliness. Eric seemed to be the tonic I desperately needed. Since he worked during the day, I had my usual time for writing. Many days I would meet him at the beach during his leisurely lunch hour for a picnic and swim. With his scuba diving equipment he introduced me to the underwater world of beautiful moving and living sea life just beneath the water's surface. He spoke fluent French, his native German and quite good English. Speaking the same language does not mean understanding each other's meaning of the words. It is only in a situation like this that one realizes just how much we misuse our language or use words in slang, changing its true meaning.

On Eric's day off we would go by train to Cannes, Nice or Menton. One day we explored the coastline of Menton. I would never have been able to do this alone. Being with Eric was like being children again, exploring, running and playing together. It was so much fun and I felt very alive. At last I had a friend I could at least converse with. Walking at night with a man was so much less awkward than as a woman walking alone. Eric had never owned an automobile and was accustomed to walking but I was not. Normally, when I would have taken taxi, he insisted on walking. We were forever walking! I enjoyed it to a point but at times I felt I could not take another step. Eric was constantly doing favors or errands for me, I could not help feeling obligated to him. He was a great help in communicating and translating. It was easy to become dependent on him.

As August grew to a close, tourist began to disappear. Now sitting in the evening at the Café d Paris there was no one to watch walk by, apart from the usual locals. Then came the overcast skies and fog. The beautiful summer days slipped away suddenly. Very few people dotted the beaches with little or no sun. Monte Carlo seemed to be going to sleep, to rest before her winter jet-setters arrival. Eric was planning to leave Monte Carlo for Munich where he said he had a job. I asked him about the film industry in Munich but he had no knowledge of it. If I wanted to come along he would help me find accommodations, help me investigate the film companies as my translator and guide. It seemed like a good idea since Monaco was like a bear beginning its winter hibernation with the tourists gone and the streets empty. That pulsation that gave Monaco life was now gone. All the excitement had drained away. It was strange how it changed so suddenly.

The idea of having someone - anyone - to travel with was enticing, especially since Munich was my very last hope for potential work. The fact that Eric was a German citizen with knowledge of the country seemed significant. I had grown accustomed to Eric's companionship. When I met him, Monte Carlo was alive and bustling with tourists yet I had been miserably lonely. Now with Monaco empty, the cool weather and the fog setting in, how would I manage alone for another month or more? If the trip to Germany turned out to be nothing more than a sightseeing venture, at least I was delaying time so that I could meet my friend in England when she arrived. She especially planned to be in Munich for the Oktoberfest. If things worked out for me in Munich, I could simply await her arrival there and travel with her afterwards.

I foolishly hoped the rental agent could be talked into returning part of my money even though I doubted, in typical French fashion, I could retrieve any of it. If not, I just had to consider that it would have been the cost of a better hotel. When I had asked (through Eric's translations) the rental agent said it was not up to him, the owner of the apartment was in Paris. He gave me his address if I wanted to write to him. As a foreigner, I knew I was at their mercy, which was nil and void toward Americans! Summer ended and so had my fairytale hope of finding Prince Charming and his castle. Grace seemed to have snagged the only prince and palace. Eric could hardly be described as "princely" even less "charming" but he was always there helping me when I needed it and a companion if nothing else…

CHAPTER 22

As I packed to leave my little apartment, again, I was faced with the over abundance of luggage. I did not know what to do with it, to store it in Monaco or ship it to England or Munich. Eric assured me he could manage both his and mine. Once we got on board the train, we would remain on that train all the way to Munich, or so he thought. The thing he did not take into consideration was crossing the Italian border! As the train pulled away from the station, I had mixed emotions--there I was, traveling again loaded down with luggage; headed for a country where I knew no one or even a few necessary words; nor did I understand the money exchange. Along with traveling with a man I hardly knew nor understood, I had left the security of my own little apartment that I dearly loved. The excessive loneliness had driven me to cling to Eric's companionship now, without my apartment and certain independence; I would have to totally depend on Eric. Oh well, no use creating possible unnecessary fears. Just as my mind was getting a bit used to enjoying the beautiful Riviera scenery, the train came to an abrupt halt. We had arrived at the Italian border. The customs inspectors insisted we take each piece of luggage off the train for inspection. In all my travel I have never seen this happen nor ever been exposed to so much irritation going through any customs inspections. Later, I would realize it had nothing to do with me. Eric could speak no Italian and what few words I knew were totally inadequate. We simplified the loading and unloading luggage by opening the train window and the passing of luggage through to Eric waiting outside. Finally the luggage was all aboard and the train was on its way once more. By late afternoon, it was growing into darkness. I would not be able to see any of the scenery along the way to Genoa, Italy.

It was an overnight ride to Munich. Sleeping while in transit has always been nearly impossible for me. During the night when the train pulled into Milan, Eric got off the train to find something for us to eat. I thought about David living there. If he had reacted differently in

England, perhaps I would have had a totally different summer. Maybe we could have begun writing together as a team. David had telephoned me in Monte Carlo. Unfortunately by the time he called, Eric had come into my life rescuing me from my isolation. I returned David's indifference as I had received from him in London. Nevertheless, if I was not so loaded down with luggage I had an overpowering urge to jump off the train while Eric was gone and stay with David in Milan. Having known and dated David for several years, while Eric's friendship was only a few weeks old, plus the lack of communication from totally different backgrounds and conditioning, I sat there ready to "jump out of my skin!" Was this another psychic warning? Eric was gone for a very long time. The train began to move -- I did not know what to do, suddenly Eric appeared all smiles loaded with snacks.

When the train finally pulled into the Munich train station around ten in the morning, I was exhausted and all I wanted to do was find a hotel room and collapse. Eric telephoned and located a room. We stored the luggage at the train station but we were taking more than I cared to carry and walk. I insisted on paying for the taxi but he insisted that the hotel was just down the block. "Just down the block" was at least six or eight blocks. Europeans have their way of life walking that can easily over fatigue and irritate spoiled Americans with constant transportation.

The hotel and food prices in Munich were comparable to those in the United States. Eric took me sightseeing through the beautiful Bavarian city. Streets were torn up everywhere, even through the main part of town preparing for the upcoming Olympic games. Without a male escort, I would never have dared go inside one of the famed beer gardens of Munich. They were gaily alive with singing and drinking of what appeared to be the laboring class of Munich. They were interesting to watch but not really my "cup of tea." German people were generally coarse, robust, steadfast, determined, and direct, and of all the nationalities I had associated with, they were the ones I had the least affinity.

Not only was Munich a massive confusion readying for its forthcoming Olympic games but also confusion reigned supreme in my life. Eric thought I should rent an apartment and save the expensive hotel cost. I had also been unable to get him to find out any information regarding the film companies. He thought I should get settled in an apartment first. We visited several rental agencies, none of which spoke English. I had to rely entirely on Eric's translations. We looked at a number of apartments. Their rents were outrageous plus according to Eric's translation I had to sign another lease and put up 3 to 6 month rent in advance. I was not about to obligate myself for that much money not knowing how long I would stay, especially after just losing the advanced rent in Monte Carlo. Prices on everything in Munich had skyrocketed because of the Olympics. Everyone was out to make a "fast buck."

Eric interviewed for the job he had been told in Monte Carlo was definite. He was very vague regarding the results of his interview. Sometimes he was not vague at all, like a small boy "pulling out his empty pockets" he informed me, that he had spent all the money he had saved taking me out. Until he went to work, he was completely broke--dumb or devious, I was beginning to think - BOTH! Maybe NOT "dumb" since he knew I was totally dependent on his help in Germany. I had absolutely no affinity for the language of the people. I could not ask a question or even say "left or right" or "yes or no." Eric was pouring on the guilt for all the help he had given me. All he wanted was a "small loan" until he received his first pay. What to do--should I trust and believe him? I realized it was looking like I was getting the American female tourist "hustle." I could not believe I had allowed myself to be taken into a beguiling ruse! He probably knew he had a "pigeon" from the beginning and carefully set me up for his plan to use me for a ticket to his homeland! Maybe that was the only real symbolic message from the dove - that I was a dumb pigeon! We had such fun in Monte Carlo where Eric had been a really great help to me. Much of the confusion I had experienced before and in Munich may have been part of his plan to get me in a position for further obligations to him and to also be dependent on him. Eric seemed always in a confused state totally disorganized. Wary as I was, I did not know what to do but give him a small loan. Possibly, I was overly suspicious and not being fair, misjudging Eric from observing young hustlers in Monte Carlo plus my unfortunate experience with Jude and Al.

Sightseeing or going out for dinner was far less fascinating once realizing that I was paying for both of us! I knew, just as the money I had loaned Jude and the deposit on the apartment, I would probably never see the loan to Eric paid back either. He said he had no friends or family in Germany to call upon for funds. There were still a few weeks before my friend was arriving in London. To keep from feeling I was being taken I looked upon the situation as though I was hiring Eric to be my tour guide and translator even though my small savings could not justify such services. Disenchanted with the idea of seeking work in the confusion of Munich, Eric mentioned that he had lived and worked in Frankfurt and was as sure of employment there. The thought of moving on deserved consideration since Munich was so expensive. At least Frankfort would not be as costly and was one step westward toward England. Of course, it meant as another "small loan" to Eric!

Frankfurt was just another hectic noisy city. I could see no European charm. As always there was much hassling with the luggage only this time I took a taxi to the hotel. When Eric left to inquire about his potential job, I wondered if he would ever return. I also wondered if I really cared! Up to now I had managed to get by alone. It was beginning to look as though I was far better off ALONE!

Most German cities had been completely wiped out during World War II, as far as I knew there was nothing of antiquity in Frankfurt that I cared to see. I was sick of packing and unpacking, hotels, foreign languages, foreign money and confusion in general. I really did not care to sightsee anything anywhere.

When Eric returned he was sure he had the job--there was only one problem. (Here came the pitch I had expected ever since he ran out of money)--I knew Eric was born in Düsseldorf. In order to get the job he had to return to the place of his birth to obtain certain papers. With my typical American do-it-by-phone attitude, I could not understand why he must go there in person but in Germany he told me that was the only way it was done. Who was I to argue, only a dumb foreigner with a LIMITED pocketbook. There seemed to be something mysterious regarding Eric's papers! All these things only gave me one more appreciation, piled on the heap, for the American way of life.

Düsseldorf had to be more charming than Frankfurt. The train followed the Rhine River. I had taken the train trip years before in April before the spring brought lovely green fields. That previous trip along the Rhine River was vivid in my memory. Everything about the train ride was gray, the train was gray, the people were gray, the sky was gray, the fields were gray, and all things were just various shades of gray. Summer comes late in Europe. The Valley of the Rhine River was now green. Again, this trip would require a small "loan" to Eric. He seemed genuinely honest about his intentions to repay the loan.

The train ride along the Rhine River was beautiful. This was wine country. The village we passed through seemed quaint and untouched by the war or modernization. Interspersed in the green grape laden hillsides were old, small castles. The train track hugged the hillside above the river. From miles away when approaching Cologne, the lone towers of the Cathedral could be seen long before anything else came into view. How well I remembered my previous trip to Cologne. I had asked the hotel clerk what sightseeing could be done in Cologne. His very curt answer was that I was too early. The tourist season had not started. The tour boats were not running. The one thing to see was the Cathedral – so I saw the Cathedral! People were taking the winding stairway up, so I thought "why not" and UP I went--up and up and up. I thought there was no top to those two towers. When I finally reached the top, there was a fantastic view of Cologne below. No surrounding buildings were anywhere nearly as tall as the Cathedral. I looked down upon the city that had once been completely flattened by American and English bombs years before. As I started down the stairway, eventually I had to sit and rest because of getting dizzy from the circular stairway. Cologne had been my departure point from Germany on that previous trip. There was no reason to stop in Cologne – I did not care to see the Cathedral or its stairway ever again. Next stop would be Düsseldorf, which would be a new experience. All I wanted to see and find was a nice clean, quiet, peaceful, reasonably priced hotel room somewhere to wait for my friend's arrival from London. It was time to just stop for a while for a nice rest.

Cathedral of St. Peter is a renowned monument of German Catholicism. Its Gothic architecture is a World Heritage Site, Germany's most visited landmark. The construction of Cologne Cathedral began in 1248, was halted in 1473 and left unfinished. Work restarted in the 19th century and was completed to the original plan in 1880. Its towers are approximately 515 ft tall. It is the largest Gothic church in Northern Europe and has the second-tallest spires. The two huge spires give it the largest facade of any church in the world. (As I recall, equal to 10 stories, round and round and round!)

CHAPTER 23

The conductor finally announced Düsseldorf. While we watched the city flash by the train window, suddenly the train was stopping at a station before we had gathered the luggage from the rack above. With our usual efficient method Eric opened the window, went outside and I handed the luggage to him through the window. Just as I handed him the last few pieces, including my luggage-sized purse, the train began to move. In my purse were my passport, money, travelers' checks and all identification. Without it I would not even have the money for a phone call. Trains in Europe make frequent stops. Since they are electric, they move rapidly. The compartment was in the middle of the car; I raced to the door where the conductor was blocking the exit. As the train quickly picked up speed, thoughts raced through my mind. If I had to stay until the next stop, what would I do then? Hardly anyone spoke English. Where would I reach Eric in Düsseldorf or would I ever be able to locate him? Maybe he wanted it that way. I was terrified. Eric ran alongside the train. Pushing the conductor aside, panic stricken I took a huge leap and landed on my hip, twisting my ankle. Fortunately there was no serious damage, only a few scratches and bruises, torn slacks and scuffed shoes and emotional terror that sent me into a crying spree. THAT was a close call! Now I really didn't know whether to trust Eric! Since he was always disorganized and did nothing hurriedly, it could have been an accident. I just didn't know for sure. By now I really did not feel Eric had the intelligence to be too devious. More than the physical pain I experienced, I was terribly shaken plus I was so very exhausted from pushing, pulling, packing and unpacking luggage that my impatience had just about reached its ebb. How I regretted leaving my lovely comfortable quiet apartment in Monte Carlo. If we learn from our mistakes then I had made enough to be brilliant.

I realized if I wrote to the owner of the apartment I had rented In Monte Carlo attempting to retrieve my money my chances were one in a million. I had no idea that I would run into this little "loan" situation with Eric. Even if I walked away now I knew I would never see the money. My planned budget was shot to hell. If I was to do any traveling with my friend or have any money to buy a car when I returned to the U.S. I had to cut expenses drastically. If I could just find a nice hotel room for a week or so and relax it would also give me time to see if Eric intended to repay the loans. Eric helped me find a hotel room in a convenient location. However, as generally found in Germany the prices were comparable to the United States and two or three times more than expected. Every time I turned around, I was cashing another Travelers check. There weren't that many left.

Eric did put forth effort to secure his necessary papers and looked for employment. After his trips to the official's offices, he would show me around Düsseldorf. As a war industry center, it had been severely bombed during World War II. It was rebuilt as a very clean and modern city. Düsseldorf is a pretty city with many wide thoroughfares. Between one of the major streets, there was a wide park area dividing the street. On one side there are expensive exclusive shops. On the other side is the old city that consists of a few blocks of what Düsseldorf once was. Somehow the city had survived the ravages of the war and time. The city was chartered back in 1288. From 1411 through 1609 it was the resident of the Dukes of Berg. On one of the sightseeing ventures, we took a trip outside of Düsseldorf to the Old Castle of Berg, where I bought a souvenir necklace for Debbie. With all my psychic intuition and in my foggiest dreams I could never have envisioned that she would never see the small silver heart that had an angel within it. That day was probably the happiest and most interesting day spent in Germany. I loved the very old houses and castles even though I knew most everything had been restored for the tourist trade. Hollywood could produce settings with equal authenticity but it was good to see the real ones.

By this time Eric had lost his beautiful Riviera suntan. In his native Germany he blended in with all the others, not as nice looking as I had once thought. He no longer stood out as someone very different and individualistic. While his artwork may have been unique, there seem to be no great commercial appeal for it. At best, it was a nice hobby for him even though he envisioned himself as a great artist. The reality was that Eric, by profession, was a construction worker rather than a unique artist.

Meanwhile Eric located a nice inexpensive room in a home for me near his work. His employer provided sleeping accommodations for him. He came by after work and we usually went into Düsseldorf by bus for dinner. Since he was working he paid for our meals and seemingly intended to repay the loans. The better I got to know Eric the more I realized I was a poor judge of character. I had been in severe loneliness in Monaco. What had seemed a lack of communication because of language and heredity barriers was, for lack of better words, what I might call a "class" challenge. Concerned with my own dread of being alone in Europe, I had not realized how attached Eric had become to me--almost like a child to a mother. Heaven forbid! Some of the strange things he would say began sounding as though he did not have quite all his "marbles!" To top it off, I finally realized why his papers were such a problem. He was an expert in judo and had accidentally killed a man in a bar room brawl in an argument over a girl. Those circumstances were not likely to create much apathy from the judicial forces. He had served time in prison, been paroled, deported and lost his passport privileges. Dear God! What had I gotten myself into this time!

As time neared for my friend to arrive in England, he became very possessive about my every move. He kept insisting she come from London to Düsseldorf to meet me rather than me go to London. Needless to say after his confession I became more alarmed. He seemed to guess that I might pack up and leave without his knowledge. To prevent this, incredulously he had involved me in some small white lie related to renting my room. In a semi-joking way, he promised to report me to the German authorities in - "Do you know what I can do to you?" From what I had observed, German authorities were very definite regarding proper papers, almost to the point where one had to have correct papers to breathe! Eric had gone from slightly irritating to downright infuriating!

There was the evening when I was still paying the tab. Many times in the old city we had passed a unique coffee house. Finally I insisted we go in. Eric became furious over the prices on the menu. I quietly tried to explain that I did not mind, and in a place like this one, one pays for atmosphere. To quiet his embarrassing grumble I hurried to finish my Turkish coffee. I had seen fortunetellers turn a cup upside down, then turn it three times and wait for the grounds to settle. I turned mine three and waited for the grounds to settle. When I looked into the cup there was nothing but a horizontal line halfway around the cup but very surely etched in the coffee grounds were two pictures - one of an airplane above the flat horizon - on the opposite side of the cup was a woman with long hair kneeling with her face lifted upward and hands in a praying position. Not convinced that I knew how to read coffee grounds, I flippantly said, "Well, here's the plane, I may be going home soon." The woman praying bothered me as I had a feeling it represented me. With Eric's continued griping over the prices I did not dwell on the symbolism of the coffee grounds.

My curiosity toward religion, philosophy, psychic phenomena, ESP and meditation concentration also included working with an Ouija board. It had progressed from game playing to sometimes exceedingly prophetic advice. I needed no more than an alphabet scribbled on a piece of paper and with my finger mid air, it would guide swiftly over the alphabet. I received messages ranging from confusion to revelations that amazed even me. This was always done with a protective prayer, since I really don't know what may be just beyond our conscious comprehension. People say my messages come from my subconscious but what exactly is the subconscious? No one really knows for sure. People only know their own personal convictions and conditions. If people, including members of my family, choose to think that I and people like me who seek the unknown are a little nuts, that's okay--for everyone including me has a tendency to condemn that which we have never experienced personally.

I received a letter from mother telling me of the senseless murder of a young woman from a neighboring community. The Sheriff investigating it was a high school classmate of mine. The investigations seem to be at a standstill. Mother wondered if my psychic communications could bring through any information that might be helpful. My mother, Debbie and my niece were the only family members that I could discuss subjects like psychic or channeled messages as they were aware of the startling communications I had received through the years. It was never a subject to discuss with anyone as it was almost always met with condemnation. Feeling a little foolish I sat down to write the bit of information that came through to me. If there was any thread that might help the investigation I felt it was far more important to share it than be concerned about any possible condemnation. Not in my wildest imagination could I ever dream that within only few weeks I too, would be deeply involved in the same hideous investigation!

In retrospect, my friendship with Eric was a gross mistake but at the time I was caught up in the situation, be it good or bad I was too afraid to change. My past year of loneliness made me a prime target for just such a situation. With my childish lust for a fairytale world of love and romance, the child-like running and playing relationship seemed like destiny at work. Hurled into the adult world and parenthood long before I was ready for it perhaps this was my subconscious desire to recapture that youth I felt I had missed. Eric could be so endearing at times. He might bring a good bottle of wine or just as likely bring a handful of wild flowers.

Eric had talked about a surprise for several days. Bright and early one Sunday morning he hurried me to the downtown area of Düsseldorf. He had a schedule to meet, but it was terribly unusual for him to attempt to keep any schedule. He knew of my soon to arrive friend's ambition to be in Munich for the Oktoberfest. He wanted to do the next best thing he could for me as an American. He was taking me to the Rhine River community of their Annual Wine Fest. We arrived by bus. It was a picturesque hillside village without any distracting modernization. There was an air of excitement with zesty Swiss and Bavarian music playing. As we walked up the street we passed the street vendor selling their wares. Around the town square there were wine tasting booths as well as more vendors. It was such a charming setting but yet the numerous street vendors created a commercial atmosphere much the same as any cheap carnival in the United States. Again the setting was not as idealistic as those created in our motion picture industry.

There were fantastic views up and down the river that were dotted with sightseeing tour boats. We walked around the little village several times, even stopped and tasted the wine. It was a very pleasant day except for the usual aching feet from extensive walking. There were many pleasant outings with Eric. There was that seemingly beautiful day in the park when I snapped a photo of Eric feeding a beautiful white dove, eating out of his hand. That day was Sept 6th! How I could know that Autumn would forever be indelibly printed in my memory!

CHAPTER 24

It was Mid-September when the German police awoke me in the middle of the night with an emergency phone call from the United States. I just knew while waiting for the trans-Atlantic telephone connection that seemed to take forever, something had happened to one of my parents, never dreaming the news would involve Debbie. When I finally heard my father's voice on the other end of the line, he began griping because it had taken 18 hours to reach me. I knew he was covering up the real reason for calling so I abruptly asked, "WHAT'S WRONG!" I knew from his trembling voice he was ready to break into tears. He tried calmly to tell me Debbie had returned from her visit in California, arriving in Dallas on Wednesday and went to the apartment complex where she lived before returning to my parents' home about 30 miles away. Apparently she was staying with a young man and did not want my parents to know. They didn't know she was in Richardson (near Dallas) as no one heard from her. It wasn't like Debbie to not stay in touch with them or even Sharon. The family had been at a nearby lake on Labor Day. Perhaps Debbie had tried to reach them by phone to come and pick her up. At the apartment complex she had been seen around the pool Monday and Tuesday in good spirits, happy to be back in Texas. The last time she was seen with him was 7:30 PM on Tuesday, September the 8th. Less than two weeks had passed, not long for a teenager nearly 19 to be out of touch - but inconceivable for Debbie. I knew my parents tendency to overreact but I also knew that Debbie, since early youth, had been taught to always stay in touch in case of an emergency. Just a year before, when my brother's son was killed in a car accident, no one could reach my sister's family as they had been on vacation. All the more reason for her to stay in touch which we had thoroughly discussed! Yet there was an unanswered question why she would not have called the family by Tuesday. If something dreadful had happened to Debbie, my first instinct flashed to Rob, the young man living in the apartment building. I had discouraged her from dating him. I felt he had an uncontrollable jealous streak. She had stopped dating him shortly after my visit in Texas and had dated another young man in the same apartment complex. Between seven and eight o'clock that Tuesday evening Rob <u>said</u> she had sent him out to get hamburgers. When he returned with the food he claimed she was gone. He went from apartment to apartment asking Debbie's whereabouts. Was it on the pretext that he setting up an alibi?

After the German police had gone, naturally I could not sleep. It was a matter of waiting the endless of hours of the darkness until the American Express office opened at 9 AM. As I attempted to pick up mental vibrations halfway around the world, just as clean as a bell, in my mind I could hear Debbie's voice saying, "MOM! I AM ALRIGHT!" It repeated several times. Hours dragged slowly by--what was this all about? Was it real or were my parents looking for an excuse to force me to come home? Maybe this was all happened merely to give me a good excuse to get away from Eric and go back to the states. I would not become panicky. I knew nothing could happen to Debbie – me, perhaps, not Debbie. She was destined to have a good marriage and about three children. I had always known it since she was a small child. The primary psychic feeling I always had for her future was a solid marriage and family, without the frustrations, confusion and failures of mine. There would be no divorce for her. No, the whole thing was just an excuse to get me out of this seeming captivity by Eric. Yet, IF Debbie was all right, I really did not want to leave Europe just yet. I so sincerely wanted to see the countryside of England, Scotland and Ireland then spend some time in New York City. What to do! WHAT TO DO?

I arrived in downtown Düsseldorf before the American Express office opened. I would try to calm down over a nice breakfast only it did not dawn on me that Germans did not have coffee shops as in the states. They have street restaurants where one stands to eat various sausages. Finally, in a nearby department store I found a restaurant where I could be seated, to be served a roll and coffee. Each minute of the 30 minutes, seemed like at least five hours in my mind of total confusion. Finally, the American Express office doors opened. I attempted to get a flight out that day or as soon as possible. All flights to London were booked. The only thing I could do was to go to the airport and standby. The house where I stayed was a long taxi drive from the airport and with my luggage that seems impossible; perhaps this was an omen I was reacting too hastily. If I waited until Monday, maybe Debbie would show up and I would not have to return to Texas. There was really nothing I could do on Sunday in Texas anyway except comfort my parents.

With all my psychic intuition, ESP. etc. surely if Debbie were dead, as a mother I would feel it and know it – – I felt nothing! Debbie was all I had; I could not consider death as a possibility. She was the only thing in my life I could measure with some success. I followed what I believed to be good guidance in my life. I knew money could make life comfortable but I could never put material pursuits first. I had made a vow to write and be open in every way I could toward understanding my own spirituality and deep spiritual enlightenment. Maybe in a more "down to earth" way it was as many might say to do - "God's work."

"THE-POWERS-THAT–BE" would not allow Debbie to be taken, it could not be so cruel – it must be ONLY to scare me to go home.

I decided to try to calm down in order to make a rational decision. I was dead tired by the time I returned to my room and spent the rest of the day resting and attempting to cram more into my luggage than it was willing to accept. I was glad that my folks had not gotten around to sending the winter clothes I had requested. That Autumn in Germany had been bitter cold. Thank goodness I would not be around to experience the coldest part of winter. Under the circumstances I knew Eric could not prevent me from leaving. Yes, underneath it all, I felt sure this was only an excuse to get me out of Eric's grasp.

On Sunday Eric wanted to take me sightseeing to get my mind off of Debbie. We went to an old hunting lodge where royalty had once played. Much of its riches had been stripped away by Napoleon during his march toward Russia. Several years before I experienced an unusual dream in which I spoke fluent French as well as understood it. It was such a stirring dream. It was one of the first acceptances of reincarnation being a reality with memories of past lives being deeply planted somewhere in my subconscious mind. In that dream I stood within the courtyard speaking to a young man attending the horses. This hunting lodge had just that kind of a courtyard. While I felt sure I never lived as a German citizen I wondered if I had lived as a French woman and visited this German hunting spot or a similar one long years before? There seemed a familiarity with the thick forest surrounding the lodge. It was absolutely gorgeous, so dense daylight was dimmed.

Monday came with no word. Even with my fears and suspicions regarding Eric I had grown accustomed to him. It was never easy to say goodbye to someone you know you shall never see again. I had accumulated more than my luggage would hold and had to leave things, which Eric promised to ship to Texas. There was much rushing around to get the luggage in the taxi and to get to the airport early Monday morning. I was flying BOAC to London. From London I would make arrangements to fly to the states. As usual, I was carrying several small pieces of luggage on board the plane with me. One was my typewriter. The ticket agent demanded I weigh the typewriter, and then he charged me almost $20 for it on the short flight to London. It was the first time any airline ever charged me for excess luggage. I swore never to fly BOAC again. I was in no mood to hassle with the ticket agent. Even way back then, I am reasonably sure that airlines in the USA give consideration to a person flying under distressing circumstances.

Eric and I sat in the lobby until departure time. I had mixed emotions about leaving. Eric promised to repay nearly a thousand dollars in loans. I preferred to ignore the feeling of being an American woman tourist taken by a European gigolo and chose to remember the pleasant moments we had shared. There had been such fun and innocence (or so it seemed), in our companionship in Monte Carlo. We had walked, talked, skipped, jumped, run, sung and had so much laughter together. There were times I laughed until I cried. After the disheartening years of what I perceived then as failure it had been good to feel like two children full of fun and adventure. We had walked in the woods; enjoyed the smallest of nature's wonders. We strolled in the parks. There had been excursions to castles, the old hunting lodge, the Wine Festival, the constant exploring in the beach areas of Monaco and -- the white doves! They had seemed such beautiful omens at the time. Little did I realize the Sunday one dove ate out of Eric's palm was the day before Debbie's disappearance, possibly the day of her death! Our time together was now only moments from ending forever. With the many misgivings about Eric, we had still been together so much that parting was not easy.

When finally we said our goodbyes, I hurried through the gate and for the first time in my life met with a female guard who was insistent on frisking me. This was the beginning of the aircraft hijacking. To top that off when we arrived at the plane, there sat all the passengers' luggage on the ground near the plane. I could not understand what they wanted us to do. Finally someone who spoke English explained, because of security they require that each passenger carry his own luggage to the plane. It seemed if one was willing to carry the luggage to put in the luggage compartment, and then board the plane, they felt fairly certain that luggage contained no explosives. There was no way I could manage all of mine. A man offered to help me. Settled on board, as the aircraft exited toward the takeoff position, I felt terribly sad as I saw Eric's childish act of desperation, waving his white handkerchief from the airport balcony. Had I been too cold and materialistic? Had I misjudged his intentions? So many memories as well as anticipations and fears for what I might be facing flashed through my mind. In one way it felt good to be soaring in the air.

It was very short flight to London. I found I could take a charter flight like the one I came over on but there were only prop planes going to New York. I would have to wait until midnight. It involved traveling many miles across London to another airport and then there was no guarantee I would get the flight. It was another standby situation. There was an excellent connection on a 747 leaving shortly with seats available. All I could think of at that point was just getting to Texas as quickly as possible. Handing the ticket agent an American Express credit card for a much higher fare was less painful than counting out travelers' checks.

The interior of the 747 was beautiful and more spacious than I had imagined. As the flight time approached I fasten my seatbelt only to wait and wait and wait. Eventually a man's voice announced the delay in departure was because someone had checked two pieces of luggage that was loaded on board, but no passengers boarded. The plane could not take off until the unattached luggage was located and removed from the plane - the bomb scare again! Because of the delay the crew invited the passengers to feel free to inspect the different parts of the giant 747 and have a drink. Everyone headed for the circular stairway for the first-class section that led to the bar above. Finally, we were airborne. The flight was the most delightful I had ever experienced. There was a movie, a couple of nice meals, drinks, snacks, music earphones, everything to make the trip a pleasure and a seemingly short flight. This was the beginning of the more luxurious airliners.

In New York I simply went from one terminal to another. When I explained the emergency situation I was rushed through customs and my luggage through the gates without being inspected by customs. I had a very tight schedule to meet but made it. In a very short time I was in the air heading toward Dallas. For such a long time I had looked forward to spending time in New York City. I had not been there since returning from Europe while filming "Cleopatra" in 1962. There I was high over New York City and could see nothing but clouds below. It was disappointing that I had to miss visiting there. After many, many hours of flying, I finally stepped off the plane in Dallas, Texas, 9 pm the same day I had left Düsseldorf at 11 A.M. I had been following the sun but was too concerned, confused, tired and dazed to stop to count the actual flying hours. NOW, with the sudden realization of what I might have to face - being in Dallas was total reality!

CHAPTER 25

Greetings and farewells with my family were always tearful emotion packed experiences for all of us. This day, the joy was marred with great anxiety and fear. Arriving in Dallas and seeing my family again began to bring a more real possibility that something terrible had happened to Debbie. In Europe I had more or less settled in my mind that the whole thing was a reason to get me out of Europe and away from Eric. When a possibility of reality took hold of me, I still could not accept it. Debbie was all I had! God could not be so cruel. There I was, blaming God for our miseries when for years, I had "preached" we must not blame God for our misfortune. It is our own accumulation of religious credo; I believed our retribution came to us through karmic debts, through deaths and rebirths - through reincarnation. I thought I understood why Debbie and I had come together in this life, through karmic debts, but a youthful death for her was not a part of any of my strong intuitions!

I just could not accept that anything really serious could have happened to Debbie. It was just a misunderstanding, a lack of communication somewhere along the line – yet how well I knew Debbie's dependability for staying in touch in case of emergencies. Debbie was a gentle soul. Fortunately, she had not inherited my temper or capacity for holding grudges. Because of my own weakness in those areas, perhaps I had over compensated in her training, always attempting to talk her out of any situation that might have create those suppressed emotions. Debbie had never been vindictive. Why would anyone want to take her life when she was such a sweet, compassionate dear young girl? As for Debbie just running off without letting anyone know, it was not like her to so severely hurt those who loved her the most. She had not been out on the streets where strangers could assault her. She was in the apartment building among friends. I could not believe anyone who knew Debbie could take her life. She was charming, kind and able to beguile her peers, children and adults with equal charm. Rarely did she dislike anyone. She had learned compassion and understanding well, especially for being so young! Why would anyone want to snuff out her life just as it was blooming so beautifully?

As we drove to my parents' home, my family tried to fill me in on all the information that they had. Awaiting my arrival, they had not yet reported her as a missing person to the police. My niece, Sharon, knew Debbie's associates far better than I did and had already done a tremendous amount of investigation of Debbie's whereabouts from coast-to-coast. She contacted everyone with whom she knew Debbie had any former association. When I checked over Sharon's list, I could not think of anyone she had not already contacted. Our conversations were repeated questions; "What time was Debbie last seen? Where was she last seen? Had she said anything to anyone regarding going anywhere? What was her attitude when she arrived in Dallas? Had she said anything about any situation in California that could have upset her? Why had she suddenly decided to return to Texas? Why did she call Sharon from California and tell her to meet her at the plane on Wednesday but had arrived on Monday and never called to tell Sharon that she changed her plans? That was the big question. It certainly was not like Debbie to have someone drive all the way into Dallas to pick her up at the airport, and then not be there!

Tuesday morning my sister and I drove to Dallas to attempt to report Debbie as a missing person to the Sheriff's office and then to the Dallas police--neither wanted to take the report. With a blasé, nonchalant attitude, they hesitantly did their paper procedure routinely and warned me there was very little they could do. Treating me like an overwrought mother, they reminded me that she was over 18, of legal age and had the right and freedom to do as she pleased. It seemed all missing young women at that time were lumped into three categories: 1. She ran off with her boyfriend. 2. She ran away to a hippy commune (very popular in the 1970's) 3. She was on drugs and probably a prostitute - PERIOD! They seem to refuse to consider a nice young woman could have been Abducted. The FBI would not even talk to me in person unless I could give them positive proof that she had been taken across state lines, plus they also required her exact location. I told then if I knew that why would I need the FBI? My sister and I were terribly discouraged. I could not afford a private investigator and did not know how to locate a good one. Even if I had the money, those super-sharpies seen on regular TV were not located in Dallas or anywhere else for that matter. What could an individual woman do with a personal tragedy involving the police? The real mysterious tragedy is just not like on television on the "cops and robbers" shows. There is no police investigator, no private eye that rushes to your rescue, putting his morals, righteousness etc. above all else. The police were just too busy on what they felt were more important matters to be bothered.

What could I do? The first logical thing seemed to be to go to the apartment complex and asked questions to as many people as possible, "Who was the last to be in contact with Debbie?" I questioned the few people I could locate during the daytime. Everyone's story was about the same, they saw Debbie around the pool Monday afternoon and most of Tuesday. She was in a good mood, happy and friendly. She seemed delighted with her decision to return to Texas and was awaiting my arrival from Germany. She was last seen crossing the parking lot around 7:30 pm and I assumed she was alone in the apartment where she had been visiting. The next-door neighbor was at home and felt sure if there have been any struggle between Debbie and an assailant, he would have heard it. Debbie was not an exceptional beauty but she was attractive enough to warrant the numerous beauty trophies she had won. She did have a very good figure. She generally had plenty of male admirers and preferred to date several young man rather than being tied down to one. She scoffed at jealousy with indifference. When Debbie's best friend at her apartment told me all that she knew, I felt a cold sweat come over me. The chilling fact was that she now confirmed Debbie had been involved in several arguments with Rob. The last words she ever heard Debbie say was, "I'm just going to have to have a little talk with Mr. Rob!" Did she have that talk? Could it have cost her life? Had she insulted his male ego? Could he have been one of those neurotic men who felt if he could not have her no one else would? If Debbie was dead I could not help believing Rob was the only person who might possibly destroy her life in a jealous temper rage, perhaps unintentionally. For Debbie to take off without letting anyone know was just not like her. None of it added it. Something was wrong. Ron was not the only young man Debbie dated in the apartment complex.

The one she had the most interest in was the airline co-pilot and it was in his apartment where she was last seen. I was never able to talk to him in person, only by phone. He seemed beyond reproach and terribly concerned about Debbie.

In a few days we heard the police had been investigating the same people at the apartment building. My sister's husband had a friend who was formerly with the FBI. They decided to take a ride to Dallas and see if they could talk to her last boyfriend. Rob told them the same that he told the police earlier, that Debbie was on drugs and he felt sure she had returned to California. Both men noted a bit of eye shifting between Rob and his roommate. Rob's absurd accusation made me even more suspicious since I felt sure I knew Debbie's attitude toward the use of narcotics. On the basis of the parents are always the last to know, I made telephone inquiries from New York to California seeking any thread of information. Each time I asked those who had known Debbie best for years about Rob's accusations regarding narcotics, I insisted on total honesty. The same answer came from all who really knew her. That was just not Debbie's style. Debbie had always encouraged friends to stop or not start any form of narcotics.

It was peculiar that Debbie had supposedly taken her luggage, too bulky for her to manage alone, from the apartment where she was visiting without one person seeing her on that warm still daylight summer evening. She had left a tee shirt and a pair of cut-offs lying on a chest of drawers. There was also a pair of shoes with a dress hanging in the closet and a hairbrush had been left on the bathroom floor. It was not like Debbie to leave things behind plus not turn off the stereo. It was also noted that the dial had been moved from her usual setting to a different station, which I was later told she never listened to. There was no note. It was not like Debbie to leave without saying goodbye to anyone. She cherished friendships too much to ignore such a common courtesy.

Friends and relatives came with condolences of death – none came with hope for my daughter's life! As long as Debbie's body was not found, it meant there was a 50-50 chance she was alive somewhere under circumstances not yet explained. I felt I had to be the positive force within my family. I had to maintain a positive attitude and hope, at least for appearances sake. My parents were closer to Debbie than their other grandchildren since she had lived with them part of almost every year of her life. Since I was the youngest of three children and unmarried, they felt Debbie was like their own child rather than grandchild. Everyone in the family also accepted the fact that Debbie was their favorite grandchild. Outwardly my father admitted Debbie was probably dead but inwardly hoped he was wrong. My mother, sister, niece and I maintained that there was just as much possibility for her to still be alive. I came on strong with everyone's doomed attitude with, "I choose the fifty percent odds that Debbie is alive!" That was what I "said" but when alone in my room at night I would sob with such deep, indescribable heartbreaking pain that cannot be understood nor communicated unless experienced. It was a horrendous grief and pain I pray never to experience again! It was more than losing my only child. It felt like a death within myself.

A small macabre incident that really upset me was a black chiffon headscarf which had blown against the telephone pole in the front yard, that I could see from my bedroom window. Each time I looked out the window I could not avoid seeing it. It was too far up the pole to be removed and a morbid reminder that Debbie might be dead. Also, I recalled the dream I had in London regarding my parents' 13-year-old dog. In the dream she tried to jump a high fence but dropped to the ground. She told me she was dying of a heart attack. The dog had been Debbie's when it was just a small puppy. Not long after Debbie's disappearance the dog seemed to wander out in the street to nap, seemingly intentionally to be killed after running around freely in the neighborhood for many years. Was Debbie calling her from the other side? Was the dog just too tired to face another cold winter? Or was she jealous of the tiny black puppy Debbie had placed in mother's hands just before leaving for California. She asked Mother to take care of it while she was away. Would Snuffy intentionally give up life not caring to compete with the new puppy named Rover?

There was still another morbid memory that haunted me. While Debbie and I were living in Hollywood just before moving to the mountains a rather eerie experience bewildered me. At the time I was attempting to correct my own thought patterns. I never really seriously believed the devil or an evil spirit could possess us. I did consider the possibility of that when we are not in control of our conscious mind through drugs, alcohol or another strong influence. Perhaps momentarily, we could be possessed or influenced by some sort of evil or lower force. In case that was a real possibility, I felt one should not leave her or himself open to such forces. A protective prayer was always given. One evening after Debbie had gone to bed, I was mentally working very hard through meditation and attempting to control my own thoughts. Through mind control, if there were any evil forces surrounding me, I was attempting to drive them away. Suddenly Debbie bounded into the room her eyes bugging out of their sockets explaining she had just had a horrible nightmare. The devil or some hideous thing that she could not describe was chasing her. After I soothed her back to sleep I shuddered with fear that the evil spirit or power might really exist. While I was attempting to drive it out of my life, was it possible that this force tried to attack the person nearest and dearest to me?

While living in that same apartment, I came in exhausted from swimming and lay on the sofa. I had read of many forms of the materializations but had never personally experienced or seen one. On the ceiling above me I saw a bright red spot that seemed to be blood. I squeezed my eyes closed. When I opened them it was still there. When I repeated it, it disappeared. Could it be from being in the Sun and was it a delayed reaction? Did it have any meaning? Did it represent blood? The neighbors above my apartment fought frequently so I thought it might represent a bloody fight between them. I could not prevent these memories from popping up. Pondering over them only left me in more fear, more confused and apprehensive as I have always searched for meanings of things that happened.

Shortly after noon one day in October, I was in the house alone when the phone rang, a male voice asked, "Are you Ann Palmer?" It was the police in Plano, Texas. My heart jumped. Here was the next thing I expected to hear, that they had found Debbie's body – so far they had found two suitcases in the woods that they believed were Debbie's. From the description I knew it was Debbie's luggage. They wanted me to make a positive identification in person. They had found no identification in either, only an address book of mine that Debbie taken to California with her. There was a telephone number from a nearby community. They called that number, which turned out to be

Debbie's father. He referred them to my number. Plano is just a few miles north of Richardson where the apartment complex was located. I hung up the telephone feeling paralyzed. What do I do next? Did it now begin.... was this the beginning of a grim reality - that Debbie was actually dead - murdered?

As was the recent custom, we each ran to the telephone when it rang. My Dad came rushing in from outside when I turned to tell him. I remember him standing in the doorway, exhausted, with one hand leaning against the door. He burst into tears crying, "I KNEW IT! I KNEW IT! That boy killed her! She is dead!" At that moment all hope, faith and any positive reaction was impossible to muster. When we both regained our emotions, I telephoned my sister. She and her husband rushed over to drive us to the Plano police station. She tried hard to console me but the realization that Debbie could really be dead hit me and hit me hard! All my life's work seemed suddenly to disappear. Trying to keep my wits about me, I asked my sister when and if they found Debbie's body, would her husband identify her? That was the moment I could not face nor did I think my mother, father or sister could do so. My brother's oldest son had been killed in a car accident just a year before. I did not wish to expose him to any more grief or horror than absolutely necessary.

When we arrived at the police station, there was a long wait and gross anxiety. Finally after my insistence, they ushered me alone into a room where the luggage was kept – it was Debbie's, just as I knew it would be. They called the Dallas police and were awaiting their arrival. I asked if I might go through the luggage, hoping to find some small thread of evidence to give us a clue.

During the previous week there had been extensive rain. Heat and humidity had mildewed the contents. No words can describe the pain that I felt as I leafed through these moldy, smelly clothes. The horror stricken realization came over me that Debbie's beautiful youthful body could be in the same condition in a shallow grave or deteriorating at the bottom of some lake. Without a doubt it was the deepest and most horrifying grief I could ever know or imagine I could ever face - but there I was... totally engulfed in it. The best way to describe the depth of my grief was the feeling of blood twisting from within my intestines.

With each piece of mildewed clothing I picked up, the years of motherhood sped through my memory.

The tiny soft infant stranger so easily held in my lap – the discoveries and growing in all ways of the baby - the learning years - three - five - ten - thirteen - seventeen - the heartaches, the joys, the fun, the problems, the worries, the love, the companionship, the sharing. Now at nearing nineteen, the beautiful, so healthy body and attitude, my pride and the one really right thing in my life...now gone - dead - mildewing - rotting. The human flesh I had given birth to. Rotting! What horrors had Debbie experienced that Tuesday evening? I hated gruesome, morbid, shocking dramas. I never read about them in the news or watched them on television. As a lover of fairytales, idealism, beauty I was now suddenly totally ensnarled by hideous mysterious murders, police, and crime, et al. It was an experience I could never have considered facing. "Why me God?" Why hadn't it been given to those who thrive on lust for the repugnant? The life I had chosen in the film world had been filled with its very high highs and very low lows. To act, one must understand and relate to all emotional experiences, but dear God, I did not need this excessive grief experience.

Finally the Dallas police arrived; one was the same detective who had so lackadaisically filled out the missing persons report. Now with the case possibility becoming a homicide rather than a missing person, his attitude showed noticeable change. At that point I felt I should leave the investigation totally in the hands of the police as they insisted I should do. I might do something to interfere with their investigation. I trusted that they were putting their full effort into the investigation. They searched every inch of the woods where the luggage had been found. For several days, even helicopters searched the area but her body was never found. Each long day I lived in horrifying dread and fear that her deteriorating body would be located.

Until someone is involved in a personal police investigation such as this, a person is never aware of how many dead bodies of young women are found. When you are waiting for one of them to be your only child, it becomes unexpressed agonizing anxiety. My heart beat rapidly each time I heard the news report. It seemed almost daily the news reported another young woman's body was found, then the wait until the body was identified--each time knowing that it might be Debbie's. It was always some other young woman, but it was only a matter of time until it would be Debbie. The police kept assuring me that a body generally had a way of turning up. If Debbie had been murdered, her body would be found. I urged the detective to question Rob further. One rather passive detective gave Rob a lie detector test without informing the most aggressive group of investigators. Rod passed that lie detector test. There was nothing further they could do nor did they feel they could question him further. As long as Debbie's body was not found there was no proof that a murder had been committed. My suspicions of Rob mounted when I heard he had put forth effort to become good buddies with the copilot Debbie had dated. They had never before been friends, suddenly Rob was insisting that they double date. Shortly thereafter, one at a time, each young man moved to a different apartment in Dallas.

I felt totally helpless. I wished I had the money to hire a private detective yet I did not want to interfere with the police investigation. I did not want to be an unrealistic mother who denied any faults or character weaknesses with my own child. I tried to be objective, honest and consider any and all possibilities thrown at me, from drugs to forced prostitution. White slavery seemed to be a preposterous idea to most yet that possibility grew greater with rumors from reliable sources. There were no pleasant possibilities offered to me. Yet as far as I was concerned life was far better than finality. When one's faith, belief in God, eternal life, etc. suddenly is brought out of the ethereal into the very real basic physical senses, what seemed like "solid as a rock" becomes putty or rocks crumbling under pressure. With all my inner strength that had been the strength and solace for so many friends through the years, I felt totally empty and void. All of my faith felt like a child feels when he had a devout belief in Santa Claus, then suddenly was told it was only a myth. Life just could not be so cruel – but the weeks that followed only grew worse. My inner religious beliefs were personal and far stronger and deeper than most people's superficial ceremonial acts expressed once a week by attending church. This strength had been tested and tested severely--but would it hold up THIS time!

CHAPTER 26

After Debbie's photograph appeared in the newspapers and television news, many people reported sightings of a young woman answering to Debbie's description. The police followed one girl to a nearby community. She turned out to be a young German housewife who looked quite a bit like Debbie. My daughter had a look not uncommon to many healthy all-American tall blonde young ladies. It was easy to mistake someone else for her.

When the issue of White Slavery kept coming into the realm of possibilities, people would come to me and say, "Oh you would rather have her dead than living in White Slavery." I vehemently disagreed! I knew Debbie had so much charm and whatever possible situation she might be in, she would make the best of it. Even if she could be in that kind of situation I refused to imagine anything morbid or gruesome happening to her.

Before leaving for my European trip, I had placed both of parents' names on my checking and savings accounts in case of my death. If there was any emergency that they might need the money, I told them to use it, assuming my credit cards could always get me home. The one thing I had been very definite about was that I did not want any part of it spent on a car for Debbie. She had wasted away the proceeds in Dallas from the sale of her car in California. I was annoyed that she had left me stuck with the job of getting rid of her car in the first place. Sure enough it was the one thing that my father did! He took part of my money and part of his to buy her a nice used car in an attempt to keep her from returning to California. She left immediately after he had purchased it and never even drove it. With this money spent on the car my savings account was just about finished. At least I owned the car to drive, even though it was not a car of my choosing.

Through a friend of a friend I was contacted by a private investigator. In no way could I afford his services even though he offered to work for "expenses only." He certainly was no investigator as seen on TV crime shows! The expenses he wanted me to pay were for him to hang around bars in Dallas to pick up information. Debbie never hung around bars! She was too young to even be admitted. I strongly suspected it was just an excuse for this pathetic little married man who had a house full of children to get out of the house for some social hours at my expense. There was something about him that I did not trust although he had been recommended from a friend whose judgment I trusted. He had convincing tales of investigations involving young women who had also disappeared. If his stories were true it seemed some of the girls had been drugged, placed in forced photography, kept drugged and to who knows what fate followed. The connection with him was so secretive and mysterious that it eventually fizzled out like all the others.

I had returned home but for what reason? My presence, in no way, helped to turn up any information on my missing daughter. My hands seem to be tied. For some reason there was an underlying strange fear that something might happen to my parents or me if we pried too deeply. I don't know if it was an intuitive feeling or something an investigator said. The word "Mafia" kept creeping into the investigation conversations. For all intents and purposes I could just as well stayed in Europe for all the good I had accomplished since returning to Texas. Naturally, I could not stay away!

The police investigation seemed to be getting nowhere. They were willing to grasp at straws. I discussed with them my strong belief in the realm of psychic phenomena. Psychic communications had been possible for me and for many of my friends. It was simply a sense that we all have but most never bothered to develop. When someone approached the police volunteering the services of a psychic they knew I would be willing to experiment. The detective and I went to see a man who was a psychic, taking along Debbie's personal things. After some explanation he lay across the bed and went into a psychic trauma as he and his wife explained his behavior. He seemed to be living an experience that amounted to Debbie's being dead at the bottom of a lake. He gave the approximate location. It was a very nauseating experience for me. Perhaps his intention was well meaning but if he was only seeking publicity for personal gratification, it was a cruel hoax for me! I had been around many psychics and read many books on the subject – somehow this one seemed a little too dramatic; and he was not a very good actor at that. I did not believe him. Presumably in a trance, somewhat in a fetal position, he acted out what was supposed to be Debbie hugging her stuffed toy, recalling many years of youthful attachment with great affection for THIS stuffed toy. In reality, Debbie had received the unusual stuffed animal only the preceding Christmas and had nothing similar to it in her youth. As far as I knew the police did check the area he described to no avail. He was the only psychic of many who had predicted that Debbie was dead. When I did visit others and suggested to each that they contact Debbie on the other side, they all hesitated with the same reply, "This person is not in the spirit world as she is still in the physical world." It could have been because they knew me, or was it impossible for me to receive that kind of horrible news, as they knew I needed to maintain hope.

One psychic seemed to think there had been a threat against my life or my parents' lives if Debbie tried to return. That rather confirmed my own fears. If alive, this would be the one thing that could keep Debbie from contacting us. One psychic I visited in another city was right out of an eerie novel or morbid movie script. Her house was literally crawling with all sorts of creepy, crawly things! It was filled with cats and their droppings that were never removed. The stench and filth was unbearable. If I hadn't heard that she was quite good and felt so desperate for a lead, I would never have stayed to see her. The room was covered with spiders and filth was everywhere and on everything. How could any human live like that? If so, how could her communications have any validity from any worthwhile source? "If cleanliness is next to godliness," she had to be at the opposite end of the pole but then it was not mine to judge.

What of my own psychic ability? When one is deeply emotionally involved one's own psychic abilities seemed to turn off or be influenced by emotional ties, plus I knew what I WANTED to believe. My best results for others had been when I knew nothing about the person in question. To act as a medium one must not be emotionally involved, instead rather detached and pliable so that the information can flow through freely.

Weeks went by; the police still came up with nothing. Occasionally they contacted me to let me know that they were still working on the case. I was in a quandary as to what to do. The longer we waited, the colder any evidence became. If I stuck my nose in it, would it do any good or would it interfere with the official investigation? There seemed to already be enough confusion between the metropolitan and suburban police departments investigation. The Dallas chief investigator was fired for some questionable acts he had committed unrelated to Debbie's case.

It always disturbed me as to how Debbie's luggage had been discovered in the first place. A man driving down a seldom-traveled road said that a rabbit ran across the road in front of him. As the rabbit ran into the woods he spotted something unnatural. He stopped to investigate, found luggage and notified the Plano police. They failed to get his name. There was no way to interview that man. Maybe it was a true story but it sounded a bit "fishy" to me.

Debbie's disappearance was more or less lumped into the unsolved murder cases of several young women in the Dallas area even though her body had not been found. The irony of my Psychic investigation for the Sheriff of a neighboring community, which took place while I was in Germany, was that Debbie's disappearance was linked to that murder in their investigation. That girl had attended a party in Richardson and was on her way home when she had been murdered. Her body and car were left to look like a robbery but an investigator told me the odd thing was that the window glass on the driver's side had been smashed yet no broken glass was on the girl's body. That indicated she had been murdered, then placed in the car after the glass was broken, and set up to look like a robbery and murder.

Several of the girls who had been murdered or disappeared had some link with the community of Richardson which had grown rapidly with Dallas' expansion and was filled with young apartment dwellers. The girls had worked, lived or attended parties in Richardson. The murdered girl who had been left in her car had attended the party of an associate of the man Debbie knew who "used to be in the Mafia." Coincidence - maybe but we had to look into anything that might have a small bearing. There were many other areas around Dallas filled with apartment complexes where crimes had not been committed.

The Texas Rangers were also involved. It seemed the police were putting forth great effort on Debbie's case but would give me little or no information. On one of two occasions an investigator came with a few bits of burned clothing for me to identify. One small piece appeared to be nothing more than the back of a black vest. I told the officer Debbie hated black and I never saw her wearing it. He did not bother to explain where the burned clothing came from except in the woods, which left me to imagine all sorts of things. Naturally because he avoided explanation I thought these were bits of clothing found on an unidentified cremated female body. That gory thought crept into my mind for a long time. It was months later that I accidentally discovered that it was only from a transvestite destroying his female evidence.

I was experiencing the greatest possible tragedy of my life and so few friends were concerned about Debbie's disappearance or my well-being enough to even call. It is at times like that; one can really count one's friends. It is shocking just how clean the slate had become. A few of my friends from California called at first but no more. None of my former school chums or Debbie's bothered to inquire or write with concern or caring. I kept asking myself what would I do under the same circumstances but I knew that I would have made an effort toward consoling the person. Men I had dated for several years, work associates, girlfriends and buddies through the years--all those people I had been there for them when they had needed help, yet where were they when I was desperately in need of warmth, compassion and encouragement?

One day I listened to the nonsensical chatter from a group of Debbie's friends. The more I looked and listened to them, the more disdained I became -- "Dear God, why Debbie?" She had more purpose in life than most. Except for my niece, Sharon, who gave me the greatest comfort and compassion, I resented being in the presence of girls Debbie's age. Debbie, Sharon and I had many discussions regarding psychic areas, pros and con. Sharon thought much the same as I did, a bit more so than Debbie. They had known each other all their lives; Sharon loved Debbie like a sister. They had always been very close. She was deeply involved in getting information on Debbie's disappearance. She more or less turned her love for Debbie toward me and I, in turn seem to turn my love for Debbie toward Sharon. We became far closer than we had been. I could share my innermost feelings with only Sharon, who gave me a sounding board. Her innocence and youthful counseling was the most mature and honest communications I had with anyone.

When my nephew was killed in a car accident in 1969 the family members commented that he had told someone he did not believe he would live to be 21. Later, Debbie confessed to me that she felt the same. I assured her that everyone in his or her teen years felt that fear. I told her I had never believed I would live through childbirth but I did. If one believed in the lines contained in one's palm, Debbie's lifeline was solid, strong and unbroken. A few friends who studied astrology looked into Debbie's chart. There seemed to be confusion in her life at the time when she disappeared but there was nothing to indicate death.

Time moved along. My savings account was gone and my pretty furniture had been sold. My car, including everything I'd given up in California to begin a new life in Europe, were now gone and the money was spent. There was no job in my parents' small community. Dallas had film work but toward the end of the year, everything came to a standstill. My state of mind was not conducive for locating employment or being interviewed, etc.

One thing I could count on was my California unemployment insurance. I had made good money while working at the advertising agency that now put me in the qualifying period to collect the maximum benefit. It would not be much but enough to carry me through since I was living with my parents. Every Wednesday two men from the Texas unemployment service came to town. Each and every Wednesday I stood in line waiting my turn to fill out my interstate claim, which was slow to be processed. Weeks went by, my claim never came through. Faithfully each week I appeared. Missing their Wednesday date meant I had to drive to a suburb of Dallas to file the weekly claim but I did so in pouring rain and hail so that I did not miss a week. It had built up to over $600 due to me. The Texas office sent inquiries, then a hearing was demanded, finally my total claim was refused by the state of California. This was because the man in Los Angeles at the watch company whose office I had so obviously organized, even finding my own replacement before leaving. He supposedly trained her, but didn't spend even five minutes doing any training. He told the California state officials I had quit my job against his will to vacation in Europe. He knew about Debbie and what I was going through. His supervisor in New York had always been pleasant to me, even offering a new job in New York when I returned from Europe. I wrote to him explaining my situation. The claim was based on my work at the ad agency prior to working for them. I reminded him that the firm industry was my profession and I had gone to London with the understanding I had a job in my established profession. His very hateful answer hinted that I was "cracking up," and denied any help in correcting the claim.

Typical of the materialistic people involved in the wholesale industry--as long as you are doing something for their gain you were wonderful but if you ended the connection, you weren't even a person who deserved normal human compassion. As a boomerang returns to the sender, I hoped their indifferent attitude would someday be returned to them. It was such an unnecessary petty vicious act. The state of California Department of Employment office perfunctory attitude was just as cold and indifferent. The state of California was always there to take from you but fought against returning any money to you. That was my last source of money. Never in my life had I been so desperately in need of my unemployment insurance which had now been cut off completely. I was refused any further consideration. All I could think of was the memories of those bright new Cadillacs often seen pulling up in front of the Hollywood state employment office with their owners collecting their weekly benefits.

One of my goals in life had always been to help support my parents in their retirement years. Now when their only income was retirement benefits, I was totally dependent on their support. A situation that galled me totally considering the money wasted because of my stupidity and poor judgment. Living in the upstairs of their home was cutting into their livelihood even more since it could bring a small amount of rent. Being back in the states under such extraordinary circumstances, surely Jude would repay the loan. Each phone call to him brought the same response, "Oh, yes I'm getting some money in the mail to you today." But it never came nor did the letter I requested asking him to write to support my state unemployment insurance claim. He knew the fact that I had gone to London under the impression I had employment with his dear friend in my normal profession of the film industry. It was such a small favor to ask of him.

If I thought I had reached a desolate low point in Monaco, it was minor compared to that forlorn era of my life. Everything in life seemed to be crashing down on me. What was there left? Was life only to be a downhill accelerated fast pace for the rest of my days? Even my weak consolation "at least I have my health" did not work. Migraine headaches drained me to the point I really did not care if I lived or died--1970 was coming close. The new decade had only brought my most horrifying battle. Was life so precious? Was it really worth hanging onto?

CHAPTER 27

Nearing the Christmas holidays, there was nothing for me to do but keep as busy as possible to keep my mind off of the ever present, never ending questions that had no answers. Fortunately 20th December would be my parents' 50th anniversary. My sister and I planned to give them an open house, inviting over 100 guests. I wanted to do all that I could to make their home as pretty as possible for the celebration. In all their married years, this one by far was the nicest and largest home they had ever owned.

Before I went to Europe I had purchased exterior paint for the entire house assuming that if I paid for it surely other members of the family would do the work, fool heartedly as that was! I now took on the pending project of painting a two-story house alone in December. I soon learned exterior paintbrushes are designed for a man's hand and wrist strength. Some days I painted until I felt my arm and hand would fall off. I painted when it was so cold that even with gloves and warm clothing my body became numb. I was obsessed with getting the job finished. Even with the taller ladder, there were areas too high for me to reach. After I had painted everything I could reach, my sister hired painters to complete the job. The new two tones of the gold paint gave the old house warmth that it never had before. There was the inside painting and cleaning, curtains to be hung, enough work to keep me completely occupied from the time I arose until I exhaustedly fell into bed. To drop with exhaustion was the only way I could cope at that time. Of course, there was no stilling my mind during the long hours of physical labor. The memories of my entire adult life with Debbie flowed through me with each brushstroke.

The 50th anniversary came and went with joy and sorrow. The rain kept some guests away but there was a busy flow of people through the house continually Sunday afternoon. Again, to each negative attitude question regarding Debbie, I responded with a definite positive attitude stating that there was still a 50-50 chance that she could be alive but not truly understanding if I believed my own certitude. There were awkward moments when people did not know if they should ask questions or make comments. A town of petty piety would choose to believe any awful rumors rather than choose the innocent truth. In this situation with publicity as it was, rumors were plenteous, especially Debbie being the daughter of a divorced Hollywood actress. Most were forgotten or ignored but I do recall a couple of rumors stating that we knew where Debbie was. I wondered why we each spent so much time in tears and sadness if that were true! The other one was from my sister's mother-in-law who said it was only to get publicity.

After the anniversary there were but a few days until Christmas. Everyone superficially had their joyful Christmas celebration with family gatherings--still there was an obvious void. Debbie had been somewhat like a special angel atop the tree--a bright, cheering light to everyone. The Christmas before, it had been my brother's eldest son who had been killed the previous August. My sister must have silently had a prayer of thanksgiving for her four beautiful healthy children but with a certain anxiety, wondering if she might be next struck by tragic grief for the loss of another one of her children.

Debbie and I spent few Christmases apart, only two that I could recall. The one when I was in Rome working in "Cleopatra," the other was only the year before when neither of us could afford airfare. Naturally my mind raced through the last Christmas we were together, possibly the last one we would ever have together. It had been a day to remember! We managed to turn adversity into humor. Since it was our first Christmas not only to be alone, but with no invitations, except for Christmas dinner with a man I was dating in Palm Springs.

For the past several days the weather had reported snow for the mountains of San Bernardino. Debbie had said she would really like to go skiing. Her new ski equipment had hardly been used. She would set the clock alarm to go off before daybreak. When the shocking alarm went off Christmas morning the whole thing seemed like a terrible idea. Nevertheless, it was Christmas and my child wanted to go skiing, so skiing it would be! We hurriedly opened our gifts that were under the tree. It had been many years since I celebrated Christmas morning with children awaking before daylight. We decided it would be fun to have a nice breakfast in the mountains and we hurriedly dressed in our warm ski clothing.

To start the day my gas tank was empty and Debbie's car had only a quarter of a tank, plenty to get to a gas station. We drove through Palm Springs and not one station was open at that hour. Along the highway headed toward San Bernardino we still could not find a station. I didn't dare go up the mountains without a full tank of gas. We had to pass up the back short cut road and drive all the way into the city of San Bernardino until we found a station open. That was about a thirty-minute delay. We were still early. We were very jolly as we drove up the mountain. We both loved the area. As we approached the snow line,

I noticed only a few thin patches of snow--it wasn't long before Debbie commented, "Mom there doesn't look like much snow here." I assured her there would be at the ski lift but really doubted there would be if it was so sparse at the snow line. However, as was often necessary, the ski lifts were equipped for manmade snow. As we drove toward the first lift, we saw only one or two cars at the usually bustling parking lot. There was no snow nor were weather conditions right for making it! Never mind we would have a nice breakfast and drive up the mountain to the higher altitudes of Big Bear. In the restaurant, there was no service except the cafeteria line. The only food being served was burned rolls and cold coffee. Never mind - it was Christmas, it was still early and we had a big day ahead of us.

    I always loved the drive toward Big Bear--finally the ski lifts were in view and they were running! What luck! I parked the car and Debbie took out all of her equipment. I planned to rent mine. As we approached the snow, it was packed with firm ice. One has to be an experienced skier for that kind of snow. I wasn't about to tackle it having been on skis only about two or three times. Debbie wanted to try. I told her she could, although I felt she was not experienced enough for that type of snow. She was going into her final semester of high school, a bad time to be wearing a cast. There were other ski lifts we could check out to see if there was softer snow. She decided on a more cautious approach. As we drove each one looked worse than the last. We stopped to look at one where there were skiers. By this time we were ready for lunch. We stood in line over 30 minutes to end up with a very dry cold plate of meat between cold buns. They called it a hamburger. Oh well, by that time, we had come to expect the worst, that way we weren't disappointed.

    Debbie came up with the idea of skiing in the terrible snow so that it would not be a total loss; I suggested we take the back roads down the mountain to the desert, a drive we had never taken. It seemed like a good idea at the time. I drove and drove and drove! Not only did the road down the mountain seem endless but also the drive through the desolate desert was even longer. We drove over 100 miles, twice the distance as the way we had come earlier in the morning to get to Big Bear. We joked about our special Christmas day--what else was there to do! We could gripe and be disgusted or make fun jokes of it as a memorable unusual Christmas--never did I realize just how memorable that Christmas Day would be. We had a delightful Christmas dinner with my friend and weren't the least bit upset when the waitress announced that there were no more cranberries nor candied yams.

But Christmas 1970 was quite different. I was definitely not alone but with many members of my family. Yet I was alone. The day after Christmas I drove from my parents about 75 miles away to visit an uncle. Toward evening, when we started home my mother felt very ill. Shortly after we arrived at their house she collapsed, unconscious onto the floor. Being unconscious and quite heavy, my dad and I could not lift her. We did not know what to do for her or what was wrong. We called the ambulance which rushed her to the hospital where she stayed for the next several days. I don't recall if we ever knew exactly what was wrong with her, perhaps some sort of intestinal disturbance. Perhaps I, too, should have been in the hospital or at least given some sort of medication to help me through this mental, emotional and physical exhaustion. When one loses a loved one in death, there is a tremendous grief but there is finality. In this case we had the never ending grief of death constantly with us, plus the ever-present anxiety of waiting to hear if Debbie's body would be found in and who knows what condition--the anxiety was indescribable.

Another New Year was upon us. 1970 had been a new decade but it certainly had not been the beginning of a new mystical life for me. Instead it had brought me more and more heartaches than I ever thought I could bear. I had read and reread of Job's trials and tribulations in the Bible trying to muster faith to go on but at that point everything in my being was at the lowest ebb. In privacy I cried and cried with excruciating inner pain ...and I prayed! I prayed to God that if my life was never tuned to know any fulfillment, if merely existing, breathing air, taking up space on this Earth was all I was capable of, then please release me from this physical life. "Dear God, if this is all there is to my life--if it is to be one of constant trial, with hope only to be followed by one disappointment after another--if everything I did was to fail--if the one person who had the most meaning in my life was taken--if this was all there was ever to be for me, then let me be free of the physical life--just let me out! While I certainly considered it, I had no intention of committing suicide. I knew too well that one day or one hour of one's life could totally be reversed in a moment but I did pray to die if the "All Seeing Eye" knew nothing better was ahead for me. Recalling those days, perhaps my prayers were answered for without the physical death perhaps, I did die and life began again but ever so slowly. Ever so subtly only now can I look back in retrospect and realize the depth of myself that I experienced as 1970 came to a close...

CHAPTER 28

The entry in my diary for January 1, 1971 reads: "Thank God 1970 is over! What a year! Someday, maybe I shall look upon this as a learning lesson, only now I'm too near it to see anything but horror! Europe should have been a triumph, it should have represented excitement, satisfaction, etc. but those memories are of loneliness, frustration and beauty. As usual what I enjoyed most of all was nature, which can be found most anywhere. Nature holds God's beauty but his "likeness" "man" had created so much ugliness all over the world. Was it too late for me? Surely, it was not. Is it over? I felt at long last, maybe I would step into work suitable for me. I could not divorce my first love, television and film. I could not turn away – I must find a way, some kind of outlet this year. A new year always made me feel that there was a new beginning!"

As usual, with the beginning of the New Year, I dug deeply into my soul to dig up renewed vitality, quite in contrast to my entry toward the end of 1970. I always seemed to write in my diary when I was the most depressed. I thought I had conquered my enemy--myself, but I had been going down--down--down screaming "Help!" to everybody and ignored by all--including God! I just didn't know how much more my physical brain and spiritual soul could take! I had reached the "bottom of the barrel" - I was drained more than I had ever been. "God, what is this lesson all about? Will this stripping ever taper off? Will there ever be any success or happiness for me? Is this all there is?" I wanted to finish this earth cycle with contribution--I didn't want to come back! I was overdue for fulfillment, contribution, a bit of joy--I wanted to write but felt so empty and fruitless. What did I have to give when was I so unhappy myself? How could I help others when I could not help myself? I prayed to accept this damned aloneness! Why could I not accept and then adjust to it? It was my one real handicap. Everything I attempted had gone wrong. Where could I get the energy to do something of worth? I felt like I was at the point of tears constantly.

Hope - disappointment - why when there were moments of happiness, that it seemed I then paid for it by the hours, days and weeks of pain, sorrow and grief? Would I ever see Debbie again? Sometimes when I drove alone in the car, I cried so hard I could not see the road. Thank God for Mother and Daddy and their home. I just could not have made it if it were not for them. I needed them so much now. I wish I didn't need my Prince Charming (who did not exist)! Year in and year out, same hope, then charged up "my battery" only to fall flat on my face "in the mud." If I am to be reincarnated in the future, I had been in the mud so much I'll probably come back as a frog or water lily! At least a water lily can close its pedals, which is what I would like to do! (Written sardonically as I do not believe we return in lower forms of evolution.) This time last year I was miserable, same the year before! Life seemed to be nothing but one miserable disappointment after another! No matter how hard I prayed, called for help, it seemed to be ignored, thus I could not help but come to this point.

    I had been in my own little world communicating with a "source" that I had trusted to be of higher spirits. Was this all nonsense? Was this all there was, I kept asking. With what source could I have been in communication? Was it some source or force or plot playing tricks on me? Would God desert me when I needed love and comfort so desperately? Was there a good loving force in the Universe or was it all evil? I didn't know--how could I create or contribute when I didn't know! July, August 1969 seemed an upswing then down--down--down--stagnant, then, June and Europe, an INSTANT down via Jude and friend, Al! Even though I loved Europe so much, what did I accomplish there? I prayed I could get in forward gear. God bless my family, I prayed never to hurt or cause them any pain or worry, only joy and happiness. Debbie's disappearance caused them so much grief and pain – WHERE is Debbie! With Christmas I leaned toward giving up all hope that Debbie was alive. These past four months really made me feel burned out of any spirituality, doubting my own strong faith.

    With the beginning of 1971 came the realization that I must get hold of myself--at least attempt some discipline of my thought patterns. Inwardly, I knew I had the strength to handle anything that life would dish out – I had to! <u>No, I would not be conquered now!</u> First, I had to make a change. Being around family was living in a continual grief. No one intended it to be that way. There were no peers for me to share, to laugh, to live among in that town. There was no way to go forward to bring about any newness in my life at home with my parents in the pious, petty, hate-filled community that was their "hometown," not mine.

A woman who knew me was a friend of Joyce, a longtime friend who I made my first trip to Europe with when I worked in "Cleopatra," owned a nightclub in Dallas. In those days, mixed alcoholic beverages could not be served except in private clubs, which was what she owned. While visiting with her I told her I had to do something, I was rapidly going crazy and needed desperately to make a change in my life pattern. She offered me a job working evenings at her club. At least, it would keep my evenings occupied, which were the most remorseful time. It took two staff members working the door to assist each guest to sign in and then receive a guest card. At that time, it was one of the busiest nightspots in Dallas. The job totally consumed my mind. By the time I got to bed at 3 AM, I slept well. She insisted I stay at her house during the nights that I worked since it was too late to drive 30 miles to my parents' home. This became inconvenient for all concerned, as her place was a mad house. The best thing for me to do was rent an inexpensive efficiency apartment. I only planned to spend few nights a week in the apartment, spending part of the week with my parents.

The job was a monotonous one; I sat at a desk night after night, somewhat unconsciously writing down people's names and addresses, never really seeing their faces. The important thing was that I was busy and making a little income. There was laughter, gaiety, music and dancing. It helped keeping my mind off of grief. The faces were only a blur - I never noticed individuality. One evening I glanced up said "Your name, please?" This time I looked again, for the first time a man worth a second glance. He was clean cut, good looking and with an Adonis physique. He was an airline pilot stationed in Dallas. There was a bit of twitter in my seemingly dead emotions with the beginnings of our little flirtation. Now there was a little spark in my drab existence and I found myself looking forward to seeing him come in once or twice a week. Finally we had a few totally unpredictable dates--it was an ideal experience and he was fun to be with having a Walter Middy mysterious unreachable attitude. He wasn't married, he was much too devoted to bachelorhood for that. For a while I felt "in love," which gave me a lift and joy but it was totally one-sided.

I was kept busy on my nights off by dating men I met in the club, plus a few from bygone years. There was nothing with any real substance, just something to keep me busy. My primary life unfulfilled goal always included a satisfactory marital relationship. Every day I would look around and see only married people. Why was this "normal" state consistently denied to me? There had to be some psychological imbalance, since those who wanted me, I never wanted. Somewhere along the line, I had simply "missed the boat." I wish I could give up on wanting a mate. Regardless of how hopeless, I couldn't stop looking.

Promiscuity was supposed to be synonymous with Hollywood but men in Dallas seemed to have more insatiable appetites for non-involved-emotional sexual lusts. At least men in California seem slightly more refined and subtle about it - just slightly. It became a bore to be subjected to their stupid petty passes. I needed love, friendship, male companionship, and compassion and understanding, not their grabby attempted lust. I was dumbfounded to realize some men would stoop so low as to try to use Debbie's disappearance to achieve their goal. What a cruel appetite men can have. I was sick of being the Rock of Gibraltar for everyone. It was my turn to need someone to lean on, even if only momentarily, but alas, that too, seemed impossible. Life seemed a pointless "point of no return" merry-go-round.

When checking in guests I realized that there were several men's names associated with Debbie's disappearance. Men I did not know but wanted to question regarding their association with Debbie. A strange set of circumstances took place while I worked at the club. One by one at different times, each signed in. Each time I read the name I was startled since he was another man I wished to question. One was from New York, another from Los Angeles and a couple from the Dallas area. One man, in particular, had a telephone number that had appeared on the phone bill of the apartment from where Debbie disappeared. The call was made to his number the hour before Debbie was last seen. He irrefutably denied receiving the call. He insisted that the answering service answered the call and never gave him the message. I knew professional answering services rarely failed to deliver messages. He was with his lawyer who immediately rushed him away when I tried to question him. The lawyer refused to allow his client to talk any further to me and spoke very rudely to me.

The salesman from New York for whom Debbie had modeled knew nothing nor had even heard from her for several months. Another night, the importer-exporter friend and former employer of Debbie's from Los Angeles signed in. Debbie had tremendous respect for him. He spoke several languages, was quite intelligent and had daughters close to Debbie's age. He had given Debbie an opal birthstone ring surrounded by diamonds that had made me suspicious of their friendship. Both assured me it was a father/daughter friendship. I knew Debbie sought "father" friendship since she didn't get much from her own father. He said he knew nothing about Debbie's whereabouts nor had he heard from her since she left California. He claimed he loaned her money to fly to Texas with her promise to go directly to her grandparents' home. He told me very hurtful things Debbie had told him. In one of the tales he told me, I had to stop him with a chuckle saying, "Don't you recognize this story - it was from an old movie shown frequently on TV." It was Debbie's Libra trait of playing in the middle by seeking a sympathetic response by telling lies about me. After my talk with this man, I wondered, with all the pain and grief he knew I was experiencing, why would he attempt to add to it by repeating these sordid tales, seemingly pointed to hurt me. My psychic instinct gave me the feeling neither of these men were telling me the truth but how could I coerce the truth from them? It was one fault I did not like about my child. Parents of her friends were often cold and indifferent toward me and did not know me at all. It took me time to realize it was Debbie's seeking their sympathy, trying to turn them against me. There really wasn't anything I could do about it. I don't know IF there is a perfect parent child relationship. I DO know that being a single parent is no easy task, especially for a woman who must work. I felt the freelance work I had always done gave me time to be more of an "at home" Mom than other working mothers. I wished that I had some of the beguiling ways that I had observed her girlfriends successfully used.

When one is going through a mental-emotional experience that seems to possess the mind every waking hour, my solution and advice to others, is to get involved in reading, which was exactly what I did each and every day until it was time to go to work. Between sitting at the desk writing all evening or sitting reading all day, I kept a stiff neck. I enjoyed my small retreat I had rented only two blocks from work. It had a large living room where I had my sofa that made into a bed, a nice large bath, a dining room and kitchen. I liked being alone, it was only way I could recharge my battery. I wanted to return to the writing that I had begun in Europe but could not get my mind back into deep concentration necessary for its continuation. The very basis of the book had to do with spiritual beliefs and I was too involved in questioning my own at the time to make any positive written statements.

Joyce, who was a friend of the nightclub owner, returned to Dallas to live. I had mixed emotions. On one hand with her bubbly personality, she always managed to keep me busy when I would have had a tendency to hibernate. On the other hand, I could not trust her as the years of our friendship had proven. She was also a Libra like Debbie. She had always professed a profound friendship for me yet, in her underhanded way, she continually managed to seduce guys I was dating. Only Joyce would jump in the sack with them knowing I was not sexually involved. Maybe she did it because I lived what seemed a "glamorous life" and she inwardly felt inferior; having sex with my beau made her feel superior. I felt guilty for thinking it, as it was always hard to prove, but prove it I did when we were living together in Rome. While I was at work on "Cleopatra" I came home early one day. There she was dressed to go out on a date. The date wasn't to come to our apartment; she was to meet him downstairs. He was an Italian I had been dating and owned an Alpha Romeo that was so loud, it could not be mistaken. I knew that was her date and the reason why she didn't want him to pick her up at the apartment. There were also other proven times. I wasn't going to bed with them, so she did it for me, NOT with my blessings! I acknowledged her friendship with a skeptic eye.

When my sister heard Joyce had returned to Dallas she asked, "Aren't you afraid she will try to cause you to lose your job?" It seemed in Texas as in California someone was always warning me about her. She was one of several female friends through the years who I marveled at their ability to manipulate men. Joyce was the type who bounced around with an attitude that she was the cutest thing ever invented. Often I said if I had her confidence and ability to maneuver males I probably would have been far more successful as an actress. Years before when I first met her in California we had one thing in common, we were both from Dallas. There was one word to describe her – "cheap." She was bright, self-educated and held a good secretarial job. With ever a constant outstretched wing I hinted at grooming suggestions that she readily adopted. She knew I taught at several modeling schools and she took any and every opportunity to improve herself in any and every way that she could – several ex-husbands could attest to that. Regardless of the facts she would lie, cheat and steal from her own mother if necessary, and I had to give her credit for that.

She had a knack for bouncing into my life when I hit the lowest downs and she forced me out of my natural hermit tendency. She was clever enough to take advantage of my tremendous loyalty. In some ways she entered my life like a needed tonic but always laced with a bit of arsenic! Women "friends" can be vicious, MEN greedy with lust. I had this "thing" about rescuing people and helping them become better in any way that I could. In later years I heard of an "enabler" via A.A.; that seemed to be what I was and my pattern with friends!

CHAPTER 29

Toward the end of March 1971, my brother heard the end of a radio news report that included something about Debbie. He thought her body was found. I assured everyone in my family that the police would notify us before releasing it to the news media. Again, moments became hours as I tried to reach the Dallas radio station. Unable to get through, I called the Dallas police. They informed me another piece of Debbie's luggage been found along the roadside only a few miles from where the two suitcases had been located. When I asked why I was not notified the answer was "I don't know." The police released the overnight bag to me a few days later, as it contained no evidence that would help them, plus they were doing little or nothing on Debbie's case anyway. This was peculiar that the bag had never been found in all those months. It lay along the roadside of the heavy traveled street. Young boys looking for bottles to sell found it. I asked the police if there was any sort of chemical analysis that would tell them how long the bag had been there but there was none.

In the bag was some jewelry including her high school graduation ring, a treasure she would never willingly part with, as well as other mementos. No young ladies who enjoyed being attractive would throw away their makeup. This discovery was proof to me that Debbie had not flipped out and run off as many chose to believe. There was nothing in the bag with her full identification. Her personal IDs were never found and where was this missing diary she kept religiously? Did it hold incriminating evidence and had been destroyed? Her beautiful opal ring she loved was also never found and she would have been wearing it. The bag proved that Debbie was either abducted against her will or she was dead. If she had been murdered, I felt sure it was not at the hands of some unknown maniac but by someone she knew well. It was an expensive bag that I dearly loved. It was a different shape than most and it was an item I left in my closet and had given strict instructions NOT to use! An old friend in the film industry had given me this unique bag as a Christmas present. At that same time, he had given Debbie a red dress that was one of the cutest she ever owned. This was another act of defiance toward me, invading my things I had told her not to use, plus, she had also found my credit cards my mother had hidden and used them, leaving me with debts. There were certainly times I did not LIKE my daughter but it didn't affect the deep love I had for her.

One of the television stations' news department sent a female reporter out to interview me at my apartment. I hoped the new interview would bring some thread of information. A few days later, there was a knock on my door. I was apprehensive toward allowing a stranger inside my apartment. The young man identified himself as the brother of another young woman who disappeared only the month after Debbie. There was no trace of his sister. On his own he had done quite a bit of investigating. He told me that a number of girls disappeared around that same time, which had not made the news. From the information he obtained, he told me that all the girls were similar types, All-American, longhaired, good figures and pretty. He believed these girls might have been put into some form of white slavery. He looked through Debbie's address book which had been found in the latest piece of her luggage. He was trying to find just one name in common with his sister's associates. He found only one simple name like Smith that might not be a link. He assured me he would contact me if he uncovered any further information. His visit made me realize there were people with far greater grief than mine. Shortly after his sister's disappearance, his brother was killed in a boating accident; then another brother and his father had been hospitalized for months from an automobile accident. How could that family stand so much? No matter how grievous our situation, there is always someone much worse off. His family's tragedies sounded too weird to just be accidental or coincidental. It seemed there could be a link with the numerous disappearances.

I could never find a way to call Rob. The discovery of Debbie's overnight bag made it even more imperative that I confront him. If he had murdered Debbie and I faced him alone, I wasn't sure what he might do to me. As far as I was concerned he had proven himself to be quite psychotic from the things he had told police and others. A news reporter from one of the radio station seemed to take an interest in Debbie's case and kept promising me he would go with me to talk to Rod, as well as the co-pilot that Debbie had dated. If I could just face Rob I felt I would sense the truth. I knew he had lied to everyone. Was he only trying to make her look bad because she jilted him or the important question, was he covering up his own actions?

I asked every male I knew to go with me to talk to Rob. Several were going but never seem to get around to it. Finally one day the news reporter did take me to interview the co-pilot. I had never met him but I knew that Debbie had been very fond of him. We visited with him for quite some time and he was willing to answer any questions we asked. I felt he was telling the truth and did not feel he knew more than he had told us. I definitely did not feel he had anything to do with her disappearance. I did feel that he, too, suspected Rob. After living in the same apartment complex for a year or more, he and Rob had never been friends but after Debbie disappeared, the co-pilot told us that Rob suddenly insisted they double date and acted as though they had been long time friends. The news reporter assured me we would deftly go to see Rob but it never happened. I was sorry I had not insisted I go the evening when my brother-in-law went, for the opportunity never came again. What a helpless feeling it was to be a woman alone, regardless of what Women's Lib was trying to prove.

About the same time I read that a well-known psychic Peter Hurkos was visiting a department store in Dallas to promote the sale of his book. I had been an avid admirer and kept up with him through the years. When he appeared as a nightclub entertainer in Palm Springs, I had been on stage with him. At that time, he suggested I should never have left my chosen profession. He advised me to have some new photographs made, to go back into the film business. I did eventually-- to no avail. That never daunted my faith and respect for his phenomenal ability from all that I had read about him. Perhaps fate had brought him to Dallas when all else had failed. I was so excited at the fateful event. I was the first to arrive at the department store auditorium and waited-- then was lucky enough to be one of the audience members selected for him to answer a question. I was so positive this was the help for which I had so long prayed! I handed him Debbie's photograph. He asked, "Could you stand the truth?" I said I could. He said he did not think I could and asked me to see him after the show. Afterwards, I waited and waited through the entire autograph session. Suddenly, he was being hurried away. I reminded someone he had asked me to see him after the show. His young wife, who seemed to be his business partner said, "NO!" I could talk to him no further! I still could not accept that ending. I found out where he was staying and telephoned the hotel all afternoon until I finally got through – whom else answered the phone but the business manager wife. Now over the telephone she was far more receptive. She informed me he would be available for consultation one day two weeks hence for the fee of--$5,000! There was no guarantee he could provide me with any information. If that was a sample of monetary rewards for psychic ability, I should have worked harder to develop my own psychic ability rather than pursue acting or film production. The whole illusion presented on television and in the news media of this brilliant psychic, the private eye, the detective, the newspaper or Good Samaritan coming to a person's rescue was only mythical and just does not happen in real life experiences.

Just after the news report of the discovery of Debbie's bag, one evening at work, the nightclub's part-time hostess started pointlessly telling me what to do. In the same harsh manner in which she spoke to me, I suggested she do her job and I would do mine. I had put up with her overbearing, pushy attitude and was distraught enough to speak up to her. Rumors were that she was a lesbian. If so, I had never had much association, except at the Advertising Agency and in general I didn't think I got along with them very well. Being strong willed and totally female, I must have posed some sort of threat to the aggressive type lesbian. The next day I was caught totally off guard when the club owner called to say that she had to dismiss me as I was causing "dissension" at the club. What a hell of a time for a "friend" to fire me! Couldn't she have let it ride for a couple of weeks? Why was my point of view against the hostess being totally ignored? Why did she have so great an influence on the owner? Suddenly, I was confronted with a passing remark made by the owner, which made me wonder about her. I dismissed it because she had a husband, a "milk toast" one added to the fact that I could also be overly conscious of homosexuality and bisexuality. I thought I had left that sensitivity behind in California. In my heart, I knew that Joyce had something to do with the so-called dissension I was supposed to have been responsible for at the club. No way did I suspect my Libra friend Joyce, of lesbian activities since her choices were quite the opposite obsession. No, her involvement would be the fascinating way of sowing seeds of dissension with flowing flowery complements about me. I had seen her do it so often in front of men. She was the only person I knew that could "stab you in the back" with a compliment! She almost always included a subtle but vicious stab. What vicious animals women can be, just like cats, their claws come out with deadly aim. I could not deny vicious thoughts myself; it seemed a part of the female mystique, but the difference being I never carried through the thought into action - perhaps by nature or by my religious conditioning from childhood.

I had not planned to spend the rest of my days working in a nightclub, signing stupid pieces of meaningless paper and had been there longer than I intended. Maybe being fired from the club was to push me into doing something else - but what? Since I had been in Dallas I contacted various film production companies, advertising agencies and modeling agencies. Now and then, some work came in that I loved but there just was not enough to live on. As always there was production work coming up in the future but how well I knew the future never gets here. A full-time job seemed essential for now.

With the continued investigation of Debbie's case, leaving the Dallas area seemed an impossibility. Even if I could leave where would I go? I had no desire to go back to California - enough was enough. If I had a place to go, I did not have the money to make a move. I would just have to seek employment in Dallas. I really wanted to find a job in which I could become 100% absorbed. Newspaper ads that sounded interesting with a future were always ads from employment agencies. To list with one required the best hours of the day spent filling out the papers, testing, typing, waiting to be interviewed, then a job was never available for some reason or the appointment to be interviewed was never set up.

Finally, an ad appeared for a job training to be an assistant manager in a lady's specialty shop. God! How far had I fallen! Success certainly had passed me by. Before my glamorous years in Hollywood where I was so sure I was destined to win an Academy award here I was back in the city where my fashion photography modeling and TV commercials had all begun. I was now scrounging for a job that I would have refused almost 20 years before. I applied for the job at the dress shop and got it. The salary was horrible but the position offered the promise of a commission after the first week or two of training. How aggravating to waste all the knowledge I had acquired in the film industry, to be a sales clerk in a dress shop. Oh well, it had happened to actresses far more famous than me. The job was something else! Right away I learned everyone was hired "in training for the assistant manager's job." The employer would not allow the sales girls to sit, except on their morning and afternoon break. You had to stand on your feet all day even if there were no customers in the store. It was a constant shuffling of dresses, hanging garments, straightening the entire rack, sometimes helping ladies to zip and unzip, smiling while lying about how well that the dresses looked on the customers. I was ready to scream when I went home in the evening. The job proved there was something worse than writing people's names and addresses on pieces of paper.

The storeowner suggested it would be a good idea for all the sales people to wear the store's merchandise. He was willing to allow a small discount but he still made a good profit. This left me with no choice and took a big hunk of my small salary the first week. We were selling fall and winter clothing but the Dallas weather wasn't cooperating. I was miserable and sweating profusely while wearing the required new dress. Standing on my feet all day wore me out. With very sore feet, one morning I appeared in clothing more suitable for the temperature that included comfortable thong sandals without hose. My employer quickly noticed my hose-less legs and suggested I return home and put on a pair of hose. I said I would do so at noon. He suggested since his store was not busy that I do it now. Driving home with each block, the more furious I became! Had I come to this? Had I reached the point that my intelligence, ability, personality and workability no longer mattered and I was being judged only on the basis of whether or not I wore a pair of hose? Instead of putting on the hose, I just sat there and thought, reassessing my values. I had become far too independent to live like this. Hose today, what tomorrow? I was no one's unintelligent slave. Years ago I had not compromised myself in attempting to attain success in the most glamorous profession in the world. In Hollywood where the stakes were the highest and where few jobs for women paid the possible salaries of actresses. All of this left me wondering why I was compromising myself now. Would I even give up a small measure of independence and individuality by putting on a pair of hose to indulge the idiosyncrasies of a small time merchant? I never put on the hose or returned to work that day or any other!

The two experiences in Dallas had convinced me I was incapable of working for someone else in full-time employment. I have become far too independent to bend to the petty, immature attitudes of people whose ability was far less than my own. The thought of going back and trying to live in my parents' hometown was depressing. However my only hope seemed to be to go ahead with the original idea of opening an artsy, crafty little shop. That had been my decision in Europe when I had purchased a few small antique items in my travels for just that purpose. The garage I had planned to convert had since been torn down. On one side of the front of the house, my dad had enclosed a covered patio and made a sunroom out of it that was used for storage. It was a long narrow room but for a gift shop I would not need a large area. Their home was situated only two blocks from the downtown and the town was growing in that direction. The area had already been zoned for commercial use. The street the house faced was the second heaviest traveled in town. There would be no great expense in opening a small shop. If I could just close the world out and be satisfied to live and work there, I knew it was something my parents had always wanted and at least I would be making them happy.

CHAPTER 30

In Autumn I gave up my small, cozy apartment in Dallas. Again, as many times before, made up my mind I would force myself to be content to live in my parent's hometown. It was never my "hometown" -- for me it was only a town where my family lived. From the moment I entered that high school mid-year of my junior year, that town had been vicious toward me. I believed it had been my own persecution complex until years later, the same thing was happening to my daughter whose personality was totally unlike mine. There was never anything but heartaches and disappointments for me there. My father said that I imagined it but I saw my parents hurt many times as well. I don't know if I ever had a gypsy past life but I did have a gypsy spirit to keep "moving on."

In that town, resentments flourished and always had. With a glamorous Hollywood lifestyle and a divorcee, I suppose I was prime target for jealousy and gossip. After the traumatic experience of Debbie's disappearance, I just could not believe any community would express jealousy and resentment before compassion and kindness, especially considering most of the town's social life revolved around its churches. It was not only my grief but of my whole family, especially my parents who had so much love for Debbie. Not knowing how this attitude might affect me, even financially, for years I had borrowed and paid back loans promptly from one of the town's local banks. When I approached the banker for a loan, he was quite willing--only this time, he required my father's signature. After all those years of establishing credit, why now was I treated like a teenager applying for a first loan? What the hell, it was only a piece of paper and my father was more than willing to sign. I had no time for petty pride; yet, it should have been a warning sign.

There was much to be done. I began weeks of exceedingly hard work. It seemed when I was in a "down" period; I always buried myself in hard physical labor. Thus, when I went to bed at night, I was completely exhausted, too tired for self-pity and the reminders of none of my life's goals accomplished. I was plagued with migraine headaches. Often I was so sick I could not work. I blamed it on the Texas heat and prayed I would never have to spend another full summer there. I never intended to be totally tied down to this little shop, feeling that my mother could take care of it part of the time. The first big job was the ceiling. If it had just been a matter of ceiling tiles, I could have installed those alone. It had to have 4' x 8' sheetrock put up, which I could not handle alone. There was electrical wiring and other jobs that required my Dad's help but he was usually busy when I needed his help. Except for those few necessities, I did create the soon to be a gift shop alone. I had painted the walls, the trim and the cabinets three shades of soft orange because I had found a bargain remnant of carpet in those colors. The shelves were also up and in front of the house, the wrought iron decorative sign holder was painted and placed in the ground. I painted a shapely wooden sign with the store name - "Ann's Et Cetera." The name had no connotation and I could change the shop's merchandise as business dictated. I had also managed to save most of the bank loan for merchandise. I began bargain hunting in the gift market and wholesale areas of Dallas. I stocked up on unique items and pieces that I thought would sell. A few years before, my sister had attempted a gift shop but with four kids, she had little time to run it. She still had some of the stock that I would sell on consignment. I had also bought floral supplies to make dried flower arrangements. Since I did not expect to be deluged with customers, while watching the store, I could keep occupied by making new artsy creations. I had many ideas for making clever items to sell. When I used my creative ability, life always moved into more contentment, as my mind seemed to go blank.

As the time neared for the Grand Opening, I wrote and recorded my own radio commercial and tried to use clever newspaper ads. At the same time, the newspaper happened to be running a promotion. Each merchant was encouraged to have customers sign up for free gifts and have a drawing at the end of the week. I had my Grand Opening and how "GRAND" it was! My first sale was 30 cents and anything that followed not much better. After six days I had sold less than $10 worth of merchandise. During the week little old ladies would hustle in, sign up and leave without not so much as a glance of my merchandise. The only regular customer was a young boy who bought dried flowers, 10 cents at a time. I think he had heard that I had worked in motion pictures and television and spent his dime just to see me. Every time I had visited there from California and when there had been a new store opening, I always made it a point to drop in to compliment the new business and try to buy something to encourage the new merchants. A few of my mother's friends came to look and also had a visit with her. Almost none of the people in town that my sister or I knew ever came to see the shop. I could not believe the people that had known my family, Debbie and me for years could be so cold and indifferent toward my plight. In the back of my mind, in spite of the petty piety, I always believed in times of trouble, people in a small community responded in warmth and loyalty, but instead cold indifference that was not unique to metropolitan areas like Los Angeles.

It takes the tragedies and emergencies in one's life to prove who and what kind of friends you have. I could count mine on one hand - "out of sight out of mind." I left California after some 15 years of friendships--during this most horrific time of my life, hardly anyone had bothered to even call or write. I had chosen to leave Texas to seek fame and fortune in Hollywood. Therefore the attitude in Texas was that I thought I was too good for Texas, so I should be ignored. Thank God, I had witnessed and been turned off to pious, sanctimonious, hypocritical and organized religious groups for years. I had felt more real communication with God and the Universal power in nature rather than in man's structures. If I had to depend upon ministers and the church family for my personal strength, I would have been plowed under long ago. Just like any other business, as long as you are a good customer - "You are a welcomed brother or sister!"

The earnings from my shop would not buy one meal a day - much less restock the merchandise. I had the ability to be very patient and also very impatient. That may have always facilitated my downfall. There were passed opportunities I wish I had handled differently or with a greater patience. A few weeks were not a fair trial for my gift shop. Anyone knows new merchants should be prepared for at least six months of drought. I could see no future hope for eking out even a meager livelihood and had no desire to become a liability for my parents.

A Texas Ranger stopped by to assure me they were still working on Debbie's case. When her overnight bag was found, I tried a bit of psychometry by holding Debbie's ring in the palm of my hand, closing my eyes and endeavoring to sense something. Very clearly, at the top of a plateau, I saw a crescent shaped structure with a very wide veranda. I had the feeling it was in an area of Northern Mexico. I felt there was a flat area or maybe a small landing strip. It seemed to be a very large home or very small resort. When I described it to the Ranger, he told me he had been to a similar spot in Mexico on a hunting trip. He wasn't sure of the exact location, as it had taken them hours to reach it in a car driving on a dirt road. Could it be an illicit spot for White Slavery? Even if I had more than a psychic hunch to go on, he told me it was next to impossible to get any reciprocal cooperation with the Mexican authorities. Again, I had the helpless feeling that my hands were tied.

Ever since I opened the shop, thoughts of returning to California kept creeping into my mind, yet consciously I had no desire to return. There was nothing there, not even friends yet the thoughts kept popping in, almost like an inner force pushing me. It was ridiculous. I had just settled once again at my parents' home and I was totally determined to make it my home. Plus my intentions were still to complete the book I had started in Europe. With all of the emotional eruption - my foundation had crumbled and it would take time to rebuild. Questioning my own reality or illusion did not put me in any frame of mind for the deep mental searching necessary to complete my book. In time it would come, but this wasn't the right time.

I had sold the car my father bought for Debbie and replaced it with a sporty Mustang. I began covering many miles in it for the next few weeks. I took on a sales representative job part time promoting a new type of carpet. There wasn't much money in it but better than my merchandising venture. I also took a job as a hostess in a nightspot in Dallas and stayed with Joyce when I worked. The two of us reminisced over California living and before long we began planning to go back to California together. After we got to California, I figured we might go our separate ways. Joyce wanted to return to Palm Springs. I was considering new territory such as San Francisco or San Diego and I began hoarding every penny in order to make the trip. Money was not a problem for my sister. She had been using my once new large cabinet stereo since 1962, plus my sewing machine. I suggested she considered buying them to glean a small bit of money.

With all the reconstruction work on the little store, I had managed to stay very busy during the first year's anniversary of Debbie's disappearance. The Thanksgiving holidays were approaching and there would be another Christmas to face without Debbie. I hated the holiday season and now cool weather had hit. Even though I did not like living in Palm Springs, the thought of warm desert sun in the winter months began to appeal to me. Any change would be a welcomed one. That had been the most miserable year of my life, filled with grief I never believed I could live through. On top of that – the loneliness, the sense of failure plus the awful accusations, the mystery, the constant questions, the confusion. Yes, I had hit some downs in my life but never as completely nor as long as this had been. What could possibly be worse in California? I needed a bit of joy and happiness for a change. My married friends whom I stayed with prior to departing for Europe had invited me to come and visit them for as long as I wanted. I felt I had been in negative vibrations for so long, if nothing else a vacation from it all was more than justified. I knew my parents would be disappointed and disapprove but the urging persisted so strongly I could not ignore it. Regardless of how foolish it may have seemed to others to have opened a gift shop and then shortly thereafter return to California it was the right move for me. For the tiny amount of business my shop brought in my mother could handle it with ease and still watch her soap operas. It might also give her a little mental stimulation that she could use, since she had always worked outside the home. With me out of the way, maybe her friends would give her business. Any profits would be hers. If business picked up, maybe she could save a little money to help repay the bank loan.

I told my family I was going on vacation, that I just had to get away from it all for a while. I did not know how long I would stay. It would depend upon what fate had in store for me. If nothing worked out in California, I could always return to Texas and continue to try to make a go of the little shop. What cross-purposes plagued me! The past few years in California had been nothing but continual heartaches and disappointment. There had been a few accomplishments. Why was I returning? No inner feeling had pushed me so strongly as this--I knew I must go!

It came as no surprise when a few days before we were to depart for California some guy came along and Joyce decided not to go. I really didn't have enough money to handle the entire expense plus I desperately hated the long cross-country drive alone but my plans were to go - SO GO I DID!

CHAPTER 31

I packed my little car not knowing if I would be gone for a few weeks, months or indefinitely. My poor little blue Mustang was bulging at the seams when I had finished packing. My plans were to leave on Sunday morning preceding Thanksgiving. Early Sunday is a good time to travel across Texas, especially since the first hundred miles of my journey was through the congested Dallas-Fort Worth area. Since I was born on Sunday, I hoped this too would be a new birth, a new beginning – just another beginning even though the end of 1971 was at hand. If I had any serious trouble, I always knew I could call my parents for help, so I was leaving on my new venture with only a couple hundred dollars, my dad's gasoline credit card and a whole lot of faith that things would work out far better since it couldn't be much worse for me in California. After all, on my first trip to Europe, I arrived there with only a one-way ticket and $200. The one thing I could always count on was my Dad's reassuring me that I always had a HOME to come back to, which I never heard from my Mother, although I did not feel she had any objection.

That November Sunday morning, I was pulling out of the driveway at 5:40 am wearing my Sunday's child necklace for good luck. The night before I had backed my car into the driveway so every move made Sunday would be in forward motion. With our overly sentimental nature, goodbyes were always painful. If my parents did not awake with my scurrying about, I would leave without a tearful goodbye. I was happy to start the journey without sadness. My parents usually awoke early, this morning they seem to be sleeping. I suspected they dreaded the departure more than I did.

The dawn was just breaking in the East behind me although ahead it was still dark. I felt a surge of joyful energy as I drove through the downtown area of Dallas. I was on the freeway heading west. The thoughts humorously came to me that when Debbie was born, I was still under heavy sedation. I told my family I would be happy when this freeway bypassing the downtown area of Dallas was finished. They sort of chuckled since there was no plan for any such a freeway at that time. Here I was gliding across the downtown area just as I had said all those years ago. It was years later that I realized I had a bit more psychic ability than most. Off in the distance loomed a tall brown brick building, the Methodist hospital, where Debbie had been born 18 years before. If Debbie was dead, perhaps that life of mine had also died and now I was going forward into a new one. Just then a popular song played on the radio "Just call me angel of the morning" as the sun was rising with all its splendor. The earth around me had an eerie glow – at that moment everything became a beautiful glowing gold. The edge of the clouds were also gilded with shimmering gold. It was easy to understand how man once thought this was his God speaking to him. Was God speaking to me? I was too enthralled in nature's beauty and wonder to be sad as I passed Debbie's birthplace. It was only a few days before I was driving through East Texas, the birthplace of most of my family. During the fall season each year it was a sight to behold; the leaves were a rainbow of fall colors. It was the time of year when everything died or went to sleep for a while then fell away to return another day as a new growth - a new beginning. I was identifying with my own old dead leaves - negative destructive habits - and thoughts that were falling away. Also I prayed to die, perhaps I did not see it at the time but to look back I believe my prayers were answered--there was a part of me that also died with Debbie.

 I was so totally alone as I drove along the barren highway. It was a wonderful aloneness. How I hated and loved being alone. There were few cars along the highway at that hour of the morning. My only travel companion was my tape recorder. During the long lonely stretches between West Texas towns I would talk, sing or recite anything I could remember, then laugh when I played it back. There had been so little laughter for me for such a long time and it felt good to laugh at myself. On the first playback, there was no doubt my stay in Texas had left its mark on my voice and diction. After hours of chatting to the recorder, playing it back and then arguing with myself, I sped through West Texas much sooner than I expected. I had planned to drive no further than El Paso but it was only three o'clock in the afternoon and I felt very alive and refreshed. By the time I crossed into New Mexico, there was a marked difference in my accent. Not only was the slow, negative accent disappearing but also there was a noticeable change in my voice. It became bubbly and blissful. So many times I had taken that long drive to California alone. I had expected to be bored and tired but in searching for beautiful scenery and having the tape recorder along made the time pass amazingly quickly.

If it had not been for having to replace my shock absorbers that I was told was necessary, I would have been able to drive all the way through to New Mexico but as it grew dark, I stopped for the night. As I began driving the next morning, the realization came over me that I had now gone too far west to turn back. Desert scenes had never been my favorite form of nature but in the early morning off in the distance were beautiful Arizona jagged hills. As I drove through Arizona, more than halfway to California, fear filled my happy thoughts. What would I do when I got there? Would I be friendless? Would I be able to find a job? Jobs were always so hard to come by in California with so many people to fill them. Yet, memories were far too painful and unhappy in Texas to ever make my home there. I knew that leaving Texas was the best medicine I could possibly have. I wish I had a new area where I really wanted to go, around San Francisco or San Diego? I assumed I could get some sort of work. Maybe it was a blessing that I had long since been forced to give up that glamorous side of my life. I had observed that it seemed to force some beautiful women into high-class prostitution or to marry some old guy with money rather than face the less glamorous world of unemployment.

When I crossed into California, just as I had always experienced on previous trips, a sudden jubilant intoxication came over me. Far more exhilarating than the feeling of the tight band removed from around my head as I drove across the border out of the state of Texas. It was a long drive across the California desert. In the far distance, I could finally see Palm Springs nestled against the mountains. I felt I should stop in Palm Springs but my car was so adjusted to rolling along the highway at high speed, I could not get my foot off the gas pedal to make the turn when Palm Springs road signs appeared. I drove on into Los Angeles. As I drove along the freeway into Los Angeles it was much dirtier than I remembered. Even the foliage along the roadside was black from the exhaust fumes. The air was thick with smog. There was a depressive feeling in the air and the city was even more congested than I remembered. There was no feeling of being home, no joy to be in Los Angeles again. It was the first time for me to drive into the area without a thrilling feeling. It had never before appeared to be so ugly.

When I finally arrived at my friend's home in Hollywood, they informed me that they were leaving for the Thanksgiving holidays and the house was mine. I made a few phone calls to people I felt were still somewhat friends - all were very busy, some leaving for the holidays and would see me in a week or so. I was pretty let down after my long drive to find everyone was too busy to see me even for a few minutes. The next morning I picked up the telephone and called a friend in Palm Springs. The person was not really my friend but an acquaintance I had met through Joyce. I was met with an enthusiastic welcome, insisting I drive to Palm Springs immediately. This seemed to be an omen I should have stopped there in the first place after that non-enthusiastic reception in Los Angeles. Back into my bulging Mustang, the usual long 120 mile drive to Palm Springs seemed nothing after my cross-country drive. I often wondered what would have happened if my Libra friend, Joyce had come along. Actually all of the people I was first surrounded by in the desert were her friends. The little group of people was exceedingly friendly, fun and full of encouragement. I found myself laughing and having fun for the first time in such a long time. They showed a natural concern for Debbie but when I expressed a desire not to discuss it after the initial explanation they respected my wishes.

Sooner or later each one of them told me gossip Joyce had shared with them about me. All of which were out and out lies to turn them against me, to strengthen her position in their eyes. Just like Debbie! Joyce's birthday was October 17 and Debbie's was October 18th. With a chance to get acquainted with me they were not blinded by her evil slander. When each realized her lies they wanted me to know what sort of "friend" she had been. Never before had I been able to find such open and obvious admission to her viciousness. Even in my most agonizing tormented time and grief over Debbie, she still managed to use her ever-present handful of daggers, even causing me to lose the Dallas hosting job. Through the years, I had been put in a position of being guilty of ugly suspicious thoughts regarding her behavior and subtle actions. This time I had the proof I needed to justify ending that friendship and totally without guilt.

One of the women invited me to stay at her house and use her extra bedroom for as long as I wanted. I was so much more at home with my new friends than the people I had left behind. Another woman whom I had grown to know was a delightful, fun loving, happy-go-lucky friend who insisted I go everywhere with her. She was a successful dog groomer and told me she needed someone to work at the front desk. If I wanted the job, I could have it until I found something better. Within five days, without seeking employment, I had five jobs offered to me! This was definitely an omen that I was meant to stay in Palm Springs. My new friends knew I had been to hell and back. Each tried to do everything to keep me busy. One by one, they shared my thoughts and ideas making me feel like an individual who was wanted and needed. I shall always cherish that time with much gratitude to a handful of strangers with whom I have long since lost touch.

The job I decided to take opened a whole new career for me and that was exactly what I had wanted. I was trying to face the fact that I had reached the point of no return. There would be no happy marriage and I had to support myself for the rest of my days, like it or not. My glamorous youth was gone and with it went a large percentage of any pursuing males. Maybe I was conquering that obsession, too. The exciting active year was subsiding, best I accept and live with my present conditions and not long for or think about bygone days. I was weary of the extreme of highs and lows and welcomed a more even keeled life. I truly wanted to get down out of the cloud of dreams and unfulfilled ambitions into the world of reality where I could live a "normal" life if such a thing existed, just like other people. With my child-like faith I believed I had enough intelligence, maturity and ambition to make a good life for myself.

CHAPTER 32

The new job I accepted was to do interior decorating for a base salary, plus sell mobile homes on commission. This was a perfect arrangement to replenish my dwindling $200 and still have an opportunity to make an income equivalent to a man. To me, mobile homes meant very little, dinky homes like the one we lived in temporarily during World War II. Those were actually travel trailers. Little did I realize the size and luxury of mobile homes were comparable to a regular house. The mobile homes on the lot had furnishing arranged by the owner and salesman. They were in dire need of a woman's touch, especially me with professional decorating experience. After a week or so of shifting furniture here and there, accessorizing, digging out lamps and accessories from the junky storeroom, the model village finally showed a much-needed feminine touch. Again, I was involved in very hot, hard and very tiring work that did give me a much-needed positive creative outlet.

There was so much to learn about selling mobile homes; also there were new and used travel trailers to sell. The new ones were Airstreams, a luxury traveling trailer I did not know existed. How perfect one of those would have been for Debbie and me to travel like sophisticated gypsies after her graduation. A pipe dream, for they were as expensive as a small doublewide mobile home, neither of which my financial status could consider. For years I have been involved in many shows and Expos that were nothing more than memorization of sales presentations offered by an attractive female used as an attention getter. Through those shows and my prepared commentaries, I thought I was good at selling. The only problem was that while I knew I could sell, I had never been left to <u>close</u> the sale - which is an art of its own. That personality quirk had cost me money through the years by not collecting money owed to me. I was a terrific salesperson as long as I didn't have to ask for money and that was when the owner took over the closing. That was all right at first but as the only saleswoman, when a sales equaled or surpassed those of the men's sales, I knew I had to learn to take the sale through to its completion. It became obvious to me, no matter how much I enjoyed the interior decorating, the money was definitely in sales. Decorating was just hard work for a minimal salary. I wanted and needed a job to be totally absorbed in and I had one. It was interesting and exciting to be learning a new career, one in which age would not be a handicap. Selling homes is a natural for women. Previously, mobile home sales were a male-dominated profession with licensing similar to that of auto sales. It was still considered a "man's world" by most sales organizations, thus it was awkward to have a woman as a salesperson.

There was no one to date in Palm Springs, although I had a social life with much fun and laughter with my new friends. In a small resort community such as Palm Springs, knowing many of the owners of better restaurants and bars made it possible for women to go out unescorted without being thought of as hookers. The dog grooming shop owner, Cindy, and I often went out for cocktails, dinner and after dinner drinks. We shared many of the same ideas, attitudes and opinions. What a joy she was as the first single female friend I had ever had on a noncompetitive basis. It was not me that was competitive! On one of our evenings out I was shocked to see a handsome young blond male with a familiar face – it was the young man Debbie had dated in Palm Springs and considered marrying when he got out of the Marine Corps. He was now out of the Marine Corps. How I wish they had married in spite of their youth, another one of those "if only" that bugged me. I had talked to him by telephone when Debbie first disappeared. He seemed quite distracted talking to me as I was bringing back memories he probably was trying to forget.

For the first couple of months, I worked seven days a week. I came to work early and stayed late. Totally work involved was the best medicine for me. With construction costs soaring, new mobile or modular construction seemed to be the coming trend. Very few women were in the field so I was getting a head start. I could be realistic about growing older – I did not mind growing older as long as I could do it gracefully in every respect. I did not want to be in any type of job that hinged on women's youthful good looks.

The girlfriend whose house I was staying in had a teenage son who had rock music blasting at full volume all the time. I longed for peace, quiet and solitude. Some aloneness was essential for me. There was a damaged new 12' x 52' mobile home on the lot which I kept eyeing. It was a one-bedroom with large rooms and I could see its potential with a little TLC (tender love and care) by now I was sold on mobile home living, especially with my vagabond soul. By having furniture and personal belongings in one of these, idealistically I thought it was simple enough to have a truck move it from one location to another. To have a home where everything could be moved without packing and unpacking seemed ideal for me and to have my own little home interested me. Knowing how unbearably hot Palm Springs becomes in the summer, in the back of my mind, I thought I could have my house moved to the beach area toward San Diego where there were many mobile home dealers. By then, I would have enough experience to be able to find employment in that area. Since business was so slow in Palm Springs in the summer, perhaps the winter months I could return, house and all. Yes, a portable home was much to my liking. It would certainly solve my disdain for packing and unpacking. Little did I know that mobile homes are not moved from place to another quite so easily, as I had imagined. When it is moved onto a lot, there it stays fairly permanently.

The deal was working out so that my payments were reasonable. My employer agreed to allow me to park the mobile home in the back of the sales lot where there were two other occupied mobile homes. There was a small stable next to the location under the protection of tall trees where I wanted to park my mobile home. I asked if there was any chance a horse would ever be put in the stable. "Not a chance!" he assured me. Shortly after the house was all set --there came the horse! No wonder he never charged me rent – no one would steal the horse with a horse sitter adjoining the stable. That was not my first exposure to my boss' deviousness. I had seen him pull some business shenanigans I did not like, however, in general I thought he seemed quite fair to me. My commissions earned were growing day by day. I liked the idea of receiving one big fat check. My fellow salesmen subtly warned me that I should collect everything I was owed and keep drawing against commissions! In addition to my salary, my boss had paid me one commission check for several hundred dollars. I really did feel I would have no problem collecting the commissions due to me. I never learn--after being taken repeatedly. Here I was again - full of trust or stupidity!

There was something pleasurable about being away from family when Christmas time rolled around. Strange how an event can changes life's patterns. It had always been a special joy to be at home with family during Christmas holidays. I was happy to work on Christmas Day. To treat it as just another day was necessary. Sentimental memories were too painful to be brought up and I did not wish to discuss my previous year's experiences. When I arrived at work Christmas morning, there was a little black bundle of fur in my chair, a tiny baby poodle. I said, "I don't know who left this here but if it was meant as a joke you just lost your puppy! It's in my chair and I am keeping what's in it!" I was never really sure who left her or if they meant for me to keep her. I suspected it was my boss, a friend of Cindy's. Since Cindy knew all about dogs, she could advise me on my precious little pet's care. This was a pleasant surprise, as was the sale I made that day of the most expensive home on the lot. I could never imagine that I would never see the commission for it. One of the nicest things about Christmas was that I had managed to pay off the bank note in Texas and was free and clear, except for my new home which was hardly more than an automobile payment and less than an apartment rent. I finished Christmas Day with a nice dinner at the woman's house of where I had been living. Christmas came and went fairly painless by keeping my mind occupied with my new life and friends. They all knew I was determined to begin anew and did not want to discuss Debbie and they honored that wish. With fondness I shall always remember their help when I had needed friendship the most. Work was my life with no datable men around. If there were any my age, they were busy chasing 20-year-olds. Sometimes I would go out with some older guy just for an opportunity to go somewhere special. However it was always boring with their totally materialistic viewpoints and empty conversations. It was a struggle to converse. I certainly did not want the companionship to progress beyond conversation only!

Finally I began making excuses to collect large sums of commissions due to me. How appalling to have to ask for money owed to me. That was the one in advantage in the acting profession. An actor must belong to the union and have an agent. The agent dickers for the money above the required union scale. The union requires payment within a certain period of time, so there was rarely any problem getting one's pay.

My employer kept postponing paying me. The "last straw" was when a customer of mine came in one day to pick up a travel trailer I had sold. The man had given us a month to do a couple small repairs like putting on better tires for his trip into Mexico. He had taken time to call to make sure it would be ready. When he arrived he had several people with travel trailers with him to make the journey into Mexico. Each week I had requested the work be done. For several days I left notices on the owner's desk to remind him of it. He was notorious for taking the customer's money and never following through with his promises. The amount of the sale was meager but it was practically all profit for the owner. I went storming into his office and said nothing more than, "Mr. Baker is here to pick up his trailer" - he blew his stack using every four letter word known, no doubt his guilt had taken over. I had heard them all in Hollywood and was not offended at their use, except if they were directed towards me. He ended the conversation by saying that he would run his business the way he pleased and if I didn't like it I could get the (blank) out. I did not like it so I went storming out, back to my little mobile home. Being female in a male oriented job did not justify such total disrespect. I did not have to accept it. I knew if I "tucked my tail" and went back he would have me in the exact position he had his other employees. No job was worth selling out one's integrity. I would not go to work nor speak to him and he would not speak to me. One salesman suggested I go to him and apologize. "APOLOGIZE FOR WHAT?" He warned me that I might never collect the money owed to me, but that did not scare me. I had kept copies of the sales contracts as well as the commissions that had been paid and those yet to be paid. If I had to, I would go to the Labor Board. Everyone had told me how California State Labor Board really forces the employer to pay or they can close the business. Being sure I had the State Labor Board behind me, I never doubted he would be forced to pay the commissions he owed to me. With that I considered myself no longer employed.

Through this job I had an opportunity get a pretty good idea of what the mobile home industry was all about. Very few manufacturers used professional decorators and their furniture packages were horrible. With a little taste it would be possible to put together inexpensive furniture without it looking so cheap. For some time, I had given a lot of thought of starting a furniture packaging company. Then after numerous requests from a very wealthy oil man who had offered to help me start my own business in Palm Springs, my plan seemed to be in reach. He wanted investments in Palm Springs for tax purposes that made sense to me. I had been at his home with his wife and had assumed his offer was legitimate. Plus he was originally from the same town as my family and was acquainted with them. He was a friend of my sister's husband and his mother was a friend of mine. On that basis with the usual trust, I set about putting together a presentation with facts, figures, goals, etc. The furniture packaging would not be limited to mobile homes. There were apartments, condominiums, and motels to sell the service. It was a good idea and there was no one doing it. I took the time to contact the major mobile home dealers in the area to be sure there would be a market for the furniture packaging. In the meantime, I had managed to rent a lot in a mobile home park. For a while it didn't look as though it would be possible to move my home. My former boss began parking other trailers as close as possible to mine. He was blocking me, but why? I had bought my mobile home, was making payments to the bank and it was registered to me. At least I had the sympathies of his employees. While the boss was away one day his workmen moved the homes that had been blocking mine. They pulled my house out and moved it to the park to my rented space. What a relief it was to be out of that dirty, stinking place. I felt I was out of a "den of inequity" - often I had said that if my former boss had a choice of doing something legal or illegal he would choose the illegal method just for the challenge and intrigue. Perhaps it happened for the best, as I had become familiar with his business ethics I wasn't and was not happy to be associated with such a questionable operation. I could ignore this middle-aged man chasing 20 year-old girls but found it appalling. It was like his business practices, irresponsible attitude and business ethics I feared might eventually involve me. I felt much stronger in every way and realized the job was only a stopgap. I did not feel the usual defeatism for the short-lived jobs. It was time to move on to bigger and better things.

CHAPTER 33

When I called on major mobile home dealers in the area to see if there was any interest in furniture packaging, I had gone to the sales lot next door to where I had worked. I was introduced to a tall nice looking gray-haired man who was the sales manager. When I presented the furniture packaging idea, he seemed receptive. Instead of involving myself in all that work, he suggested I come to work for him as a salesperson. He had just received orders from his home office to try and hire a female salesperson. Feeling confident of the wealthy man's sincerity in backing my business, I thanked him, took the application and agreed to fill it out but never intended to do so.

The day finally arrived to present my furniture packaging concept to the oilman from Oklahoma. I then drove out to his other home in the desert as he had requested that I stop by his house. When I arrived I realized his wife was out of town. I sat down with my all my papers and information together in presentation form. Enthusiastically I began only to sense there was no longer any interest in the business from him. My heart sank when I finished as I awaited his reply. He stated that it did not sound like a profitable investment for him at this time, however - he was planning a trip to Japan in his new jet airplane. Instead of attempting to start a business, why didn't I just drop the whole thing and come along with him to Japan. DAMN! Foiled again! How many years and how much "spinning my wheels" does it take to see through men's words and intentions! So went my potential furniture packaging business. At a time when I was fighting to overcome life's greatest grief, this man's empathy and compassion seemed sadly lacking. I just knew that my sister's husband would never believe me. He would think I had "come on" to the guy! Since Debbie's disappearance, everyone I thought to be a friend and people I thought I could count on; one by one seemed to drop away. There appeared to be no one left on the list, even God seemed doubtful. Life's up and downs--I had been in an "up" since I arrived in Palm Springs, it was only natural for a "down to follow."

The pertinent fact remained that I had many years before retirement age, yet age became more of a factor in locating employment with each passing year. The disillusionment of finding that one right man, falling in love, marrying and living happily ever after was nothing more than a fairytale from youth and must be faced as an impossible reality. Regardless of my need of marriage fulfillment, time, circumstances and conditions demanded total acquiescence. With Debbie gone, the one success of my life was also now gone. I did change my request to God though. I no longer asked for Mr. Right to be a famous star, director, writer, not even in the film industry, nor rich or famous. It wasn't necessary for him to share my interest in the metaphysical fields, spiritual research or psychic and phenomenal studies.

In the quiet of my little home I felt quite dejected. Even if I had the money to start a business I knew I needed a partner to manage the money end of it. As I flipped through the pages of the presentation, I thought to myself, "When will I ever learn?" The concept and the presentation were very good. It was sad that I had no financial way to carry it through. Just as I had known I would have been a very good producer at the Ad Agency if I had been given that chance! I had managed to pay off the bank note in Texas, furnished my new mobile dwellings and paid my current debts and lot rent but since I had been unable to collect any of the commissions due me, I was growing short of cash. I hated to be forced to borrow money again but I still had the application form the sales manager gave me. There seemed to be no choice now but to fill it out. As I read some of the ridiculous questions, I gave equally ridiculous answers. It was a gamble to answer in such a manner but, sooner or later if I was hired the statements I might make would be also ridiculous. Better they know from the onset. When I took the application form back to the sales manager, he all but hired me on the spot. "Shouldn't you read the application?" I asked. He agreed and promised to call soon. When he did call, he appeared to be amused by my answers and agreed the questions were ridiculous. He then gave me a date to report to work. I was not very excited at the thought of strictly selling on commission but the people with the organization seemed pleasant enough and business-like which was a totally refreshing atmosphere compared to the one I had just departed.

While their general sales format and contracts were similar, as with any new job, there were many new things to learn. Their system was altogether different as well as they used different manufacturers for their mobile homes. I had to become familiar with everything as quickly as possible if I was going to earn commissions which I needed in a hurry. The sales manager was charming, a gentleman but he had moments of fairly strong worded instructions. I was a bit apprehensive after he reprimanded me one day for a minor error. Right after I began my new job while alone in the comfort of my home I had a strong fisted and shaky talk with God. I said I just had to have help and have it now! If there was any ethereal guiding force in my life, it was time to show me a little consideration by answering my needs and prayers. I must have gotten through to someone up there because within 10 days I had sold over $50,000 worth of mobile homes with an ample commission due to me that allowed me to draw against it. At the time I had been just about to the point of counting my pennies. For me it seems there are times when it becomes necessary to come on strong in our prayers almost demanding attention rather than the namby-pamby begging. Perhaps it is necessary in order to get through the heavy layer of negative vibrations surrounding us that may stifle our prayer requests. I had to believe my prayers had been answered when my sales jumped above the seasoned salesman. Again, I was having difficulty closing sales. My new boss was a master of sales closings and I would listen outside his office trying to learn his closing techniques. He seemed pleased with my work and having a woman salesperson was a whole new experience for him within such a male dominated profession.

The better acquainted I became with the sales manager the more I really liked him. Jack seemed to be a very special person, kind, gentle but could display a very strong manner when he needed to with customers or employees. Yet, he seemed to be tolerant, generally friendly showing a warm attitude toward everyone. He was 50 but looked older because of his gray hair. Most men I dated were a bit younger than me. There was quite a contrast between them and him. I had never considered dating him but realized he was one of those really good men and there is definite truth in "a good man is hard to find." The first girlfriend I had lived with when I initially arrived had dated an older man. I began trying to get the two statuesque people together. I even planned a party, especially to arrange for them to meet but it fell through. Neither could be pressed into meeting the other.

From Jack's conversations I had assumed he was a bachelor. Although not too anxious, he was somewhat receptive toward meeting my friend. One day I overheard someone talking to him with reference to his wife and this came as a shock. I dropped the conversation regarding dating anyone. Jack obviously did not take care of himself. All he ate all day was coffee and cigarettes. Each day when I went home for lunch, I would usually bring back something for him to eat. He always seemed surprised and appreciative. I thought my actions were only being seen as compassion for such a nice man yet each and every day, I could feel the chemistry building up between us that I chose to ignore. I did find out that he and his wife had been separated for months and were planning to dissolve their marriage. To mix business with pleasure would have been totally disastrous and might end the only job opportunity I had. It was getting hot in April and the need of a cooling system for my home became necessary. With Jack's okay, the company allowed me to purchase a water cooler and disposal unit against commissions due to me. Jack was always considerate about sending the servicemen over to make installations and repairs to the damaged interior of my mobile home.

I took over rearranging furniture in the 12' foot wide mobile homes. Most of the doublewides had been professionally decorated through the manufacturer. In no time, there were obvious improvements to them through my efforts. I wanted the company to allow me to do more decorating as well as selling. I could not tolerate ill-arranged furniture. I had to restrain myself to keep from grabbing heavy pieces of furniture and shifting them for better coordination. Everyone seemed pleased with the changes I made. The servicemen who had helped me move the furniture complained to Jack - why not, I could out work them and out lift men.

One Sunday the Mobile Home Owners Association was holding a meeting. Jack needed to attend in order to keep current with information as to any action applicable to mobile home sales. Any information I could gain would also help me with my sales ability. Jack and I agreed to meet for breakfast before the meeting. That morning as we sat having breakfast while sharing some general conversation about people, I told him I really liked him as a person. He was the one of the nicest men I had ever met. I told him that I just loved him for being the kind of person he was – friendship love not romantic love. He seemed startled with my outspoken attitude and was at a loss for words. At work that day, I contemplated what I had said to Jack and hoped he had not misunderstood. Being outspoken had often got me into trouble in the past. As I thought about it well into the evening, I questioned myself - was this just a friendship kind of love or had I overlooked something much more. If Jack was such a special, wonderful, warm, intelligent, strong man - I realize was a rarity so why was I trying to pawn him off on a friend? What was wrong with Jack for me?

That Sunday evening I did a lot of thinking about this man and realized how fond I was of him. He had told me about his wife. It had not been a lengthy marriage and they had been separated for months. A dissolving of their marriage was just a matter of getting around to it. To encourage a dating situation with Jack or instigating a romance could mean the end of my promising job yet I knew how hard it was to find a really good man. A psychiatrist advised a friend when she asked how to find a good man, was to find an unhappily married man. A good man rarely instigated divorce unless he has a reason - usually another woman. I knew Jack was a marrying man, not to his estranged wife but a man who needed marriage. He was definitely not a confirmed bachelor type that I had dated these many years. Most women have a need to be married regardless of Women's Lib, at least in my generation, and many men have the same need. I had to really weigh the situation before I opened the door to a possible romance as I felt he was ready. It could ultimately lead to marriage, the impossible state of being I had longed for so many years. With a younger man, I was still young enough to have children but would I want one after all the years of struggling to bring Debbie into blossoming womanhood only to - POOF - lose it all. Jack's age difference was more socially acceptable than being with the younger men I had dated even though I had far greater mental compatibility with them. Jack and I did not see eye to eye on many subjects. I could not discuss my inner search for spirituality.

I had been single for such a long time and I had been in and out of love many times. I had grown accustomed to the idea that I could never fall in love with a man who could truly love me. Hence the men I did fall in love with had never really loved me. I assumed that most relationships consisted of one person really loving the other. It seemed to me that one more or less only tolerated their spouse for ego satisfaction or security. I came to the conclusion that love relationships could never be mutually shared to the same degree. Wishing for that to happen to me was my idealistic fairytale like so many other of my ideas. Did I dare gamble with my newfound career for a romance that would probably be disastrous? Yes--a lot of thought and consideration was needed as I fell asleep that Sunday night with the thoughts of Jack filling my mind.

CHAPTER 34

That Sunday seemed to be a turning point for both of us. The following week there was an obvious hasty chemistry growing between us. Each time I stood near the desk he seemed to come unglued. When we simply walked across the sales lot together it was like a magnet pulling us closer. I looked for excuses to get Jack out of the office alone and he seemed to do the same. Finally he called me at home one evening and asked if I would meet him for a drink. I readily accepted. That relaxed social evening was the beginning of a totally committed relationship between us and without it being said we both knew it. From that evening on, Jack came by my house every evening for a drink and usually dinner.

At work we tried to conceal our personal relationship but when we were in the same room everyone in the room could see sparks flying. A well-timed business trip came up for Jack to go to San Diego. He asked me to go with him and scheduled me off work that weekend. From that weekend in San Diego, we both felt married. Neither words from each other nor a minister was necessary for us to both feel a total commitment to each other.

Usually after dinner Jack would go to his apartment although we both wanted more time together. I still had unfinished business with my former employer. I had plenty of records and proof of the $1,500 that he owed me to not fight it, even though Jack kept assuring me he would take care of me. He kept telling me I was wasting my time but I secured the necessary papers to fill out a complaint anyway with full confidence that the State Labor Board would force him to pay the commissions due to me. It was quite a lengthy undertaking. The explanation and copies of unpaid contracts consisted of many pages. Jack kept saying, "You might as well write it off to a bad experience. It is very difficult for commissioned sales people to collect money owed to them." Not only was I convinced of the State's fairness but if they let him get by with it, he would do the same thing to someone else.

The day arrived for the hearing. I asked Jack to go along in case the man conducting the hearing would allow a sales manager to explain the usual practice and basis for sales commissions in the mobile home industry. The hearing was a fiasco! We were both under sworn oath. I proved my ex-employer was lying but the Arbitrator ignored it. The employer stated that I was paid a salary and that was enough pay for me, a woman! After all my preparation of papers sent to the Arbitrator weeks before, it was obvious he had not so much as looked at any of the material. Just as Jack said the Arbitrator would not allow him to testify. The Arbitrator ignored everything I said as well as the proof that lay before him. At the end of the hearing, the state Arbitrator told my opponent he would see him outside afterwards "regarding the other case." No doubt a nice payoff for him - "traitor" he was! Jack kept telling me, "I told you so." I was very depressed not only about the money I had fairly earned but also the injustice. I could hire a lawyer but Jack kept telling me it would only keep me upset for months. It was best to forget it and he would see to all my needs. Hearing a man finally tell me he would take care of me was the sweetest music to my ears I could possibly hear. After over a year of being in the depths of depression and grief, I was very vulnerable and probably if any other man had said the same thing to me, I would have fallen for him.

It takes years to really know another human being if knowing another person IS ever really possible. When two people come together at our ages there has been a lot of "water under the bridge," past hurts and disappointments create defenses that cannot help but be reflected in a relationship no matter how wonderfully in love the two people may seem to be. Prince Charming had finally ridden into my life, only by now he was gray-haired and driving a white Lincoln Continental instead of riding a white horse. He was a little too fond of the cocktail hour to suit my taste but we all have something wrong. I had never been around an alcoholic so I didn't know the difference between cocktails and serious drinking. I had no idea what an "enabler" was, nor that for those years I was just that. At first I made excuses for his broken marriage. Only years later after we split, I found out he had never supported his four children. According to his story, his ex-wife would not allow their four children to have anything to do with him, therefore he had not seen them for years nor did they ever attempt to contact him. It was only human nature to believe if I was fulfilling a major void in Jack's life, the prior sadness would finally dissipate.

In our new relationship, there was the personality trait of procrastination--gentle soul that Jack seemed to be, he felt it was dishonorable for him to instigate the "dissolution of marriage" against his estranged wife. He waited for her to file, weeks went by with no action, and little by little we began living together with his marriage still unresolved. Jack decided to buy a doublewide mobile home for us and allowed me to decorate it. He kept assuring me his divorce would come through any day - in the meantime we could live together through its interlocutory period, and then get married. My sales dropped to nothing as I became involved in planning our home from the ground up. Naturally, I was ecstatically involving myself in the "career" I had wanted - with the man assuring me he would be the breadwinner. It was great fun to play house from its inception. It was my childhood dream of playing house come true. We selected the floor plan we liked, made many changes and additions, rented a lot, ordered the home, then I set out to furnish it with all new furniture. Now I was in my glory. Not only was I decorating again, which I totally enjoyed, but it was a creative opportunity and it was to be our home. I was very happy now - to get married and live happily ever after and it would make a perfect ending to my previous tragic years. Ah, but life has a way of never letting things be simple or sweet as the fairytales that we believed in our youth.

Before long we were living in our little love nest and still no papers had been filed. I knew the vindictive nature of a woman. If she found out our situation she could delay and create many problems that I felt too emotionally drained by the past years grief to handle. Considering that she was still his legal wife, I felt she could possibly take our new home that I had worked very hard to create. As any woman in my situation would do, I put pressure on Jack to take a definite step or I felt I would have to move out. After all we were representing ourselves as Mr. and Mrs. and I was called Mrs. I literally took him by the hand to the courthouse to obtain the necessary papers and encouraged him to get it filled out and signed and filed.

Life is "never a bed of roses." Both strong-willed, we fought tooth and toenail from the very beginning yet there was such a strong bond between us, a legal piece of paper could not reinforce that which we already had. Jack having a legal wife upset me endlessly. From what I had been told, she was not totally sane and I had a terrible fear that she might even take some sort of attempt on Jack's life.

Finally the long six months of waiting were over. Jack went into court and it only took a moment for him to be legally free. That was the main thing I had wanted, the unfinished business to be completed. We had lived together long enough to pretty well know each other's idiosyncrasies - like most women unfamiliar with a real drinking problem, I believed Jack's emotional frustration could be settled with my security of love and devotion to him. I hoped to be the antidote needed to temper Jack's overindulgences. We had a lot of very different ideas that were not compatible and there were many considerations that needed to be made. It had been years since I'd last been married and now with the reality of my long cherished dream at hand I was terrified to give up my freedom. I had been able to do and go as I pleased, making my own decisions for years. Now I wondered what would it be like trying to let a man make most of those decisions? Could I do it? Jack's generation of thinking was almost like a generation gap from my own. It was obvious that there were many areas of discussion that had to be avoided. Would Jack's Dr. Jekyll and Mr. Hyde personality when drinking destroy our marriage? Drinking is certainly a serious problem; I just never knew how serious it could be. I knew that everyone has something wrong and one must cope with some frailties in their spouse. In my years of exposure to married men chasing females, I did not believe that in current morals, a sharp, intelligent type man was capable of fidelity yet I knew instinctively Jack's fidelity was immovable. He made me feel totally a woman. My aging years would be no problem for him. He made me feel very feminine, young, pretty and just about everything a woman needs to feel. There were more good qualities in Jack than I had found in any other man ever plus we shared a great physical attraction and chemistry. There seemed at the time to be far more pluses than minuses. I did not wish to push Jack into the actual marriage since he had just gone through the dissolution of his last. I wanted to wait until he was totally ready.

It wasn't long before Jack insisted we get our blood tests and marriage license. We did both. One weekend we drove to San Diego and planned to find an ideal spot to tie the knot, but things did not go well and we never got around to it. I had always wanted to get married in the Wayfarer Chapel on the Pacific Coast Highway but that meant making reservations far in advance and getting Jack into and through Los Angeles which was next to impossible. One day Jack said, "If we are to do it, let's get it over with!" Not exactly a romantic decision. I awoke early one morning and started fooling around with numerology although I knew very little about it. I had a book that explained the various meanings of each number. As I wrote down our names, dates of birth, etc., I was amazed to find nine was a strong number and I figured we needed all the strength we could get. Further, that particular day was a number 9-day and 6 o'clock in the evening represented the number nine. Jack thought it was nonsense but little by little he had grown accustomed to my own orthodox ideas. Since we had the license and blood tests it was merely a matter of getting someone to perform the ceremony. I had never seen inside the prettiest little church in Palm Desert. It was a modernistic splendor that sat on the hillside overlooking the desert. It was designed to look as though it just grew out of the desert. We went there and talked to the minister. He had no appointments that evening but since we had no witnesses for our ceremony he suggested a more intimate Eisenhower Fireside Room that housed some of Eisenhower's artwork. It seemed fitting as we had our blood tests taken at Eisenhower Medical Center. We were both great admirers of General and President Eisenhower.

The number one priority on our list had been taken care of and next was the wedding bands. Jack refused to wear one and I wanted the smallest ring we could find as I wanted to also wear rings I already had. If I was really ready to wear a wedding band then I had no intention of ever taking it off. Neither of us were strangers to divorce. I wanted Jack to understand that this was the last marriage for me. We found the ring. We would need two witnesses. We ran across one of the contractors Jack liked and asked if he and his wife would join us that evening for the wedding. He heartily agreed so that was all set. That was one of the longest days of my life, but all the plans were set before noon. The rest of the day slowly dragged by. For years I had waited and dreamed of this day--here it was--so very simple, so unpretentious. That was our wedding, totally simple and went off exactly as scheduled taking only a few brief minutes. For a man I thought to be the strongest I'd ever met, I could not believe how mortified and frozen Jack was during the ceremony. To top it off I had purposely selected a ring a half size smaller to allow for winter's shrinkage. Jack could not get the ring on my finger - he pushed and pushed. I started to help since I knew how to get rings on my own fingers. No, I would never hear the end of it, so I let him struggle. Everyone was trying to hold back from giggling. In Jack's previous marriage, he had never been married by a minister. He wanted, as I desperately wanted, this to be the last and most successful for both of us. The four of us celebrated afterwards at a beautiful Rim Rock restaurant, built on the edge of the hillside with the lovely Desert view. The other couple left. We were alone and really married after all the waiting, all the arguments and problems, we were finally man and wife, for better for worse (and the worst was yet to come....). My Prince charming did not wear a white suit but he did have white hair, he did not ride a white horse but he did have a white flashy car. At that point of my fairytale "they lived happily ever after" but life is no fairytale and my life was never to be "simple!"

CHAPTER 35

For every pleasure, there seems to always be pain as well or a price to pay. Jack and I continued our marriage with tremendous struggles but with an ever-present binding love to hold it together. I prayed to be placed in the normal type of life and my prayers seemed to have been answered. The fulfillment of marriage was essential for my growth, as I had always known it was. My quest of inner peace, enlightenment and learning had been neatly stored away. My focus needed to be for two people striving for marital bliss. Always living with a deep-seated fear of losing one another through death, I feared ever having to face it but face it we do. Jack claimed to be an Atheist. I had lost a lot of my faith with losing Debbie so I didn't care, whereas, under normal circumstances, I would never have married a man when we shared no form of spirituality. It was just a detour in my personal spiritual growth.

Never would I ever return to my youth, even had it been possible or could be offered. "We've only just begun to live" were words from a song that youth thinks belong exclusively to them. How can they know or realize the ultimate truth in the cliché "life begins at 40." For them is seems so far away. All too soon we are there and so the day of reckoning--now in our Autumn of life! Extreme pressures of youth's dream and ambition mellow into realities and acceptances. With those acceptances, a certain peace and contentment come in great contrast to the restless years of youth.

Several years earlier someone had insisted that I read a group of stories written by Marquis de Sade. The reason was to recognize the extremes of sadism and masochism that to some extent are in all of us - mostly more of one than the other. To plow through just one story, "Justine" was quite enough. To continue through the others for me had to be a little "sick." I returned the book with the other stories unread. In retrospect I cannot help but identify with "Justine." She was a young maiden who naïvely went from one horrible experience to another, one sexual abuse to another worse one, again and again, exposed to horrible tortures, debauchery, outrageous acts while being kept in a dungeon and coping with what went beyond human endurance. Finally her sister rescued her. In the end, she found the security of family, love and a home. She was given a state pension and had a promising future while still at a young age. Everything was going well for Justine and she had found happiness. Then while standing at the window admiring a thunderstorm, she was struck by lightning and was killed.

My life had not been filled with Justine sexual abuse, still I naïvely entered friendships, romances and business ventures only to be struck down again and again. Apparently I failed to recognize that my next situation would repetitiously carry the same pattern. Finally, my protective husband had rescued me. This had been my lifelong dream although I wasn't expecting to be struck down by lightning as Justine but the constant fear of losing all still plagued me. Many nights I had awakened to be sure Jack was breathing. It was difficult to push these fears aside even though I knew they were wrong. The symbol of Justine was not the "end" but the beginning--not death of life but death of lower struggles and birth of my inner spirituality. Through these awakenings we walk in the light of our God. Without identifying it with "death" we experience many little or big "deaths" without losing our present physical body. All is well that ends well yet in endings are only new beginnings. All in life is a constant evolution. AT that time, my life needed not to be dedicated to making a living, time was mine to be striving for research, enlightenment and understanding through life's painful experiences. The choice was now mine to use this time constructively or abuse this time that had finally been placed in my life.

In retrospect most of us would make different choices had we been able to see into the future. If I had not been zonked into marriage and motherhood long before I was ready for it I might have passionately pursued a career in New York in modeling and acting. Sometimes I wonder what fate could have befallen me in New York that would be worse than the years of struggle of motherhood then, to have it all zapped away so suddenly. I had a hard time struggling with the benefits of motherhood having endured the loss of my only child. Somehow those years seemed wasted. If I could have known the future, maybe my choice would have been to allow her father to raise her full time! I would never have gone back to Texas in the first place as I know "you can never go back." Maybe in NYC, I would have learned to be indifferent toward neurotic, unsavory business tactics that I had allowed to disillusion my idealistic goals. Whatever path we choose or circumstances that are forced upon us apparently they are necessary for our individual growth and evolution.

Debbie may have needed me more than I realized, that year of 1970, but unfortunately Debbie made it very difficult to help her. She was considered "legal age" by law. She had outgrown me in height. I could not force her to listen to my opinions. I had tried to encourage Debbie to make her own decisions, although decision-making was more difficult for her than I had realized at the time. In mid 1973 I received a letter informing me Debbie's very best friend for many years had been killed in a car accident. Her death shocked me into the realization that Debbie might be "on the other side." People said, "The two girls are together again." NO! I still maintained hope that Debbie could be alive somewhere in the world. Since then, my friend who had lived on the same street as the deceased girl's family also died at a young age. She had always made me a part of her family and sadly never lived to see her son reach puberty. The little dog that Debbie asked my mother to keep for her disappeared around that same Labor Day time. In only a few short years, my nephew was killed, Debbie vanished, her best friend killed, a good friend murdered, another died. Somehow when we see elderly people pass on, we feel they are ready but to see those in the prime of life snapped up, it becomes difficult for us to accept or understand. Until that time, I had not experienced the death of friends or family.

For years hardly a day went by that I didn't think about Debbie and wondered why this had happened to her. I desperately missed my only child whom I loved as much as any parent can love. Although I had kept her old letters I still could not read them and it was years before I could display her photos and trophies. If I leafed through her photographs, letters and mementoes for more than a superficial glance, I knew I was in for a painful siege of tears. If I was as strong as everyone thought I was, knowing my struggles with grief, I could not understand how a weaker person could cope with similar grief.

There was just no substitute for the void in one's life in losing a loved one and even far more intently if it was his or her own child. It was difficult to find growth within myself through these grievous experiences. However they seemingly are only setbacks as I believe - out of every adversity comes new growth. If any growth was achieved within me, I hope by expressing this account of my "Autumns" will help readers find some small amount of courage. May they discover their strength or realize a boarding of their own and develop a better understanding with renewed compassion for their losses. These years of my work then will not have been in vain. I realize if we are to make new beginnings, we must not linger in the past, at least not emotionally lingering. It has been exceedingly difficult to express this experience on paper as I needed the lapse of time to endeavor and remain detached. To write and rewrite, to re-live it has taken over many years. It was extreme drudgery to recall everything and then to rewrite what I had written back in the 1980s. Many of these events and feelings were long forgotten. Although years do not erase them only hopefully one learns to cope with it OR they may then be destroyed by it!

If I had not found within myself the strength to continue and in my grief had committed suicide at the end of 1970, I would have missed out on many fulfilling experiences, even the false belief of happiness in a marriage. I believe I had many emotional deaths without an actual physical death. I believe we experience many births and deaths without actually giving up the physical body. The spiritual self I thought I had been building on solid ground followed by the grief from losing my daughter was such a shattering emotional experience that it appeared to have killed it. I realize now my spiritual growth had been lying dormant for years, especially those years shared with my non-spiritual husband. At that time I blamed God and since God had failed me in my most horrific time, but it was OK that Jack had no sign of religion or spirituality.

Some religionists make it sound so simple to walk down the aisle in public to commit one's soul to God and all will be answered. Many of us however have tried to make the total commitment but our efforts seemingly falling on deaf ears. Does God or a power within the Universe await our individual decision to shake our fist and say, "Just a God blessed minute! I've had enough! I can't take it anymore - it's time to adjust the books in _my_ favor for a while." We have to take a stand and with it, finally and hopefully, we will find our individual life pattern of spiritual development. Most every religion has so "brainwashed" the human race into believing one cannot be an individual but must depend on their particular religion to be the mediator for the path to God. When in truth it is the greatest lie of all. Someday, we must each learn that the Subtle Energy is within each person and in and through everything! This is the energy we call "God" - and the hard lesson to learn that the story surrounding Jesus has never been interpreted correctly and only by men of their particular time. He stated he was a "Way Shower" (to show the way) - his teachings were simple and I cannot see HOW people who call themselves "Christians" do not LIVE by those teachings when they judge others who are not like themselves so harshly. Instead of shouting "Jesus Christ" it should be Jesus THE Christ, for his showing the way was the statement "I and the father are one" - meaning you and I, the father, mother, friend and foe are all ONE. That Christ consciousness LIVES within each of us but it is up to us to reawaken and accept it. That is the meaning - born WITHIN, not "born again!" If a person does not understand what someone is going through on their individual path, then don't judge it! As I rewrite this book in my senior years it has only recently come to me that all those struggles, the pain, the disappointments, the heartache are the lessons and all part of earth school. When you pass through the door of death all of your negative experiences once you cross over have been totally reversed. What was negative then becomes positive. There are different levels in the afterlife. We go into the area where we need the most growth. For me, we are not just one individual soul, we are part of a greater soul, those soul attachments eventually merge into what we call "God" - Universal Mind or any other name that is needed. We are pieces of a puzzle and we grow emotionally through earth experiences be they "good" or bad." It is so difficult to use words when each person may read it with a totally different meaning than it is written. I believe the main lesson I have understood is that we are here on Earth to work though all emotions. When you consider the world is constantly at war, when our entertainment media is all about killing, hideous monsters, horrible things people do to each other, if not physically, hell bent on killing emotionally, then it is obvious we as a human race have a hell of a long way to go before even beginning to create LOVE - unconditional LOVE!

With Debbie's absence I had a greater understanding of why

reincarnation is fact and not fantasy! Generally we cannot recall past lives except from dreams or brief familiarities. When the memory of one's existing life is too painful to remember, how could we cope with the accumulation of pain filled emotional traumas in past lives? That is my answer for those who ask: "If I lived before why don't I remember." Actually we do remember in the form of unexplained talents or abilities, inner knowledge without awareness of from whence it came. When confronted with, "Prove to me life exists after physical death!" Prove to another that which has taken me many years of living and studying to assimilate? "You can take a horse to water but you can't make it drink." Each of us accepts enlightenment in our own time, in our own way, **A.S.K.** "**A**sk, the answer will be given - **S**eek and you shall find, **K**nock and the door will be opened."

When faced with the alternative of believing in nothingness or believing in soul evolution, a continuation of life, myth or reality--I must choose the latter for without faith in eternal life I could not have survived Debbie's disappearance and probable death. I do believe that Debbie was murdered and the murderer has gone unpunished by a court of law all these years. The Universal law of retribution will catch up with him, thus creating his own hell.

What is the secret of the child, "the child in all of us" - "be as little children." A baby is a totally dependent creature through necessity. A mature adult male or female is also dependent through conditionings or choices. If any individual male or female truly desires to evolve out of earth evolution cycle of deaths and rebirths then when ready he or she would choose to seek this necessary total independence. I don't know if total independence is possible. If one becomes a hermit or a monk seeking seemingly depending only on self for survival, one would appear independent. Yet, he is not hidden away, protected from facing responsibility of his own growth through human contact and responses? To attempt to define it still further, consider a person born into a great material wealth from birth, somewhere along the way all wealth is lost. This person discovers he could survive and be happy in spite of these losses and gains true wealth. Perhaps he goes on to build another fortune but realizes he is not owned by it. In so doing he can enjoy life's pleasures without being possessed by them. Another choice is the individual who loses it all and jumps out of the window, then there are those SO COMMON today, who have so much in material wealth they become intent on keeping it all. They will spend their entire lives harboring terrible fears that someone will take something from them and never really enjoy their prosperity. It is because he is *possessed by* his wealth. He never OWNS it - it owns him. Job, career, parenthood, spouse, religion, politics etc. are all examples of a substitution for wealth. WE EITHER POSSESS OR WE ARE POSSESSED!

Just as there is a female mystique few understand, so is there a male mystique. Many women have a deep-seated need to lean on another person. Perhaps more modern younger women are not as inclined as are the women of my generation. The male has an emotional link to his mother for all of his life. He may strive for his independent nature but the female-mother image he seems to search for in a mate is the woman he may marry. Amazing how a man may seek his God image through his mother. Hindu, a male-dominated religion, seeks God in the female mother's image, while most Occidentals think of God as a male image. The fact that a man may attend church services does not necessarily mean he is actually a believer - he may only be attending to appease his spouse, family or community image. It seems to me, a part of the male evolution growth pattern is to reject this God belief in an effort to become more independent. To believe, he must go within when it is so much easier to spend his time playing golf, attending football and other games or burying himself in his career--all outward expressions. In many cases they transform this emotional need into the lust for irresponsible, noncommittal sex or booze. To need God unless in an emergency, men seem to think of it as a weakness. I have not encountered many men who actually believe in life after death or reincarnation or any idea that requires an inner journey into understanding themselves - it is all outward lust. I think they are embarrassed to admit they need GOD! It is acceptable for him to love his own mother through blinded eyes of her natural human frailties. To him she becomes superhuman.

Through centuries Mary, the mother of Jesus has often been revered in equality to Christ. Some people look upon Mary as Mother of God. Great pity and empathy has been shared by millions of Christians for 2000 years for her suffering and the loss of her only begotten son who was hung and nailed to the cross. Was her suffering at the loss of her child regardless of his destined fame any greater than my own pain and suffering from the loss of my only child? There is also the suffering and pain from thousands of mothers who have lost one or several or even all of their children. What really happened to Mary during the rest of her life?

These precepts cannot be stated without being offensive to many. Statements I make may be total contradictions of the personal dogma twenty years past and will surely grow henceforth. We are all on different planes of soul development. Not necessarily higher or lower just different roads leading ultimately to the same goal. My hypothesis is not that a woman should turn her back on motherhood. It is a natural state of the female soul evolution. This soul evolution must eventually be a natural letting go with no emotional ties, but I don't think that is possible for the majority of human beings. The past generations of pressure on every female that is her duty or obligation to be a mother has forced motherhood on many women who may have contributed more to the world without having children. These women may have served in that stage of development motherhood in another life or in a future one. It is the same for men, except when a man's belief in God - Universal Mind - is usually limited as they are more inclined to reach outward rather than inward, much of his drive is related more to ego, to keep his likeness or genetic line forever repeating. My genetic line stops with me since there are no grandchildren. My "mothering" since I lost Debbie has been shown in counseling others, perhaps when I leave the physical body, it will continue on to help raise the consciousness of this planet. We are so far from any kind of "divinity" - one needs only to read the newspaper or Internet to see the lust for destroying others who have different beliefs or more material possessions. For me the theory of constant soul evolution through lifecycles of reincarnation exists until we are freed from the lust and greed of material possessions which are a basic necessity and there are some who may achieve it through different methods. As I said - there are many paths up the mountain! It doesn't mean NOT having comforts, luxuries, et al. but not being POSSESSED by POSSESSIONS! I believe my journey into deep research, conducting past life regressions, seeing how they connect with present life circumstances has been the most important part of my enlightenment journey.

CHAPTER 36

"Take my life and let it be--dedicated, God, to the--" from a song I often recalled from my church attendance years. In the 1960s I made a dedication after working diligently all of my life to understand the true meaning of God. Within my human limitations I contemplated religion, soul evolution in all of nature and within the Universe as well as I could within human limitations. It took many years to come to certain conclusions at this point in my life. That "point" is ever changing and expanding. Every occurrence, including every cell in our body is in constant flux creating an endless evolution of death and rebirth. On our Soul's journey in the physical body, symbolically, we live numerous lives in our present physical body.

Man may have been "created equally" but he has not evolved equally. Consider the acts of a terrorist that kills, strips the heart out of his victim and eats it (As seen on YouTube!) compared to an Einstein. Just as there are no identical fingerprints, neither can our spiritual evolution be identical. Our brain cannot do the work of the heart and all other organs. The body water cannot replace the blood or the nerve system--all parts of the body must function separately and also be in perfect harmony. When that harmony is severely thrown off by the damage or failure of one part, the whole physical body may die. Made in "God's image" I cannot see God as having our body parts! Human kind's opposition to harmony creates human's destruction, illnesses, etc. "United we stand, divided we fall" - "Where two or three are gathered in my name, there shall I be also…" HARMONY - can you ever imagine this world with all of the nations ever living in harmony? Many people make the gross mistake of thinking they have found THE way and the ONLY way in their inherited religion, usually found present in family tradition or associations. This can only be born out of ignorance in choosing to hide behind these set beliefs. Example: "The Bible is the WORD from GOD!" It is universally known that the Bible stories and parables have stayed fairly intact for many generations by word-of-mouth before they were written. The stories of Jesus The Christ were not written for at least 40 years after his death. A major event that changed various books and scriptures was during the Council of Nicaea in 325 AD created by Emperor Constantine, a former military leader. He brought together 300 various factions of Christianity to create one religion. There were many varying beliefs in an atmosphere of intolerance, jealousy, dissention, persecution and bigotry. Constantine offered to make the little-known Christian sect the official state religion if the Christians would settle their differences. He really didn't care what they believed as long as they agreed to one religion that included removing reincarnation, even the actual teachings of Christ were not in agreement among them. Also the scriptures of Mary Magdalene were removed. As new discoveries of old manuscripts are found, new information regarding various time frames of religions experiences are revealed. Not only have the meanings been changed in translation but there have been many deletions by the church or the translator, who carefully added his own interpretation, according to his own time and conditions plus the church or some wealthy or royal personage who held influence over him. In present day, one may write with a certain feeling yet, another may read it with an entirely different interpretation. The same goes for any means of communication. As Email, I may write words that are meant to convey love and understanding but the recipient may interpret the words entirely different, thus the same with bible translations and religious writings that many be taken as "the word of God!"

With regards to friendships, I have always had the typically human desire to hang on or maintain friendships throughout my life; yet circumstances change, often taking me to new areas that made it difficult to sustain communication (before Email!). Also, as my life headed more and more into an individualized spiritual journey, friends and family that thought I was a nut dropped away from all communications. My concept of friendships was that if a loving friendship was established neither time nor distance could destroy it. Through the years, occasionally our paths would cross but it seems I am often met with indifference or even unrecognized. When this happened my sensitive nature made me recoil in anguish. As the years passed I can look back on such encounters and accept that much of it was based on envy or fear. Often to friends and family, I represented an empty headed blond actress, seeking a glamorous, sophisticated way of life. It didn't matter what I felt inwardly or what my real intentions had been at times being totally the opposite of what I was or who I had been in my dedication to grow into the best spiritual evolution possible. Friendships in show business or many friendships established in transient areas like in California were based on "what can you do for me?" and "I am your friend as long as you serve a useful purpose for my benefit." It still disturbed me to lose a friendship that had existed for years. Still feeling the pangs of regret for lost friendships, it forced me to recognize that we have these brief encounters with those who have similar beliefs, direction or realizations, and then we go our separate ways. We simply grow out of each other's vibrations; such is the case with many divorces. One grows in various ways and interests while the mate stays stagnate, thus they grow further and further apart. Our friendship may have been deeply meaningful at one point. My conclusion is that those encounters were not merely by chance but just as the student's lessons are laid out in a textbook one step at a time so it is without lessons of life or what we call karma. Hopefully there will be growth regardless of how horrendous or mundane our encounters or experiences may have been.

From my many years of searching for my own answers, it is my perception that we each are part of a soul, maybe call it an "Over Soul" defined as: "a spiritual essence or vital force in the Universe in which all souls participate and that therefore transcends individual consciousness." Also Emerson wrote about the Over Soul. It seems ironic that one needs to become total selfish toward the inner self before he or she can truly love anything to anyone. We then learn to give from a selfless level. For if one gives expecting a reward, even a simple statement that is given for the purpose of expecting something in return, it becomes a selfish act rather than a selfless act as Jesus the Christ and other great prophets taught. Can a person totally commit to the Christ within, God, Angel - the word doesn't matter? In such a commitment he or she must prepare for whatever they may face. It might be flowing fulfillment depending on the individuals necessary assignments or--it might be a living hell of stripping the person, answering karma with pain and disappointment even feeling pressed to the maximum endurance. With proper mental and emotional conditioning we might live a charmed life. This is the subject I do not know since mine has been life groping and struggling through trial and error. If we are to make progress for our Soul's evolution, then we face these traumas, accepting that it is karma we set up in a previous life and now we have a chance to "right our wrong." Through understanding my own past lives, correlating them in some order has helped me more than any book, seminar, bible, church or any form of teaching, et al. that I have experienced. Finally I began understanding why no matter what I do, how hard I try, how much I create it NEVER brings me money! I have met so many successful, talented people who manage to make tons of money while I struggle to "just get by" - WHY? When I know my talents and abilities, intelligence, etc., yet I can't create this financial security. The karmic answer I believe is that I have been born in royalty, near royalty or in wealth. Apparently, I passed up opportunities in those lives to make the progress I needed for my spiritual evolution, so before I came in to this life, I must have said "sock it to me, I want out!" Little did I know what I would HAVE to face! As for fame, since I must have literally "lost my head" in one life, subconsciously, I must have been fearful of fame and influence! Regardless of how many books I read on positive thinking or how many creative attempts I made, once I gave up my will to "God," (Soul evolution) paths were laid out for me to face. If one must believe in HELL, then I would say we have created our own hell right here in our physical life. Whatever people, conditions or circumstances have been put in my path, I am thankful for my stubborn nature to SURVIVE and continually strive to conquer my own Autumns of life! One young lady said to me she did not know if she wanted spiritual growth if she had to encounter the emotional pain I had faced. I pointed out to her that this is my path (karma) not hers. We each learn in many different ways. We each "march to a different drummer." My pattern of life has always been rushed ahead attempting to pass the necessary basic learning.

The wise teacher or parent knows it is necessary for his students or child to fail and make mistakes for his or her continued growth. When classes are over, the teacher can only hope the lessons penetrated his student for the hills and valleys he must face. We are bound child to parent to child. Under God we are all equal children regardless of how bad our fellow man may accuse us of being. To me our ultimate attainment is the assimilation in the oneness of God but that maybe many life chapters ahead. Self-sacrifice that seems to be an equitable accepted necessity in most religious organizations, much more so if it includes material contributions to the church. Is self-sacrificing a necessity for growth? It appears to me, self-sacrifice is grossly misinterpreted. It is more the placing of things in their proper priority. I almost shudder to think of all the things that were "sinful" when I was a child compared to the freedom today! The more we see the more we want, the more we get the more we want until one is faced with giving up our possessions, people then fall apart - life is over and not worth living. It is then that we are truly possessed by our material things. After all those years spent as a single parent I believed that I was more or less a free soul compared to most mothers. After 25 years of vaguely maintaining hope that Debbie could be alive somewhere in the world, maybe suffering with amnesia, I finally had to come to the realization that in Debbie's absence, I was still possessed by the state of motherhood. I had a good talk with myself and said, "Ann, this soul has possessed you for less than 20 years of your life and still holds you now. It is time to let go." Many of those years were spent wanting a son. I was so certain I was destined to have a male child in addition to my daughter. Unfortunately for my destiny I remained a divorced mother in a career world struggling to provide a home and livelihood for my daughter and me. More than once in a dozen or more years a pregnancy occurred. How could I support my daughter and me, have an illegal baby, pay for medical necessities and our living expenses? The fathers-to-be were in no way willing to take any responsibility. The opportunity to have a child became a reality. I desperately wanted to fling aside conventional attitudes and have a fatherless child. But alas, regarding romanticism and what we wish to do, there is always that thing we each must live within our society - money is essential! There was no choice but to end the pregnancy in the days when abortions were illegal. No one remembers the horrors young women experienced because of that law, including deaths or mutations. The prevailing fact was that I must earn a living for my daughter and myself. I owed that to the both of us. There was no financially way I could afford this wanted child.

There are those who set themselves up as judge and jury for the would-be mothers of the world and condemn women who choose abortion. They argue that it is murder of a child, whereas, abortions generally happen within the eighth week of pregnancy. The fetus is not an inch in size! My theory is better than those who attempt to make decisions for those others when they have no concept of a woman's experience. I believe there is a karmic scene that must be played out - a man and a woman are obligated to create an avenue for a soul in the afterlife to return to a life on earth because of this karmic tie between the three of them. It IS the soul's CHOICE as to whether it wants to come into physical life at that particular time. If it chooses to not enter, the woman will have a miscarriage or an abortion which then releases that soul to a higher state of growth without living through another earth cycle of maybe 100 years. Souls in the afterlife who may WANT to come back to fulfill their lust physically or materially do so by choosing to skip the life offered, it moves up just as if it DID go through that lifecycle. It is like in school when you get moved up a grade without doing the work. The soul may have attached itself by some complicated heavenly computerized system to this female's body. Then through the passing of certain male genes there occurs similar soul growth patterns or former associations linking this same male and female in their previous lives. That coming together was necessary to resolve the karma. By releasing that soul without the necessary human lifetime bondage the woman may have assumed additional karmic debt for herself or it may be the computer's way of balancing the books. Many psychics claim to be able to read from these record-keeping systems called the Akashi records. As I see it no one really has the perfect answer or the right to judge another person's life lessons.

What is parenthood but a desire to produce a reproduction of ourselves, an extension of our own egos. Many people believe it is an internal link in the chain of physical life. It is their only comprehension of continued life after death. They live on through their future generations. For others parenthood may be playing God having someone depend on you can make you feel worthy, needed and have a purpose for living. If one needs to be needed (and who doesn't!) to serve as a "parent" can certainly be done without procreation. Almost everyone, in one form or another, is crying for help - young, old, minority groups, handicapped refugees and starving people around the world. As our world becomes overpopulated today's youth feels that producing their own genetic likenesses isn't totally necessary. Many decide not to have children or adopt orphans.

As life's irony often happens, again, I was faced with an opportunity to give birth through this female body. Only this time, I faced it <u>with</u> a husband who was a dedicated alcoholic and also over a decade older than me. A natural state of happiness had been attainted but I was also left feeling physically ill. Also beyond those ills remained my deep psychological condition. The fact was that I was nearly in my fourth decade. I had experienced many of those child-rearing years with all the love, joys, fears, worries, financial insecurities, and anxieties only to lose my daughter just as she was blossoming into womanhood. My loss also occurred during a time when I had been enjoying her the most. She was gone now perhaps gone were my child raising years as well. Physically I was not too old but psychologically I was definitely too old. With Jack's heavy drinking and smoking, it seemed a natural assumption that he would die long before me and again, I would be faced with raising a child alone past forty years of age!

My childhood years seemed to be another lifetime in the past. Just as in childhood there came a time when I became embarrassed to carry a doll with me from my abundant and dearly loved collection. I realized that I must lay down my dolls and grow up into a more mature interest equivalent to my peers. If Debbie had still been alive, I could have been a grandmother. The thought of facing years raising a child alone, I didn't see how I could do it again... then maybe repeat LOSING the child?

After Jack and I got married, he became restless and wanted to move back to Florida, which had never been any place I cared to live. We ended up selling our new home and buying a used motor home. We also sold the Lincoln and the Mustang and were left with no car to tow, meaning we could only go where the motor home would go. We drove from one place to another on the Interstate highways, while I preferred the less traveled byways; many were 4 lane highways with little traffic. He would want to stop driving around 4 pm and START DRINKING. It seemed in Palm Springs, he only had evening cocktails. I can't remember him ever getting drunk at that time so it didn't occur to me that he was a real alcoholic, especially since I did not know what qualified as an "alcoholic." He didn't particularly want to sightsee so why were we living in a motor home?

We drove to Texas, visited my parents, then he decided to visit a friend in Oregon, so off we went to Oregon. His friend lived on a ranch and during our stay one of their cows digested the poisonous plant hemlock. The poor animal was suffering and foaming at the mouth so they decided to kill her. Jack had a gun but I did not stay to see it.

One morning, Jack and his friend wanted to go fishing so we drove the motor home over to a beach area. While they got on a fishing boat I stayed in the motor home. The weather changed and became very windy and rainy. They returned after only a couple of hours as the weather was too bad to fish.

After we left Oregon, we drove south, through Northern California and saw the Red Woods and a few other sites. We went all the way to San Diego and I was hoping he would settle somewhere south of Los Angeles, but we hardly spent any time there and he was off again, back to Texas. This time he decided we would have our furniture moved to Texas and would live in my parent's upstairs apartment. I doubt that my father or mother had ever tasted a beer as there were no drinkers in my family! After we were settled in, he did get drunk. I was walking "on egg shells" to keep him from having any kind of conflict with my Dad.

Jack looked around the Dallas area for a job selling mobile homes, but he ran into the same thing. The managers were a lot younger than he was and had only half of his intelligence. They did not want him as he represented competition. After a few months, he was itching to go back to Florida. I just wanted to be a wife and live a "normal" life. We hardly got settled in with our furniture before he wanted to take the motor home and go to Florida. He was sure he could get a job with a new, very large mobile home community, as he knew the main manager of the whole construction company whom he knew from the desert. The problem was the sales office would not be ready for a couple of months or so. We parked in an RV park and paid a monthly rate. I took a job at a carpet store, selling carpet while Jack fished. We finally decided to sell the motor home and he bought a used red Cadillac (same as my second husband had!). We then bought a small travel trailer and lived in it. Although I have never been comfortable in humid climates I adapted despite the fact that it was all new to me. Finally, the sales office opened and Jack began to work. After a few months, he decided to buy a home in the park. We looked at plans and ordered one. We reserved a lot on a small lake and soon ordered our furniture to be shipped to Florida. Once it arrived, I was happy again to decorate our new home even though it was new from the factory, I wanted personalized choices of colors, wallpaper, etc. It was BEAUTIFUL!

Now he had a good job, a lovely home and we decided that I didn't need to work, so that was OK with me. I don't remember the exact time but we were there for a few years when he decided he didn't want to live in the park any longer because during his days off, residents would ask him park questions or have complaints, not respecting his off hours. By then I had attended a college passing both the Real Estate test and the State test. I began shopping for a house.

When I found out that I was pregnant, what a situation I was in. I would love to have had a child but with Jack's drinking and age, I knew I would end up raising a child alone and I wasn't 20 years old anymore. We discussed it and both decided it would be best to have an abortion. We made arrangements in my parent's town, as I knew the doctor there. We made the trip to Texas. The doctor asked me if I was sure I didn't want any more children as he could do a hysterectomy. I didn't think I would want more being married to Jack and having experienced the loss of my only child. There went my last chance for that son I thought I was supposed to have. It was a relief for Jack; he certainly did not want to be a parent again.

Ann Palmer

To skim through those seven plus years of marriage to Jack in Florida, included that first house which we sold then lived in the house at the lake in a tiny town less than 10 miles from Jack's office. Again, I created a third beautiful home for us. Seems each year the drinking got worse. I had trained myself to dress up, and wear make-up before he got home. The dinner needed to be ready within 30 minutes and his cocktail waiting when he entered the front door. I knew if I didn't get him fed within the first hour, it would be another of many drunken nights that usually ended up in a fight. He would go to bed early and insisted that I went to bed at the same time even though I wasn't sleepy. I would stiffly lie in bed until he was asleep, snoring and spewing his alcoholic breath, then sneak quietly out of bed. The house was U shape so I could go to the other side where I had a workroom and could read or do creative work. We rarely went out. He was making good money but we spent it all on living. He would accuse me of spending it all but I rarely bought anything for myself. I would shop in Orlando buying smart suits and accessories for him as well as pick up his cigarettes at the Naval Base. I kept him dressed so well that the salesmen said he looked like he'd just walked out of an Esquire magazine. When things became truly awful, I really wanted to get out of there, to Texas or anywhere but I had no money of my own to just go!

ONCE when I had convinced Jack to go to a counselor we each had a chance to tell our own story. The counselor was an ex-Navy man so they got into an ole buddy, buddy talk. Nothing changed, except the counselor called me to say that the only choice I had was to leave Jack, as there was no way he was going to change. I can't remember why we decided to sell that house after a few years, but it sold to a couple that didn't want occupancy until winter. Since I did not like Florida summers, Jack suggested I take a vacation to California. This was after my Dad died and my mother came to visit for a few weeks. He said I could take her back to Texas, and then go on to California. I did not like the idea of driving all across the nation, half of it by myself. Even though I didn't want to make my home in the Hollywood area, I had a pattern of getting tired of being away and always wanted to return to California. Driving from Florida to Texas with my mother was pleasant and I spent a few days there before heading to California again. This time, at least I had a nice newer Cadillac. I stayed less than a month, as

I was feeling guilty to be spending money while Jack was at home working. I did not know that he had an active social life or intimate life while I was away. I headed back across country and along the way bought gifts for him in Arizona. By the time I crossed the Panhandle of Florida it was still early afternoon and I decided to drive on home. I arrived around 7 pm. When I tried the door, it was locked and the night lock was also on so my key didn't work. Normally, the night lock was never used until after 9 pm. Jack answered the door rather coolly and seemed somewhat surprised. When I pulled out his gifts it was so strange as he nearly cried. Weird reaction, I thought. After opening the refrigerator door I discovered a can of Pepsi Cola. There was NO way it had been his as he had never drank one and he was also unaccustomed to having neighbors in. Around 7:30 pm the phone rang, he rushed and said, "I'll get it!" but I was closer and said, "Hello." There was silence; a woman's voice bumbling, "Oh... I've got the wrong number."

Shortly thereafter, he suggested I take the Airstream to the beach and I agreed. I will skip all the details of that time but it ended up he was having an affair with a woman he worked with. He took the $38,000 out of our savings account that was supposed to need both of our signatures. Fortunately, I had opened a safety deposit box in my name only and had all our papers which included the titles to both Cadillacs, the Airstream, house contract, etc. This left me with some leverage. Without this documentation he would have taken everything we had. For protection, I filed for a legal separation and decided to take the Airstream and go back to California via Texas. When I called Sharon, she told me that she had a feeling of my father's presence around her. This experience helped her decide to fly down to Florida to help me get going on my westward move. It was the time of a new beginning with the Airstream travel trailer, the thought of towing it completely across the United States was very frightening, yet a vicarious thrill of my renewed pioneering spirit. I had also never driven my car by towing it. The Autumn of my life came and went as much as I liked to live in California, but it is always so congested. There were maddening freeways, tax problems, yet still I knew that I must go back! I realized motherhood bound me to someone, but my marriage had held me in a far greater bondage. Perhaps, even the security that my father had always offered me in that I would always have a home with my parents was also a slight bondage, too. Sharon arrived, we hooked up the Airstream and I took my first time towing it back to our home in mid Florida. I divided the furniture, called a mover and began packing. Sharon's help was a Godsend. What seemed like a good feeling that had been missing since 1970 suddenly came back over me, as if a part of me had been missing and had just returned. The moving van came and took my half of the furniture to storage. Sharon and I hooked up the Airstream and away we drove to Texas. I went back to California to start my single life all over again. Having been out of the film business for almost a decade, I wasn't sure if I could get back in. That was in about 1978...

For a while I was living in the Airstream, in a RV Park that was way past Malibu. Then I moved it to Santa Monica to be closer to the places I needed to be and lived in it there for months. Finally, I decided to rent an apartment and store the Airstream. After being a commentator for Cadillac at many Auto Shows, I knew the car well and found a job selling Cadillac automobiles in Beverly Hills. That was really a stretch for the men sales staff to accept! I was also very involved in Metaphysics, attending classes and helping organize a major event. To put the next few years in a few sentences, apartments were soon to become condos. I then moved to Newport Beach and lived in the Airstream, finally buying a mobile home in Oceanside only to get it ready to sell. Following that, I bought a new mobile home and moved it to Newport Beach. I lived there for a few years then returned to Westwood where I had an office doing psychic counseling and also taught classes. I then moved back to Texas to help my Mother but still couldn't handle the state and headed, back to California.

Eventually in the early 1980's I got on ABC-TV's "General Hospital" as a nurse along with managing an apartment building in Beverly Hills as well as part-time managing a small hotel in Hollywood for the same management company. THEN, a cable system was opening a studio in Beverly Hills and I was urged to produce a show there. It was non-paying and at first, I wasn't interested but finally decided it might be an audition for a hostess TV show job. For a few years I produced/hosted 250 TV shows and it was the GREATEST joy and satisfaction of any work I had ever done. Although it was so typical of me, putting all that time and energy into all those shows for NO pay. I DID experience "pay" via taping 52 shows all over Mexico with free travel, hotel stays, transportation and food. Believing I could produce shows in Las Vegas and syndicate them for PAY, off I moved there. While in Las Vegas, I was ordained and began officiating at weddings as well as working as an extra in films that were being shot there. Then I moved to Mexico, then to Palm Springs and then bought the motor home which I both traveled and lived in until finally ending up in Asheville, North Carolina for about 8 years. Up until 2014 I was living in Mesa, Arizona, and then finally I moved back to California one last time later that same year.

CHAPTER 37

Now, to recap 1994 and to elaborate on the other devastating experience I had to CONQUER, it was my bout with THE BIG "C" - cancer! If I could survive losing my ONLY child AND CANCER, nothing could destroy me and was proof that I AM A SURVIVOR! Ironic that I worked as a nurse (actress) on ABC's Port Charles "GENERAL HOSPITAL" from the early 1980's through 1996. Never dreaming that the real General Hospital would be such an essential part of my life!

Los Angeles, the international city but seemingly less nationals - "born in the U.S.A.!" How things change since I first arrived in Hollywood in the late 1950s. PREJUDICE? No, not really, just longing for more of my own kind - but what was my own kind? Far removed from a Texan, I never fit in Florida and now almost everywhere I go I feel like a stranger or a foreigner. Yes, we all breathe the same air, inhaled and exhaled, we are one body in God – Goddess - Universal energy and yet, I couldn't help resenting the fact that medical expenses have skyrocketed beyond many average people's budgets but so many foreigners, including illegal aliens receive free health care. As I sat looking around the waiting room at General Hospital, there were maybe 5 white Americans, about 10 to 15 blacks, third were Orientals, but the rest of the huge waiting room were Mucho Hispanics. I was warned it was a very long wait--yes all day, after 5 pm before I saw a doctor.

My long time doctor friend Gloria studied medicine years ago when there were only three women in her class of 1970. I knew something was wrong because for months I had been enduring grinding pain and irregular bowel movements. Gloria insisted I go to a Free Clinic. When I did, their exam said it was necessary for me to have more intensive examinations at General Hospital, which I thought was for desolate people - what am I saying? I was one of them! THAT was an entire day's wait to see a doctor. An appointment was made for a colonoscopy, my first. The appointment was only a day or so later. Again, another long wait in another department. As I observed those patients waiting, a doctor came out and spoke to the old man sitting alone next to me. The doctor just whipped out "YOU'VE GOT CANCER." I felt so sorry for the old guy all alone with such an abrupt announcement of cancer, not dawning on me I was there to hear the same statement. My turn came and as I lay there watching their small camera as it went through my colon, I was amazed at how pretty the inside of the colon was. It was a pretty peachy color, seemed like curtains gently moving, and then the camera stopped! There sat about 3 nodules, milky white. Everything stopped and they wheeled me into a room where I waited. Several doctors came in surrounding my gurney and said that I had cancer and it needed to come out right away. Even though I studied a lot of healing methods and believed in holistic treatments, I said, "Get it out ASAP!" The appointment was made.

That Monday at around 3:00 am on January 17, the Northridge earthquake awoke me from a very deep sleep. For a moment I didn't know where I was or who I was, strangest awakening I have ever experienced. It felt like a freight train coming through the house or being inside a jackhammer. It was the day before I was to have my blood test in preparation for Thursday's surgery. Gloria had insisted I stay at her house before and after my surgery. Gloria's son awoke and we checked the house to see if there was any major damage. Gloria and her husband were in Palm Desert. It was amazing that there were only a few broken glasses and none of her expensive crystal ware had been damaged. I was to have a blood test in the clinic building on Wednesday. When I called, I was told that it was closed for earthquake inspection damage. The doctor told me to check into the hospital on Wednesday. The blood test could be done at that time. They would proceed with surgery as planned, providing there weren't any more victims from the earthquake.

Gloria's attorney husband dropped me off in front of General Hospital on his way to work on Wednesday morning. It was my day to check into County General Hospital alone. As I walked up those long steps into the Hospital, I remembered the same photo had appeared in the opening scene of ABC's Port Charles General Hospital. I had never dreamed that one day I would be a patient of the County Hospital. I

Ann Palmer

thought about the years that I had worked on the show and that was as close as I had ever wanted to come to the medical profession. An adult can also be scared of hospitals, too. As I walked up those steps, my heart was pounding, my thoughts were - would I walk out or be carried out in a body bag!

After checking in and being assigned to a room, the nurse was supposed to give me some medication at noon but didn't get around to it until around 6 pm. The nursing staff was unbelievably inconsiderate and seemed nonchalant about their patients. Turning a light on for an attendant became a joke. The young Candy Striper volunteers had more enthusiasm. There were a few others who attended to a patient's needs but it left me wondering how many people in the hospital actually die from need of immediate attention that never comes. I realized that the tremendous paperwork and the week's emergencies because of the earthquake had put everyone on edge. This had been the worst earthquake the Los Angeles area could recall. There was no end of the aftershocks yet, it could not compare with the inner quake I was feeling. I would look at the huge cement columns and ceiling rafters wondering if one would smash me in one of the aftershocks. The aftershocks can sometimes be worse than the original earthquake. A fellow sufferer in the room of five patients had assured me the hospital was built on rollers and was one of the safest places at the time. One of the newer buildings was condemned. The old hospital was built in the 1920s and had stood its ground ever since, with just a bit of "rockin' and rollin'."

Since it was a teaching hospital, a group of medical students were assigned to the doctor who was to operate. Each seemed to take a very personal interest in the success and outcome of my surgery. Perhaps it was because I was far more outgoing and maybe a bit more attractive than most of their patients. There were four young students consisting of three men and one woman. The Thursday surgery had been delayed, not because of the earthquake, but due to the cleansing medication having been given too late. I was informed that it resulted in my sodium level being too high for surgery. I wondered if I had been with a highly paid doctor, when the schedules could be so tight, if the surgery would have haphazardly been done anyway. At that thought I was glad to be under the care of a sharp young team of doctors. I don't think the most skilled and highly paid doctors could have made me feel any more secure about my experience than my team of doctors. On Friday the team of doctors had to attend a seminar, therefore my surgery was scheduled for Saturday. I would be spending three long days in the hospital ward before anything could be done and would share the room with four other women, all suffering from pain. The surgery delay was enough to make me want to jump up and leave without the surgery.

No one looks forward to surgery - especially "major" surgery! For three days I had to be in that hospital on a hard bed dreading, fearing and experiencing other patients' pain and suffering. Gladys had lost a thumb from a TV falling on it during earthquake. Mary's abscess on her kidney was removed, causing her tremendous pain. Crusty Jean wouldn't lose her kidney until next week. What a "hoot and holler" she let out when the doctor said she could go home for a few days before surgery. She wouldn't miss her Saturday ballgame after all. A couple of others came and went while I waited. Since I couldn't speak Spanish much of what went on was unknown to me. I knew surgery was like having a baby - once you're well on your way in pregnancy, there's no backing out, at some point you've got to go through childbirth, now cancer had come out! For weeks before, during and after my hospital stay I did not know how extensive the cancer was. It could have broken through the colon wall and spread through my organs. The cramping pain across my stomach area was a long way from where the cancer had been discovered. It was at the lower part of my ascending colon. Would I have to have chemotherapy? Would my hair fall out? How would I manage? I had to make a trip to the hospital alone, wouldn't I still be alone in whatever I had to face? Certainly no family member would come to my aid.

At 5 am on Thursday I was awaken, prepped and awaited the attendant with the gurney. It was good that I was scheduled first for surgery because the solution they gave me to clear my colon had dehydrated me to the point I thought I could not stand it if I didn't get water. They gave me a large cotton swab with lemon and glycerin to suck on, which I did until my throat burned. The green uniformed attendant appeared. Bravely I mounted the gurney for the long trip to the operating waiting room. I was the first to arrive, and then a very large overweight man arrived. He was so fat they could not find his veins. I had to witness all that, then another man... and another. What was I in, the men's ward? The anesthesiologist appeared, talked with me and then disappeared. Another man was taken out of the room headed for surgery. Hey, I was supposed to be first! Then another and another followed. After an hour and half, the anesthesiologist finally informed me that the sodium level in my body was much too high to have surgery. They might be able to operate later in the day... still NO water! "I have never seen a reaction like this," said my youthful doctor. It was no surprise to me, my body was almost convulsing for lack of water. The solution they had given me was ultra salty and my body wasn't used to a lot of salt, since I used as little as possible. Back to the dreary room to recharge my battery and prepare for surgery all over again! I had been doing as much reading as I could, considering the TV and chattering noise in the ward. I had brought some books on healing. I pulled the curtain around my bed, put earphones on my ears and listened to sweet, aesthetic music for when I attempted to meditate. I was so dehydrated I didn't care if I ever had surgery. All I wanted was water. People in the medical profession intimidate patients to the point that they assume that they are being cared for, when it is probably sheer neglect and inconsideration. Finally they came in about 11 am and told me the surgery would be postponed until Saturday, but only if they could get permission since Saturday was not a surgery day. Thursday and Friday yet to go! I was very disappointed to have to remain on the hard bed and suffer through three more days of the horrible salty bullion, jello, limited juices and indifferent attendants, especially the Asian ones, a different life routine, perhaps.

With the extra days of reading, meditating, attempting some yoga exercises, by Saturday morning I was totally calm. Maybe I needed the time to really get my body ready. Again the gurney came and took me to a different operating waiting room. This time, I was the only one there. A delightful pre-op nurse appeared and she happened to have the same first name as mine. Finally in the very cold surgery room, my arms were securely fastened and it seemed I was talking to the surgery team then suddenly I went out. One third of my ascending colon was removed. They were sure they got all the cancer. As it worked out, I wasn't going to have to take chemotherapy but would be in for frequent tests, etc. Every three months I had a blood test and after a year another colon exam.

By the following Wednesday, after the weeklong stay, I all but threatened the doctors to let me out, since Gloria was a doctor, I knew I'd receive better care at her house. Yes, there was a lot of pain in the hospital and more at home. The recovery was very slow. One day I felt normal the next day so weak I had to stay in bed all day. I planned to catch up on a lot of writing but found myself too drained to do much of anything but watch TV. At first, I could not walk up and down the stairs. Gloria and her whole family were wonderful to me. Her home was so pleasant; I stayed for several weeks, until one of her son's decided to help me get some work so that I could leave. Actually, it worked out well as he got me a job as a housemother at a sorority at U.C.L.A. where I also had living facilities. Going back and forth to Lake Arrowhead was just too hard to continue living there while working in the Los Angeles area.

The old Los Angeles General Hospital loomed ahead as I reported for my fourth month checkup at the Oncology Department. I sat waiting the long hours just to see a student doctor for five to 10 minutes. There were the audible sounds of different foreign languages that I could not understand. A buxom woman stared blankly at me; an old Asian man entered the exam room nearby, a gaunt unshaven old man shuffled down the hall, wait, wait, and wait. As I sat there I thought of the hours of waiting in the dressing rooms for my call on the "General Hospital" soap which were far more enjoyable! It felt so weird to be involved in the real Los Angeles General Hospital after working for so many years on the TV one. As I sat in the oncology department waiting room, I knew that many of these patients would soon be heading for their transition from their physical bodies. I felt so lucky and blessed that I had survived and conquered cancer! My oncology visits continued for several more months. NO! Don't call my name, Grim Reaper, I was determined to LIVE, LOVE and hopefully place a light in someone's life.

Ann Palmer

Six months later I still had not exercised as much as I should have and when I tried to lift any heavy object, I hurt for a few days afterwards. I was very determined to let this be the end of cancer in my body! I would do everything to keep myself in a healthy body with a clear mind and healthy spirit. It isn't easy in this stressful era. We all are going to die sooner or later, I prefer much later so let that be a warning to you; beware of your own stress. You can do something about it so do it now! If you have any concern about something going on in your body have it checked out. If you should have cancer as I did, just remember many people like me have survived cancer!

How we deny death in the United States. We don't want to face death even though we each know that it is not an option. Around the world other cultures make it a part of their lives, more accepting than we are, they honor it. We go through life totally unprepared for the death of a loved one or even our own. We live in such a denial that when someone else needs comfort and reassurance we avoid them, not knowing how to respond. I read all the books on death and the dying process but could not be with the three most important people of my life, my daughter, my father and my mother. When the doctors found cancer on my father's voice box with an unpredictable outcome of his surgery, I dug through every book, everything I could find, including submitting his name to every prayer group. He did live for another 10 years and played many games of golf. Medical fields have advanced so much since my cancer. Some are even opening up to metaphysics and alternate healing. His last trip to the Veterans Hospital in Dallas had been for male problems but when they operated, they found his cancer was too near a major artery to operate. The next morning when he asked the doctor, "Well, Doctor, did you get rid of my problem?" The young doctor leaned over him and said, "No Old Man, we could not..." My father did not hear the rest of the statement about chemotherapy. His body sunk, he died that night. I sat up with him the first night because he warned us to keep him on his side. From his previous surgery he had experienced trouble breathing when he was lying on his back. I would have stayed that second night but my brother had agreed to be there but he never showed up.

My father was basically Texas shy but he had been such a devout Mason, one of the five best teachers for part of the Masonic work in Texas. He gave memorized work in front of the Lodge for many years. I wondered if the two things could have created his throat cancer.

By the Autumn of 1995, the best possible gift I could receive was the doctor's words, "Your healthy as a horse, everything is normal." Thank God. I felt I needed to accept the fact that I had created cancer in my own body. At that time, there were three particular areas of my life I could not resolve. What better place to develop cancer than in the colon - stuff in my life that needed to be flushed out. I firmly believe we create our own illnesses and often without realizing it. It can be any number of problems in our lives.

In 2014, I still consider myself a healthy person. Perhaps one's health is more the mind – spirit than the body which flares up once in a while. One lengthy battle occurred when I bought the motor home in 2002 and then sold my house in Palm Springs. It was after 9/11 that I thought I could live and travel in a motor home. I wanted to see the USA and finish my book which I had been working on for several years. I bought a Saturn vehicle from a man in Palm Desert to tow behind the motor home. When I drove out to Palm Desert and stopped, the door to the motor home flung open. I quickly jumped out of the seat after setting the emergency brake but after climbing on the steps to grab the door, the three metal steps flipped up and hit the back of my leg. It was bleeding badly. I went into a nearby house and bandaged it. It was on Friday, not a good time to get medical aid without going to an emergency room. I tended to it as best I could. There was so much work to get done vacating the house and storing store my things in the motor home, then on Saturday there was the necessary mechanical work to be done.

Skipping all the details, I ended up in Montana with my leg getting badly infected with a wound that would not heal. The three cuts turned into a venous leg ulcer that required trips to the hospital in Missoula for treatments. I had to leave my friend's farm where I had stayed for a few weeks. The Doctor decided to remove the infected area and apply a skin graft after several weeks. I ended up with quite a lifetime scar, but since it is on the back of my leg, I don't have to see it.

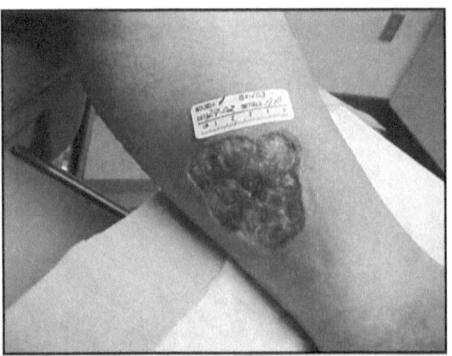

After cutting away infection

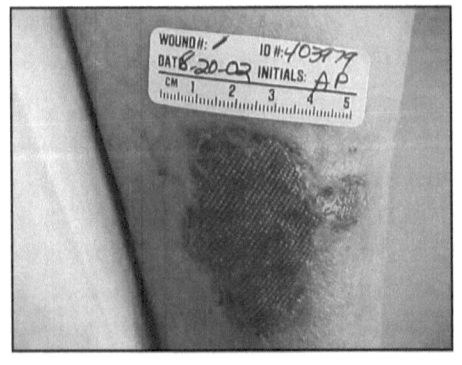
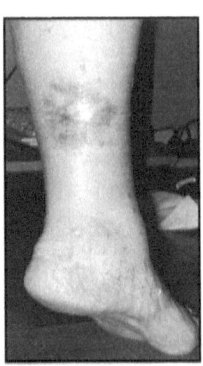

Weeks of healing

I needed a work camper job to defray expenses. While searching the Internet, I located one in a spiritual type of camp in Georgia and I left Missoula September 11, one year after 9/11. Again, moving right along briefly without details – I traveled to Georgia, it didn't work out; then Florida, then Virginia, then back to Florida for a couple of years and then to Asheville, North Carolina where I really encountered a LOT of medical problems!

Even though I still maintained that I am a healthy person I had a colonoscopy in 2006 and everything was OK. By May of 2008 in Asheville, I had been telling my doctor about my pain but he did nothing. On the night of May 11th, after throwing up all night, I stomped into his office on Monday morning and said "SOMETHING IS DEFINITELY WRONG!!" He sent me for a CAT scan, from there; they sent me for an immediate admittance into the hospital. Stuffing a tube down my nose into my stomach was a horrible experience. I guess they were trying to empty out my system and bowels completely to see if that worked--it didn't, on Friday May 16th, he sent me down for another CAT scan and did surgery that afternoon. The next day was not a Happy Birthday! I spent 12 days in the hospital. Adhesions had developed on my intestines where he also found two small hernias and he put mesh on them. As I was recuperating, fluid developed under the incision and I had to go back to the hospital to have a tube and ball to catch the fluid installed. I wore that for a week. I had one week of being OK but then pus broke through the incision and flowed for 4 weeks requiring thick bandages 3-4 times per day. Finally, the surgeon told me he must remove the mesh and booked me back into the hospital on Tuesday, August 19th. I wasn't supposed to have to stay overnight in the hospital. When I awoke, I had a large open triangle shaped gap in my belly 6" by about 2". There was also an attached tube which led to a suction machine! What followed was my wearing loose clothing, flat thong sandals dreading to have to leave my house. It was NO fun to be tethered to a machine and it was very awkward to carry the thing with me everywhere I went! Many nights, I was awakened by an irritating beep from the machine for no apparent reason. It was designed to help me heal faster but it didn't seem to work very well. Instead the hernia continued to grow until I looked like I was 8-9 months pregnant.

Intermingled Destinies Between A Mother and Daughter

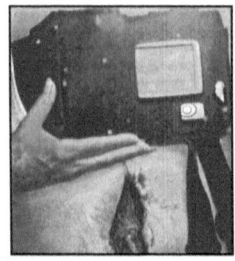
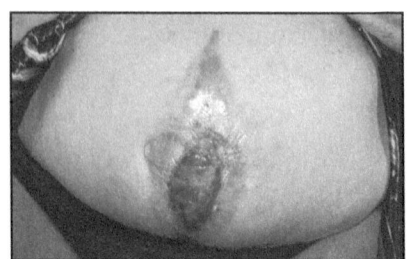
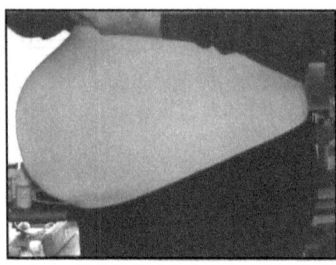

By December there wasn't a doctor in Asheville that would do surgery on my hernia. An appointment was made to see a doctor at the Wake-Forest Hospital in Winston-Salem, NC. It took me 2 hours and 20 minutes to make the 145 mile drive. Each time it took over 6+ hours with almost 300 miles of traveling to make the round trip. The doctor said he would not touch me until the wound had completely healed. That meant at least another 3 to 4 months of waiting for surgery. I was so depressed, but then I got a call from Wake-Forest saying there was a new doctor who would perform the surgery. Back to Winston-Salem I went. On January 30, 2009 I underwent major hernia surgery by Dr. McNatt, a man I learned to highly appreciate. Many trips were required back and forth to Wake-Forest as fluid called "Seroma" kept forming and had to be removed. The doctor used a long needle while watching his progress on the ultrasound. This procedure was performed in both Winston-Salem and Ashville. I've since lost count of how many times this was done, but I do remember that it was quite painful. There were many trips to the pain clinic in Asheville too, but that would not be my last bout with Seroma!

During my time in Asheville I had mammograms, a heart test and cortisone shots for a deteriorating back problem. There were more MTI or CAT scans than I can count. In 2007 lower and upper Endoscopes revealed in the upper GI track that my esophagus was causing indigestion which could be relieved with prescription medication. Then there was the day in April 2009 when I was doubled over in pain and called 911. In the ambulance, the attendant was taking so much time filling out a form that I asked if he could do that on the way to the hospital. Anyone who has passed a kidney stone is aware of the intense pain caused by this condition. After the testing, finally they gave me a morphine shot that gradually took away all the pain. By 3 pm I went home feeling quite normal. If that wasn't enough, by August I started having excruciating pain again! This time I drove myself to the Emergency Room. Within four months I had two more trips to Emergency. This time it happened on a Friday and was my gall bladder. After all the tests, the Doctor said my gall bladder needed to be removed. I felt O.K. and suggested I go home and return on Monday for surgery but he felt another attack was possible so my weekend was spent in the hospital. On Monday, by passing through my mouth and throat, they removed the gallstones blocking my gall bladder and liver. On Tuesday they removed the gall bladder. That seemed a quick recovery compared to my previous surgeries.

In 2010 the discovering of Sleep Apnea seemed minor, plus more spinal problems: Scoliosis, Stenosis and arthritis and cortisone shots to manage the discomfort. By the end of November, I had my left knee replaced and I spent almost a month in a recovery home taking daily physical therapy that was a gross pain! When the doctor would allow me to go home, my neighbor was there to take me home but discouraged me since there was two feet of snow. I told them I would not be going out of my house; I just wanted to get HOME! Weeks of home therapy followed and today – the knee is still stiff and not functioning well.

The never-ending health cycle moved right into 2011. By June, my belly was again filling out. I contacted Dr. McNatt in Winston-Salem and he found a second hernia growing. Since I had an upcoming wedding we postponed the surgery until August (still the AUTUMN!)

In September of 2011, it all began again; the second hernia surgery at Wake-Forest Hospital in Winston-Salem, NC; the LONG trips from Asheville! This time the hospital stay was the worst ever! I had so many adhesions in my belly; the doctor went in with nine scope entrances. He put in mesh that was very large. On my lower left side apparently he put a stitch in a nerve that gave me a lot of pain for a month or more. I had no control over my body. I was more miserable than I had ever been and prayed to God that it would be my last hospital stay! Again followed weeks of pain and trips to have the Seroma removed. So far, it had held out but not the surgeries. By December I decided to go ahead and have surgery on my hammertoe which was done in a clinic.

I almost began to feel that if I remained in North Carolina much longer, I might die from the bad medical care that I believe began in 2008 with that first surgery.

In the meantime, I had lower pain and my primary doctor had done a small surgery but in March 2012, the pain clinic found this:

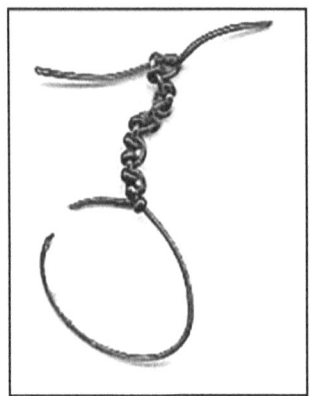

Fortunately, in April 2012, my house sold and I was able to move back to the Western USA.

By 2014, I am still here after many years of surgeries and, I can't count the number of operations I have had, yet I still consider myself totally healthy in many ways. Senior years have a way of laying a lot of ills on our bodies even though we may be trying to give it good care in the physical sense. Now, when I feel myself getting stressed out, I back up and change my direction. Even if I don't do a more formal type of meditation I think others do the same sometimes, when the TV is on and I am laying back resting not always focusing on what is playing. At other times, I do a simply short meditation of maybe 10 or 15 minutes. I am in an ever-present prayerful mode. Silently or vocally to myself I go around saying, "Thank you, God!" When I think over my life's activities and especially travel, I am so grateful for the full life I have enjoyed and plan to be living for years yet to come. I am grateful for each and every day and every night I give a prayer of thanksgiving.

I have had so many dreams, so many disappointments I have had - did I set impossible goals? Had I reached many but not interpreted them as success? I was so sure I would be successful in Hollywood since my goals were to use the media for a more positive influence on the masses. I was so sure that Debbie would marry and have three children in a well-adjusted family, and contrary to my own experiences. Even ever since my dad's death, there has been nothing but family strife. Years of not speaking and no contact with anyone except for a while, an occasional note from the wife of my nephew but eventually even those ceased, too. Family has rationalized their own guilt for greed, expressed after my dad's death in taking over all of mother's property that caused her to feel very taken advantage of and properly led to her death. She had been deserted and was alone in a nursing home where she subsequently developed pneumonia and bed sores. Once in that home, each time I called and asked for a time when I could talk to her there was always some excuse. I then realized the staff knew they had been ordered not to allow me to communicate with her. One Sunday evening, a message was left stating that she was in the hospital and it didn't look good. I called the hospital, suggesting that even if she was asleep, keep telling her that I was on my way. My experience had always been that she always got better when I was with her. I was on the plane attempting to get to her while she was alive but upon my arrival at the hospital I was greeted not by family members but a volunteer. When I asked where my mother's room was her reply was, "Oh, they've taken her to the funeral home." Stunned I could do nothing but race to my rented car, not knowing where to go or what to do. I drove to my family's home but all of the doors were locked. I then sat on the steps and cried only to be told later that I was not permitted to stay there since my brother owned it now. How happy my sister's husband must have been to have succeeded in beating me out of every possible inheritance. My brother-in-law had also manipulated the sale of my mother's house to my brother for one third of its value. It seemed to be the results of a small town sticking together with my brother-in-law on the Board of Directors of the bank. In his position of authority he had also manipulated my mother to sign an irrevocable Power of Attorney to that bank so he had full control over everything. In the realm of spirituality, we know we must FORGIVE but this has been the hardest experience in my life to find forgiveness. With two appraisals to get the real value of the home, one would think a good Christian man, actively involved in church activities and the BANK, would have to recognize the house's real value! No doubt he knew my brother would not be able to make the payments. Logically, it would seem that a good "Christian" man might have Christ-like compassion and want to see his wife's aging sister have at least one third of the property as had been stated in my parents' will.

It should not have been a surprise for me when not one phone call inquiry, not one flower, not even one card from my family when I had faced cancer and possible death. Just as I faced the grief over Debbie and my father and my mother alone, I also had to face "the big C" alone with the exception of having only a handful of supportive friends. *Yes, I do give myself credit for conquering life's afflictions, especially in the AUTUMN of my life.*

CHAPTER 38

After I left Gloria's comfortable home I was feeling well enough to tackle my new job as the House Mother at Delta Gamma Sorority, at U.C.L.A.; this position had been arranged by Gloria's son. During my two semesters in this role I felt I had come full circle in mothering Sorority girls. The girls tested me in many ways. The cooks were also testing me until I had to fire one of them. There were the house-cleaning crews, plus construction due to the earthquake with food and supply budgets to cope with. On top of adjusting to the new job, living in one room with no kitchen plus I was also still working at my primary non-paying joy, hosting/producing my TV program, which eventually numbered over 250 shows. Again, my life presented another situation of me being used as a scapegoat. One of the Alumni board members decided she wanted many things changed but I could not accommodate her as times had changed from when she had lived in the house. I did not like those things either but because of freedoms offered to the residents, legally I could do nothing about their choices. Neither could she. I even tried to teach them some table manners and how to set tables in the dining room. With girls from wealthy families, I was shocked at their un-lady-like ways, their coming in at all hours was permissible, but throwing catsup on their kitchen walls and throwing up in the bathroom that serviced the living areas was more than any House Mother should have to contend with!

(For a very short time, my hair was a deep red.)

Before they left for the summer, they had the right to reject or vote me back for the fall. The results were a unanimous vote for my return. When the girls left for the summer, all furniture and things they had left behind were to be put outside or given away. This Alumni woman could take what she wanted but had not come when a friend did great-devoted work in Peru for natives; I gave her clothing and whatever she could use. Apparently that set this woman off because she wanted many of the things for her church. In addition to that the sorority house was having many repairs during the summer months. I was not paid a salary once the girls left but I stayed on to make sure that everything was taken care of. The contractors asked if they could use the refrigerator in the girls' kitchen, separate from the walk-in refrigerator and main kitchen. I told them to be sure to clean it out when they had finished then I left for my cabin in Lake Arrowhead where I was spending the summer. I had moved more of my things into the sorority house since I was going to have another year there. This vicious alumni woman spewed many lies to the other board members and even though I was voted back, she managed to get me fired! Gloria's son had gotten that job for me and I don't think he ever knew or accepted the truth of the situation, as I don't recall seeing him since. With all that and failing to sell the cabin, I decided to move to Las Vegas where I hoped to find a buyer for the mountain cabin, which I did.

Debbie had disappeared in early September of 1970 and months later the police seemed to be accomplishing nothing. I would usually visit psychics for help but I was too distraught to concentrate on any kind of psychic readings. During the first passing years, I had been to a number of psychic friends and received so many mixed messages. Those closest to me all thought she was alive, maybe involved in some kind of white slavery or she might be suffering from amnesia. Almost none said she was absolutely dead, as I am sure they thought I could not take it. Why wouldn't I feel it if she was dead? We were so close in life; I could sense what she was doing or thinking. I knew that there was no way Debbie would take off without letting her family know. If she had been abducted, surely she would find a way to contact us. So many of these psychics kept telling me that I would see Debbie again.

Many evenings, I turned to television for relaxation only to realize there were almost no choices except crime, murder and violence. All the years hence, the same choice but with different names and they all seem to get worse each year, especially with all the special effects. For so many years my goal had been to eventually produce TV shows which would provide a good influence on the masses rather than teaching them how to commit just about any kind of crime. Over and over in my years in Hollywood I was told I was too idealistic and non-commercial. The lust for that fast buck is not exclusive to the film industry but it certainly is prevalent.

On April1st, 1977 I had to experience another loss and grief for a person who had represented a certain constant source of security and love for me and that was my father. Other than the assumed death of my daughter, the death of my father was the most painful death I have ever experienced. There had always been a very strong bond between us and his death was a deeply painful and psychological blow to me. There was a lot of life he had still wanted to live, yet his old body "coat" had grown too tired to continue. (Or more probably the bad care he had received at the Veterans Hospital.) There was a finality seeing him lying in the coffin that had never happened with Debbie. To this day, there has never been closure. Almost immediately before my Father's burial, Sharon and I became aware of his presence. Shortly thereafter he appeared many times to my sister in her dreams. A few times I had received messages that sounded so much like the way he talked, but I feel, during that time I had been living with Jack in Florida – maybe he didn't like visiting Florida even in the spiritual sense. Some of the women in our family had felt he was still very much with them at the time. I believe the spirit or soul of our beloved ones can hang around for a while, maybe because it's not easy to let go of the physical life. I also know that they need to be free to move on into their spiritual life. After being in a solid physical body, the spiritual body must find it hard to adjust to the freedom of movement.

In the early 1990s, after 20 years of living without knowing what really happened to Debbie I had to pack away all of my memories and pictures of her away from my conscious mind. So many details of her disappearance had faded until David Weiser, a TV producer became interested in Debbie's story. He began searching through old police records, Debbie's letters, phone calls, any and all information until he finally put together a segment for his television series. Time passed before he interviewed me and it was remarkable how dormant memories of grief can so easily burst into emotional tears. Over and again he asked questions that sparked my deep emotional responses. David was not a hard-nosed reporter like I had encountered in my youthful acting career, instead he was very kind and gentle. He asked what outcome I hoped to see from the TV production on Debbie. "I don't know--if she was murdered I still don't want to know. If she is alive, naturally, I wanted to know." I told David if he discovered Debbie had suffered a horrible death, I really did not want to be informed about it. After all these years I was still unable to face the possibility of a horrible or brutal death for my precious special daughter. By the time of the airing of the TV show "Sightings," she could have been a mother herself with children, and they would have been the same age she had been at the time of her disappearance. The TV program came and went without one clue offered. It had only brought back the previous pain and deep sadness. Since the time she vanished, I have never been able to identify with the motherhood of anyone beyond his or her late teens. The sorority girls did not desire any mothering! It was more of a restaurant manager, or teacher student relationship.

It seems that the more I search for answers the more questions appear. One never graduates from the classroom of life as long as we reside in the human body. Some of us are on a higher learning path than others. Because of my own life's traumas and learning experiences I have asked that this be my last Earth life. I believe we come to the point I have been in; that of being shifted to a very solo path where we can attempt to shed all our emotional ties. We just never see how so many people and things possess us. No matter how determined we may be to have a normal life, normal marriage, normal career, normal relations, friends, family, sex life, it seems a path has been set for us to see how we pass or fail. I have adjusted to whatever life has handed me with the constant, "I gotta keep going - you can't keep me down!" I have kept my goals to make life better for those that I can but mostly I cannot change anything in the world, except myself. Interestingly, psychically, I have been able to help others attain closure by bringing in communications from recently departed souls, however I have never been able to bring in my own parents or Debbie. I know the answer -

when one is extremely emotionally attached, psychic communication can be difficult and impossible for some. To finally be in a place with some measure of contentment, after living in the prejudiced, pious human race of segregated religious beliefs, it is such a wonderful journey and a peaceful place to now be.

If my sincere wish was to contribute to mankind to make the world a better place, how could I limit myself to the constant physical and emotional devotion required to raising one child? For many years I could not accept the fact that a man and a woman could not be happy without experiencing parenthood. That had been my conditioning, the same conditioning that has plagued millions of people. Who am I to judge the evolutionary path of others? Now that my Autumn has turned into my Decembers, I realize the frustration events and circumstances; failures and heartaches may have been necessary for balancing the books of the heavenly computer. Perhaps I have not lived in vain. Pursuing a career in the acting profession required a certain amount of vanity that I never really had. My humble training in youth was a strong handicap all through my life. I was caught somewhere in the middle of either retreating back into my shell or bursting forward. Apparently I had a karmic debt to raise Debbie just under 20 years of age and I hope it has been fulfilled. I am now free of motherhood. With all my broken love relations, I feel I answered to a lot of karma there, too! My training in regressions and through the years opening up to discover many of my own past lives has helped me to understand this life more than any religion, bible, psychology or anything else. I now realize there were lessons necessary for me to clear up a whole lot of my own karmic debts!

With this awakening and years of work I have done, I am free in the evolution of human soul, which is never finished until I leave this physical body. I mentioned before that our path must be individualized lessons. My lessons are not the same as anyone else's. Even in our most fulfilling experiences there are lessons to be learned at every bend in the road. Our lessons would be far more tolerable if we could develop the ability to lift ourselves out of the emotional immediacy of the situation and do it from above, a visual overseeing. If we could develop this detached ability or to project ourselves into the future viewing our problems as though they were long past, we might find that life can be beautiful and that beauty exists in all things and in all experiences life is--TRULY WHAT YOU MAKE IT! I always find comfort in the words to the song "Let There Be Peace on Earth."

CHAPTER 39

Life's challenges offer opportunities to look beyond mainstream thinking of what is "normal." It takes evolved intelligence to assume responsibilities for these past trials and tribulations. As we unravel our past experiences, it can provide us with an opportunity to reweave the patterns of our lives to become far more enlightened. Instead of going within ourselves to find answers, most people seek confirmation outsides of themselves, i.e. most religions that call themselves "Christians." Seeking to lean on a person or belief system outside is simply avoidance of one's personal responsibility. Have you lived in different physical bodies in different eras - or is it a genetic memory from your ancestors? Does it matter? (Four fifths of the world accepts reincarnation.) If you dig down into the subconscious, you will be amazed at what is there and how it affects your present life circumstances. Look to find your ultimate power and enhance it by nurturing your spiritual evolution.

In recent years there have been dramatic and undeniable evidence of a newly discovered form of energy. We communicate through a previously unrecognized form of energy that operates beyond the bounds of time and space. Our DNA influences our physical being through this form of energy. Science has accepted that it is not electronic or magnetic and are calling it "Subtle Energy" - it is everywhere, in everything, in every living thing, etc. We influence our physical DNA through this non-physical form of energy that is also directly linked to human emotion. Today more and more evidence advocates that the events of our lives, the failed relationships, broken agreements, disease and conflict of our past, as well as the joy, peace and healing of the present, stem from relationships that begin with this energy of all matter. Through energy associated with human emotion, and broadcast through human DNA, we create conditions in the realms where such events originate, past lives included. Ancient traditions, such as Kid - Chi - I gong - Prana, known forces of nature merge into a newly recognized force, the elusive unified field, that weaves into each moment of our lives. Kid - Chi - I gong - Prana Religions speak of "unconditional love" but have you ever seen anyone in or out of a church that can truly express unconditional love? This is a journey toward the ultimate union with what we call God - Universal Mind - the name is unimportant - it just IS the power of the Universe. I have yet to find a human being that can be capable of true unconditional love.

BALANCE was foremost in early Native Americans and other ethnic groups around the world. It has always been a balance between the human and nature. It is difficult to accept that the past, present and future are all one in the same. Everything that ever was, is. It takes faith to think that every word ever uttered is out there swirling in that unending energy, just as we, when leaving the physical body, return to that ever-present energy. In that in-between life, with help, we analyze our journey, recalculating what opportunities are needed to move forward again in the physical body. We then return to Earth to continue working out our emotional threads - those threads that hold us to the physical body. We can "let go" of all ties but it is not an easy path to "fly" alone! Most of us refuse to totally let go of our emotional ties.

What is referred to as the "New Age" is not a religion, nor any particular group, it is not a specific belief and it is difficult to grasp, since there is no structure, no rules, and no doctrine. Those who are attracted to New Age thought have sometimes been called the "church of what's happening now," a comical critique. Perhaps it is more of a philosophy of finding your center, your balance, listening to your inner voice, attempting to live in the moment, moment to moment. It is a philosophy of letting go, thus, accepting, exploring past events to bring them into consciousness light to reverse any negative reactions in the past. Our greatest gift as human beings is FREE WILL. You can remain stuck in the past or clinging to religious beliefs of limitations that make you dependent rather than independent. We set the course for the challenges in each lifetime to give us the opportunity to review, revoke, relive to be free of past conditions, just as our youthful conditionings by parents and others often limits us if we choose to remain in them. (Free Will equals CHOICES!) As for one who is drawn to the "New Age" thinking, one would not join a cult whether it may be an established "religion" or some far out or weird way of thinking or follow any particular leader nor continue to blame others for their present situation. It is searching for our own self-worth and connection with the Universal Energy in Oneness. The more we connect with that energy, the more we can find balance and use that energy toward healing individuals and the planet. It is achieving a place where we can look at one another and see ourselves as one-energy - disregarding race, color, religion, and limited beliefs, et al. It is no easy task to love those who dedicate their lives to destroying others whether with a bomb or stripping us of our opportunities to live productive lives and to LOVE them. This web of life is most confusing. There are many ways to kill the human spirit and it seems that rivals of good and evil are still one in the same. Do bombs and killings really resolve anything? Is it right for little children to be indoctrinated with hate and commitment? Is it right that they sacrifice their lives for a cause after being brainwashed, never having the opportunity to make personal choices for themselves? Is it right to dedicate billions of dollars toward destruction? Who has the right to judge? What can an individual do regarding politics, horrendous waste, negative indoctrinations, etc.? NOTHING, it seems! Just think! If each individual around the world would take personal responsibility to clear their own self/soul whatever name it is given - if each focused on learning to create unconditional love in their lives, what kind of world would there be?

Yes, I have survived so many "New Beginnings" that apparently were necessary for me to answer past lives karma or whatever growth was necessary in this lifetime. Now in the Winter of my life, when I look back, I would change some things? Of course, yet, recounting the many trials I have faced and survived, I have grown into what I would call an advanced "whole person." Every day, I face more challenges of the person I have become. The strangest fact is the more unconditionally loving, compassionate and understanding I have become, I seem to be far more isolated without close friends. It isn't exactly unusual as we grow into our senior years, friends and family die off; even so, as I reach out to people - they don't reach back... I have created this stage unintentionally.

Intermingled Destinies Between A Mother and Daughter

Referrals to past lives have been mentioned in some chapters. Like most people I was very skeptical and thought of it as some foreign religion. As I searched all world religions, I became more aware, and then reading books, attending lectures, classes, et al., I begin to be more receptive. Repetitious dreams are usually past life memories stored in our subconscious. I have had those, as do most people. Those dreams are never forgotten although we have many dreams at night that we never remember. The deeper I got into meditation; scenarios would play in my mind. It took many years to put them in the form of my own past lives, thus my book "Ann of 1,000 Lives" - a take-off on "Anne of 1,000 Days." It was around 1970 when I saw the movie that I got chills. I couldn't explain what was happening to me but I knew that I had lived that life. Afterwards, I scoffed at myself but the thought remained and only increased with time.

In the 1980's I did some channeling, allowing thoughts to flow through me as I wrote them down. A poem came through with seemingly old English. It was a long time afterwards while looking over some of my poems I read that one. OH! It seemed to be Anne Boleyn's death poem! As these various past lives came through to me, it was very difficult to place them in some kind of chronological order.

In my book, I don't know the exact years; I did the best I could to make sense of some kind of order. That is really not important, as I don't have the need to seek PROOF. What IS important is HOW these experiences affect THIS life. It is often years before I am able to see the connection.

Whenever I watch a TV program on the "Tower of London" - I always get eerie feelings. Early in this book I mentioned from a young adult age, I thought I was destined to have a son. For years I wanted a son, just a deep feeling that it was predestined. Watching that show, WHAM! I realized it was Anne's downfall that she did not produce a living SON for Henry VIII, who was determined that she must produce a son.

Through exploring my past lives, I have been able to understand how I have had numerous love affairs, never wanting them unless they led to marriage. I DID ask that I complete karmic connections so I understand many associations with men, women, friends, family and even short-lived associations. In one case, I dated a man named Thomas Moore off and on for over 20 years. Anne was often blamed for the death of Sir Thomas Moore.

Another longtime relationship was with a producer who I even followed to Europe in the early 1960's only to learn that his deal fell through and he was returning to California. He had been my father in one life and I was terribly attached to him. His death also profoundly affected that one past life. In this life I would end our relationship but he would keep coming back, a tie that was hard to break. It too lasted for over 20 years. Getting into his "Autumn," maybe nearing the "Winter" of his life, he ended up marrying his doctor's nurse. I figured he wanted his own personal nurse. I don't always find my past life relationships attached to my present life. The only immediate family member that I learned of our past life connection was my sister. Much of it was a carry over into this life which ended by her choice in the 1990's. In the French life when I was attached so much to my father, I ended up in Marsalis, France running a house of ill repute. There has been much jealousy and resentment from women in this life, perhaps that was the connection brought into this life from that one.

In another past life I was born into a family related to royalty. Upon running away to marry a young man who I was not allowed to marry, palace guards caught up with us and killed him. That began a lifelong resentment and guilt that I had caused his death. In my present life, I had a strange connection with a man quite a bit younger than me. It was the strangest non-relationship I had ever had, finally I realized the connection. I had longed for him throughout that life so when we met in the present life, there was a weird attraction between us. I felt the need to be very supportive and to encourage him but he kept "running" away to the point that I felt like a yo-yo. Realizing the connection from that life helped me resolve it in this one. Another helpful realization is that in a number of lives, I lived a very affluent lifestyle. In this life, I had looks, talent, and intelligence but no matter what I attempted, I have never been able to succeed financially. In past lives I had not had to accept responsibility for supporting myself. There are many circumstances I could list but many are in my book "Ann of 1,000 Lives."

I am not saying it is necessary for everyone to seek knowledge of their past lives. It is extremely rejected by many people and their religions. They can seek their life lessons elsewhere if they feel the need to evolve out of Earth lives but since they don't believe in former lives, they may believe they will go to hell or float on a cloud. It takes a lot of individualized work, aloneness and accepting responsibilities for self. "There are many ways up the Mountain." OR, they can stay stuck in possessive situations, never seeking their own independence and responsibilities.

I look back now at the time when I perceived that I was in my "Autumn of Life," not yet 40 years of age! Now I see that time period as "adult teenage" years. It should have been an ACTIVE, productive and successful segment. I did feel I was doing my best to be adaptable and seek other avenues of success. It seems that when a certain career not only attracts us but also gets into "our blood" we should accept that it is there to stay. Knowing that just one phone call could change your entire life; we hang on assuming destiny put us there. Reviewing my photographs of that time period when the Hollywood attitude of "being finished" if a person had not become a "star" by age 25, (at least that has changed now to allow a woman to reach the age of 50) it was very easy to feel like a failure. I am sure the same attitude still exists that if a person is idealistic with their hopes and dreams for creating meaningful films or TV, they are still "shot down" with: "It's not commercial," and "We give the people what they want." If the past forty plus years of the ever present violence and crime, plus now with the extreme computerized animations creating far greater horrors is a commentary of the mindset of the human race, we are in a very scary state of any progression for humanity. For me, post WWII seemed a BUILDING era, personal goals, the nation, housing, et al. Today it seems we are in a tearing down era of so much good that had been accomplished in the past.

I am convinced the animal instinct to "kill or be killed" -"survival of the fittest" IS alive and well in MOST PEOPLE, so if they don't KILL with guns, knives, etc. they KILL one's confidence and spiritual nature... at least that has been my experience. It is prevalent in the family life of many people. The older siblings physically or verbally attack the younger. Often one child is blamed unfairly and so it goes, tearing down self-confidence. In some cases, maybe it makes the person stronger. Also, I have observed that if a man or woman is quite attractive all the more reason to *kill the spirit* with fault finding, plus if reasonably intelligent or talented, ESPECIALLY if they are also a kind and good person...well, I had all so I was fair game and this applies to both men and women!! At parties, I have observed when an attractive person appears, immediately faultfinding begins, but if an ugly or handicapped person appears, immediately it develops into finding good in that person. One must have the attitude of "like water off a duck's back" to survive. Unfortunately I was more like a sponge absorbing every criticism!! When a person is very sensitive, they are vulnerable for these attacks. The irony is you need to BE sensitive to be creative in any artistic venture.

Another of my mature observations is that once a woman reaches the time in life called "menopause" and her ability to be impregnated lessens, even if a man doesn't want children, their pheromones seem to cease for women over 50 years of age. There has been research done on - some might call it animal instinct - human pheromones - "chemistry" which is that magic potion that when we see someone we feel an immediate attraction or knowingness. It can also be related to past life connections.

I am not a University trained psychologist but I have lived a very full life that includes over 50 years of directed study and research in all phases of metaphysics - the word only means "beyond the physical." It refers to the studies that cannot be reached through open-minded studies of material reality. Such concepts help to define it and our insight of it. Furthermore it explains features of reality that exist beyond the physical world and our physical senses. This includes the study of the nature of the human mind, and the meaning of existence with the nature of space and time. Few people take the time from their everyday necessities to go as deep and thorough as I have. It is my hope that my experiences are able to help convince people to be more open-minded to any and all possibilities. They need to somehow learn to BELIEVE in themselves never allowing family, friends, business associates or anyone to make them feel less than the God being that they are.

Jesus and other great spiritual guides have shown the way in Christianity called the "Christ" consciousness (It <u>IS</u> Jesus THE Christ, it was not his last name!) that we can all reach and leave Earth life for the beyond forever. Whatever method works for the individual by way of classes, some belief system, psychology, as there are many ways "up the mountain." my writings would be very gratifying. "WORDS" can be so misunderstood, even in well-meaning attempts to express a loving attempt to help people. Words, thoughts, experiences, personal growth and evolution I have expressed may offend some, so I can only hope you read my words with <u>your heart brain</u>, not <u>your critical physical brain</u>.

CHAPTER 40

Just to round out my own spiritual journey and how I hope it may help you, the reader - it began as far back as I can remember. I distinctly remember, when no more than five years old, I could not understand or subconsciously accept that the Baptist Church was the ONLY way for salvation or accept it was the ONLY way to Heaven. In the town where we lived, on the very next hill only about two blocks away, there was a Methodist Church of a similar size. All over the town there were many different dominations. Were they all going to hell if they were not Baptist. DID they each think THEY, too, were the ONLY way! NO, I did not like it! What about all the churches (religions) all over the world, did each think they were the ONLY way!

In Sunday School, the children met in a large room, then the boys and girls were separated into different rooms. WHY!! I had rather have been with the boys! Then came the Baptist baptism when I was around eight years old. I figured I had to join sooner or later, so I went through it with no feeling of "being saved." As the preacher put his big hand over my nose and face to dip me in the water, I heard him say…blab, blab, blab, and "forgive her of her sins!" For days I searched my mind to figure out my "sins" which made me wonder if talking back to my Mother was a sin and would God send me to hell for that?

My Dad understood my lack of connecting with the Baptist beliefs and by age thirteen, told me I was free to go to whatever church I wanted to attend. First I attended the Christian Church with my best friend. Later, I joined the Methodist church and was a member for years. During my teen years, as I listened to the Ministers, I became aware that I knew something they did not understand, yet I wasn't exactly sure of what it was. I wanted to dedicate my life to service but what would it be? There were almost NO female ministers at that time. I loved the idea of travel but to be a missionary didn't seem to be the answer.

When I moved to Hollywood, I attended the First Methodist

Church. I met a psychiatrist who offered "Christian friendship" and was married to a beautiful actress. He invited me to dinner at their house. I was not aware that she wasn't home. He offered counseling that I didn't think I needed--then of course, the PASS! I may have been a bit innocent for Hollywood but I was not THAT dumb! He offered to try different sexual acts with me to see how far I could go without submitting to the act of sex. RIDICULOUS! Off I went in a huff and hurry!

Later, I joined the Beverly Hills Presbyterian Church and stayed there for several years. I taught Sunday School where Jimmy Stewart's twin daughters and Errol Flynn's daughter were in my class. I was in my second marriage and we were active in the Couple's Club. Later when we divorced and I became a single woman no one spoke to me. I was then treated as though they didn't know me. Christian friendship?

Somewhere along the line, I attended the Church of Religious Science (not Christian Science), where I practiced Unity and positive thinking. I was religious, off and on through the 1990's. During my years in Hollywood, maybe when I was in Texas, I realized that the media had a greater influence on the masses than any politician or any religion. If just a few people really cared about what they produced for TV and films, it could be a good influence on the masses. My inward spiritual obligation would not go away. Early TV was family oriented but by the 1970's I realized how the focus was on crime, violence, car chases, blood and guts. This was at the time my daughter had vanished and in no way could I watch those kinds of series! Today, they have only gotten worse to the point where there are few series I watch, and those are only the old ones.

In the mid 1960's my best friend kept insisting I attend a meditation class with her. I told her that I had enough problems with not fitting in and I was still feeling out of place with religions or with "swinger." I finally gave in and attended a meditation class with her. We sat in a circle and after meditation we focused on one person in the group to see what we sensed about him or her. I began realizing I seemed to pick up more than most of the others. I had been to a number of psychics but never thought of myself as being psychic although through my childhood, I had sensed things that others didn't seem to get. Dianne suggested a book for me to read. I rarely ever read books, however, I told her that if I didn't have to be so concerned about money each day to support my daughter and myself, I wouldn't mind reading it. If not the next day then a few days later, I received a residual check for a commercial I had been in for $500. WOW! That was my "message" to take the time to read and meditate!

It had been a decade that I had not met with any success as an actress. As I look back at my life in Hollywood today, it seems I did have some success considering I had no backing in any way from anyone. What was my spiritual quest - what was I supposed to do? I had said and meant it, "Take my life and let it be, dedicated God, to thee" words from a song. I trusted that whatever I was to do in the future, I would be led.

I was surprised when Dianne suggested that the two of us work with a Ouija board when so many people thought they were evil. We always enjoyed taking rides to the mountains or wooded areas and would take the Ouija board with us. We would find a picnic table and sit working with the board. She kept her hands on the planchette, I put my left hand on it, Dianne read aloud and I wrote what was given with my right hand. Dianne had read more metaphysical books than I had, so when we began getting surprisingly spiritual, meaningful messages, I said it was all coming from her. She would say the same about me, so we were both a bit stunned at our messages and eager to apply then to our own lives. I remember one day, we were just finishing working with the board when ONE large whiff of wind blew by--just the one as though the communications through the board were being confirmed. There was only the ONE whiff of wind. I have no doubt that people might think I am "nuts" (and I really don't care) for this is my way of communicating with my Spiritual Guides. I spent years doubting their validity, as I was never given a name for my Spiritual Guides. What helped me was learning that other people who channel good information also have group consciousness guides, often a group of Angels that are merged into one.

On July 20th, 1969 I was living in an apartment in West Hollywood when the Astronauts landed on the Moon. A few years back, while living in a house that had a large picture window, three Sundays in a row, a dove flew into that window and was killed. What did it mean-- now in this apartment, again, a dove landed on my windowsill, again I searched for the meaning, if there was one?

As described in previous chapters I decided I would return to Europe and this time I wanted to see if there was any way to find work and just live in Europe. This gave me the incentive to save every penny I could and made my job at the time more tolerable. When I ended up in Monaco and discovered their patron saint was St. Devote – and again the "DOVE" that brought her to Monaco was that why I was in Monte Carlo? My intensions were to stay and be settled enough to write a book, "Sex, God and You"--I wanted to shine a different light on the act of sex and how it can relate to a person's spiritual journey.

My spirituality was violently interrupted with the beginning of the most horrific time in my life! Debbie was missing! Like many people who must live through such a horrible experience, it seemed my spirituality "went out the window!" Questioning and doubts prevailed for a few years. When I became involved with Jack and his atheist beliefs, it did not bother me in the least. Living with an alcoholic forced me to think more about the foundation of my spiritual evolution. I began to feel that "something was better than nothing" thus I began my journey INWARD rather than exploring my outwardly spiritual beliefs.

After that marriage ended, by the early 1980's I typed all the messages that Diane and I had received, plus the automatic writing ones I had received on my own, and titled it "Messages From Unseen Masters." About the same time I was to do a seminar with another couple. I rushed the typed pages to a printer, and had them put together in book form to sell at our seminar. It was a poorly put together book but the material was good.

Through the years my focus continued to be primarily on my spiritual evolution. The times I tried to get involved with the more positive type churches, I would always lose interest. It seemed "politics" were in every phase of living. I have studied about every phase of metaphysics, occult mysteries, world religions and psychology. The one area that has worked for me just about more than anything else was when I delved into reincarnation. When I read books, attended classes, lectures, workshops and also did them myself, past lives awareness seemed to begin answering so many of my "why this or that" in my life. Eventually, I put it all in the book "Ann of 1,000 Lives" – it was like the frame of a puzzle laying before me and I saw where this piece fit; others fit together to become the whole picture of WHO I am and who I have become. Ahh, the SOUL – I also did seminars on Soul Mating when I believed as others also believe that we are just one soul. For me it seemed obvious that family, friends, people we are involved with are just pieces of ONE Soul, so we are all "Soul Mates" – it seems to me that as we connect with our soul mates and work through UNCONDITIONAL LOVE on our Earth journey, we move on to higher dimensions of soul evolution.

This last chapter of rounding out my spiritual journey will not be the same as your own passage will be. My best description is about the fact that no person in the world has your same fingerprints and I feel your spiritual journey should be just as individual. The Indian Guru has described the journey as walking through a beautiful flower garden and picking only the flowers that appeal to you. Just think of the masses that never seek to find their "own way." They simply adapt to the beliefs of their family and ancestors, including their particular religion with the thinking that it is the "only" one. How often have you heard the bible described as "THE word of GOD" – "Written by the hand of God" – in that case how can you know if what I am writing now might be written by "the hand of God!"

As an individual what do YOU need? You need TRUST – we all have that inner voice that we mostly choose to ignore. You need deep seeded FAITH; no matter what may happen in your life <u>have</u> FAITH; just as I always knew that no matter what DID or did NOT come into my life, ONE phone call could change it all. PERSONAL RESPONSIBILITY! In my lifetime I have seen the past 50 years become the BLAME ERA! Everyone blames someone for some situation, be it their race, religion or something or other within their troubled lives. What happened to PERSONAL RESPONSIBILITY? OH MY! GOD is to BLAME for every misfortune in our lives, the weather, the world situation and every bad thing! EVERYTHING IS ENERGY! How can WE deny responsibility when all we do is create wars, killings, even our entertainment must contain violence or destruction of one kind or another. Even families can be so destructive to each other with constant criticism and putting each other down. The same goes for married couples, people in business situations and all walks of life so many people trying to always condemn the other.

Please! JUST THINK ABOUT WHAT KIND OF ENERGY WE CREATE! COULD IT BE POSSIBLE THAT NEGATIVE ENERGY RELEASED INTO THE ATMOSPHERE RAINS DOWN ON US IN THE FORM OF TERRIBLE WEATHER or "BAD" things happening to us?

What we know as "GOD" is LOVE! How many people do you know, including yourself, are capable of UNCONDITIONAL LOVE? I am not sure that human beings CAN be released from all possessive forces and attain UNCONDITIONAL LOVE! WHAT IS YOUR PERSONAL RESPONSIBILITY TO YOURSELF?

Namaste, I honor the place in you
In which the entire universe dwells.
I honor the place in you
Which is of love, of truth, of light and peace.
When you're in that place in you
And I am in that place in me.... We are ONE.

Ann Palmer

I would like to share some of my poems with you…

SOLITUDE

Give me but a moment of solitude.
Let me capture the quietness of the night.
Let me sit alone engulfed by the darkness here and about.
Let me enjoy the beauty of silhouetted trees and mountains
Transfixed on a starlit sky.
Let me stay away from nonsensical chatter and useless sounds
And minds saturated with intoxicating liquors.
You ask me why I draw away from these social gatherings,
Because, Oh People, can you not see
What a gross waste of time and talents
You each are so guilty of…?
Can you not realize just how much
There is for you and I to do in this old world of ours?
So may I suggest to you,
That, you, too, take a moment of solitude.

PASSAGES

Passages - Those bundle of years passing by
Growing old forces us to equate them with a sigh
Accepting old age is no easy task
Especially for those of us who wear our mask
Our mask of youth we do diligently cling
Many a decade of songs we do sing
Our songs of romance and love so dear and true
Then to awake to those passages are all gone too
A woman alone trying to stand so tall
But only reality forces us to take our fall
Some have no home in anyone's heart
Difficult to accept it can never be
And for me difficult to see
But see I must
Accept this passage is a must
Can I go on through my life complete
And ask I should, why has this happened
to me Old age - you are not my friend
You are the most evil passage of all
Or is it our country's attitude
For wisdom of age there's no gratitude
Then when death makes his call
How many are ready to go
To walk hand and hand as a friend
Has media created this sad end
Maybe it's time to see our God
Matters not what name you call
But accept that - something there is
a waiting to take our hand from death's grasp
And then to know what true love is
No longer necessary to wear our mask.

MISFIT

Do you know what it is to be alone?
To be with many and yet alone?
To be loved by many and yet alone.
To be able to give love and yet alone.
To have a child's tender love, yet alone.
Do you know what it is to be a misfit?
To be with common folk and not quite fit,
To be with sophisticates and yet not fit,
To believe in God and feel church union,
And with church folk, not quite fit.
To feel a part of those who need no church,
And, yet, there not fit there either.
Will there ever be a place for me?
With faith, I will wait and see.

GOD in ME CAN do ANYTHING

Today I choose abundance
and Universal good,
Everything unfolds for me
Exactly as it should;
God in me can do anything,
Myself - I know not how,
God in me can do anything
And I accept it now.
Today I choose forgiveness
And let my judgments go,
Christ in me loves everything,
And everyone I know:
God in me can do anything,
Myself - I know not how,
God in me can do anything
And I accept it now.
Today I choose fulfillment
For all the world to see,
As I heal my feelings,
Life is healing me:
God in me can do anything,
Myself - I know not how,
God in me can do anything
And I accept it now.

Ann Palmer

A TIME TO BE STRONG

There is time to be strong,
Even tho you feel you stand alone,
There is time to be strong,
Even when your journey seems too long,
There is time to be strong,
And enter into your own inner depths,
Where your deepest soul is kept,
There is time to be strong,
And know you are never alone,
It is time to let God in
And manage all your cares
Where you can let all fears disappear,
Where detached love is learned,
Where no words need be spoken,
That is when you know you are strong
So love with a gentle hand
And in you it once all began,
Waken your soul so each day
You know you are strong and time
Is now and endless time prevails.

ODE TO MY SOUL

Oh tormented mind and soul
What do you want of me?
I try hard to make contact
With your inner most depths.
I know you must create
But please tell me what shall it be?
You have so much to give
If only I could see it clear.
When my heart is open to you
You flow like a swift flowing stream,
But why do you fail me
When my pen is at hand?
Are you not ready to give
And give for what you were born?

Oh mind and soul of mine
Please give me contented time.
I am but your slave
All you need do is guide me
And I surrender to your will.
Please don't leave me alone
In this whirlpool existence of the mind
Or give me patience to await your call.

Ann Palmer

MY BOOK OF LIFE

When the book of Life is read
What will my life reveal?
Will yours be better than mine?
Was it better that you sought?
Material wealth and I did not?
I don't know who you are
I just know that my path was mine.
It has been so individual
No one understands it,
Nor do I.
Did I select this path?
Or was it already written in the book?
It's not that I didn't enjoy the things
Money can buy...
It's just that I thought it was supposed
To arrive when we pursued what we loved.
"Saving the world" via the media
Was my goal.
When we look at the world today,
We see how I failed.
So, what will that book say?
Will it say I did my best or
The best is yet to come?

Will it say my wealth is not measured
in dollars and cents?
Will I be credited for all my searching?
Will it show how many experiences I've had?
Will it credit me for all my travels?
Will it show how I've questioned
All accepted beliefs and searched for my own?
Will it explain to me why I've had to find my way
Always alone - always alone - always alone...
Will it tell me I had a deeply honest perception
That others or I could not understand?

I'll wait - and learn and search
I'm not ready to read that Book of Life,
Not yet - no, not yet, I'll keep searching
For the answer - but what answer am I seeking?
I know you've had more expensive clothes,
You've had grander homes - Maybe
You've had a wonderful husband and kids
And grandchildren too.
You may have even traveled more
Yet, somehow I know my wealth IS
So immeasurable and if I could do it all over
And if I could exchange places with you,
For what I feel inside myself and what
I feel in my heart, I would still choose
To live this life as it has been given
And just how it has progressed.
Oh yes, changes I would make
But that is as it is.
Maybe I don't know why some
Experiences seemed to break my heart
I've learned each only dug deeper
My capacity to love even more
To look at each person
And realize - "there but for the grace
Of God, go I"
To know that we are all one -
So hard to accept for most.
To feel deep compassion
Without being controlled by it.
To know what it is to be
Born within, not "born again."
I don't want to be born again
Into this Earth's chaos.
I want to just go home
With lessons learned well,
With wealth that cannot be
Measured nor understood by

Most who reside here on this Earth.
I hope my Book of Life is full
Of immeasurable leanings
Of unconditional love and understandings,
And know I've lived well.

END

And just one of my favorite photos…

Intermingled Destinies Between A Mother and Daughter

About the Author

From early childhood Ann Palmer questioned religions as well as feeling she didn't belong to her family or circumstances. Moving frequently did not build confidence but an early fashion modeling career did. New York City didn't seem a place to raise a small daughter, but Hollywood did where the money was in TV commercials. She realized she needed to study acting. Success through acting for ego reasons was never her goal. Ann believed that producing uplifting television was her life's goal. Commercials, small parts in film and TV followed through the years. All the while focusing on being a mother with unconditional love, plus the strength of a father. One highlight of her career was a part in the 20th Century Fox feature film "Cleopatra" that was shooting in Rome. As a Persian Princess, Ann was one of the only American women to appear in this cinematic epic. Later in her career she appeared in classic films like "Love With A Proper Stranger" and "Bonnie and Clyde." Ann appeared as a nurse on "General Hospital" for 14 years.

She always sought creative goals and worked in many areas of production - as a casting director, production assistant, and producer for an ad agency. Another milestone involved producing and hosting 250 cable TV shows, 52 of them in Mexico. She left Hollywood believing producing her shows could then be syndicated nationally. Finally giving up on that, she moved to Mexico, but that lasted only six month, then it was back to Palm Springs. As an ordained minister, Ann has officiated at over 400 weddings. After 9/11 Ann bought a 37-foot motor home and headed out for a writing sabbatical and ended up in Asheville, North Carolina. She has four published books, articles, and poems. Her ever-constant research into spiritual evolution has lead her in many areas of Metaphysics. She is an expert in many areas of the spiritual evolution, lecturing and teaching classes. Ann has never allowed seeming failures, grief or disappointment in career, family or friends to destroy her. They have only made her a stronger "survivor." Her hopes and goals are always for helping others through her efforts in writing and television. No time to ever give up!

www.ingramcontent.com/pod-product-compliance
Lightning Source LLC
Chambersburg PA
CBHW022051160426
43198CB00008B/190